# Photography in America

Edited by Robert Doty | Introduction by Minor White

# PHOTOGRAPHY IN AMERICA

A Ridge Press Book    T & H    Thames and Hudson | London

# Contents

EDITOR-IN-CHIEF: Jerry Mason
EDITOR: Adolph Suehsdorf
ASSOCIATE ART DIRECTOR: Harry Brocke
MANAGING EDITOR: Moira Duggan
ASSOCIATE EDITOR: Mimi Gold
ASSOCIATE EDITOR: Barbara Hoffbeck
ART ASSOCIATE: Nancy Louie
ART ASSOCIATE: David Namias
ART PRODUCTION: Doris Mullane

This volume was prepared to accompany an exhibition
of the same title shown at the
Whitney Museum of American Art, New York.

First published in Great Britain in 1974 by
THAMES AND HUDSON, LTD., LONDON

Printed in Italy

ISBN 0 500 54024 1

# Foreword

This book has been created as the permanent and complete record of the exhibition *Photography in America* shown at the Whitney Museum of American Art, New York, from November 20, 1974, through January 12, 1975.

Although New York has witnessed many important photographic exhibitions, notably *The Family of Man* (1955) and *The Photographer's Eye* (1964), both at The Museum of Modern Art, this is the first attempt to survey the history of photography since the exhibition *Photography 1839-1937* was organized by Beaumont Newhall for The Museum of Modern Art in 1937. The Department of Photography at The Museum of Modern Art under the direction of Beaumont and Nancy Newhall, Edward Steichen, and John Szarkowski; the International Museum of Photography at George Eastman House, Rochester, New York, under the direction of General Oscar N. Solbert, Beaumont Newhall, and Robert Doherty; and the Department of Photography at The Art Institute of Chicago, under the direction of Peter Pollack and Hugh Edwards, have for more than a quarter of a century consistently created exhibitions and publications to advance the knowledge of the art and history of photography in America. It is gratifying to bring a survey of American photography to the only museum founded for the purpose of aiding the recognition of work by American artists.

It will be immediately apparent that, while this book is devoted to the art of photography in America, it does not attempt to cover such subjects as scientific, fashion, or journalistic photography; space did not permit such a comprehensive survey. Selection was governed by the inclusion of pictures made by photographers who intended above all that their work be informed by a conscious effort toward the perfection of an inner vision or an avowed aesthetic content. I do not intend to imply that there is a distinctive "American" style in photography.

Rather, I have tried to present a chronological view of selected images by photographers who I feel have created an essential body of work, sometimes unique and always visually stimulating. I have avoided novelty and images which, although exciting to a contemporary vision, were made only for purposes of information or by chance. I have not included photographs which are important solely as the first of their kind, either in style or technique, or photographs deemed consequential by the nature or identity of their subject matter. Certain photographs have become landmarks in the history of photography and no survey could afford to omit them. However, a conscious effort was made to include as many unpublished and unfamiliar images as possible. My selection is, to a great extent, subjective. After all the aspects of a photograph were considered, the deciding factor was pleasure—the outward manifestation of a sensuous response to the photograph, which can be found only in a photograph, and which is the ultimate expression of the photographer's passion and skill.

The organization of the book and exhibition brought me into contact with many who gave generously of their time and expertise. I hereby express my deepest thanks to the following: James C. Anderson, University of Louisville; Ms. Doon Arbus; Albert K. Baragwanath, Museum of The City of New York; Miles Barth, The Art Institute of Chicago; Ms. Carol Brown; Robert Doherty, International Museum of Photography at George Eastman House; Ms. Cheryl Douglas, Friends of Photography, Carmel, California; Ms. Anita Duquette, Whitney Museum of American Art; Harold Jones, Light Gallery, New York; Dennis Longwell, The Museum of Modern Art; Miss Grace Mayer, The Museum of Modern Art; John McKendry, The Metropolitan Museum of Art; Weston Naef, The Metropolitan Museum of Art; Davis Pratt, Fogg Art Museum, Harvard University; Carl Siembab, Carl Siembab Gallery, Boston; Robert A. Sobieszek, International Museum of Photography at George Eastman House; John Szarkowski, The Museum of Modern Art; Minor White, Massachusetts Institute of Technology; Lee Witkin, The Witkin Gallery, Inc., New York.

We are all indebted to the photographers who have devoted their lives to enriching our own. I am very grateful to those who lent their work and encouragement to this project.

I am glad to have this opportunity to acknowledge a debt of gratitude to Beaumont Newhall. His creative scholarship in the history of photography has been a sustaining inspiration for many years. I would also like to thank Andrew C. Ritchie, who made possible the opportunity to organize the prototype for this exhibition and book at the Yale University Art Gallery in 1965.

—*R. D.*

# Introduction | by Minor White

Sometimes in a photographic career, we encounter the amazing thought that an archetype of photography was around somewhere before photography was invented. To preface *Photography in America* along the implications of this thought appeals to me just now, probably because art and photography historians usually attribute apparent history to individuals. So the attribution of apparent history to social movements, or forces still more remote if not invisible, could be refreshing. Exploiting this thought will not change the historical facts, but it could change our attitudes. In turn, if attitudinal changes should occur, our understanding of the phenomenon of photography could just possibly deepen. For example, the photographers in this book and exhibition could be momentarily seen as pawns in a higher plan.

Photography in America compares to photography in Europe almost like the right and left hands of the same person. The interactions of the two suggest a person shaking hands with himself. Therefore, there is no way to write on the development of photography in America without scribbling on the other half of the body.

The finest American primitive photography came to light in the daguerreian galleries of a partnership called Southworth & Hawes and their rival John Whipple. They used the process that happened in France through the medium of Niépce and Daguerre. As all users of the first physical appearance of "an idea in the air at the time," their work had the convincing power of "beginner's luck." Possibly success is a kind of gift; at any rate, it is a means of "the idea in the air" announcing itself with a bang. Certainly American daguerreotypists quickly became outstanding in the lateral spread of photography to America, Asia, Africa, and Australia.

An unusual event occurred at the birth of photography in France (1839), which we cannot overlook in this preface. The French government attended the party, but instead of giving a gift to the infant photography, it gave the babe to the world by making public the details of the process. Thereafter, the first signs of vertical expansion occurred in England between 1858 and 1880. O. G. Rejlander and Henry Peach Robinson had been inspired to combine several negatives to produce single images. Thus an interesting photographic characteristic was revealed which until recently was rarely employed in other media. American photography did not respond to this new arising. For sixty years, from Southworth & Hawes to Stieglitz at the beginning of the twentieth century, American primitive photographers adhered to detail, to straight photography. The practicality of classic photography was an asset in photographing the vast West then being civilized and exploited by whites.

The first sign of vertical growth in America was technological. The event, which took place in Rochester, New York, in 1888, was the appearance of the roll-film camera bearing the trademark of George Eastman. What happened reminds us of what happened at the birthday of photography: The human love of the snapshot was given a tremendous boost. For the first fifty years, millions could have portraits of themselves; now millions could own cameras. In the 1940s this foundation characteristic in still photography exploded again: The Polaroid system fulfills the snapshot potential in photography beyond all expectations. Any further democratization of the medium seems impossible, yet all signs point that something will occur to achieve it.

Another characteristic of the corpus of photography is a kind of anxious art-hankering. It has dogged photographers since the first birthday. Autonomous photography prophesied art anxiety also. I recall Daumier's cartoon of the French cameraman Nadar photographing Paris from a balloon. He titled it, "Nadar Raising Photography to the Level of Art." The number of "balloon" photographers ever since has been so great that a tradition has been established of photographs which are intended to emulate art but end up imitating painting. Of late the tradition has included Op, Concept, and Pop. This may seem ludicrous, but anxiety is buried in its depths. We will return to this point.

The growth of photography into art has been slow, uncertain, and painful. After the tremendous, if not glorious, daguerreian period (twenty years), "photographic art" was an advertising lure for portrait studios rather than a fact. In this country during the first decade of the twentieth century, a vertical step toward art localized in New York City in the galleries of a group known as the Photo-Secession and flowed through the medium of two men, Alfred Stieglitz and Edward Steichen. Working with colleagues in London and Prague, they "emulated" the

7

painting of the time for the expressed intention of persisting until photography was accepted as art. Ten years later their pictorial process was "accredited" in public by a well-known painter of the period. Thereupon the leaders were inclined to return to the classic photographic pictorial process known as "straight." But both being fighters, they struggled to have *photographic* photography accepted as art. The "spirit of photography" inspired others with the same incentive, and the *Zeitgeist* favored the efforts of Paul Strand, Edward Weston, Ansel Adams, and a host of followers. Yet the impetus of the painting-oriented Photo-Secession was still to swell and capture the imagination of thousands of camera-club photographers for another half-century.

The corpus of photography developed extraordinary technological, ideational, and spiritual vertical expansion in the 1920s. In Europe, Dr. Oskar Barnack's Leica appeared as if by magic. The tiny cameras took photography into every nook and cranny of the world and merged news photography, documentary, and social consciousness into photojournalism. In due time, the ubiquitous anxiety to make all forms of photography into art infected miniature-camera photography. For example, the Leica-minded Frenchman, Henri Cartier-Bresson, a determined photojournalist, caught the attention of curators and so was taken up by the museums. In America, the Farm Security Administration photographers, including Dorothea Lange, Russell Lee, and Arthur Rothstein, documented America with an honesty that has not yet been rivaled. The "best" of it hangs in art museums.

The ideational aspect involving the various pictorial processes first appeared over a century ago, as was said, in the "combination printing" of Rejlander and Robinson. It enjoyed a resurgence during the Photo-Secessionist dominance, through which autonomous photography worked in the revolt of Dada against the art establishment. At the Bauhaus in Germany, photography was but one of the new technological innovations investigated for practical aesthetic use in art and craft. In still photography this ideational revolt and aesthetic research acquired the name Experimental Photography. Along with its Sabattier effects, photograms, negative prints, multiple exposures, camera work combined with ink, pencil, and color work, its viewpoints departed from the normal eye level to the worm's eye view looking up all the way to the tops of ladders, and the bird's-eye view looking down from buildings and aircraft.

In America another aspect suddenly developed. A vertical growth of spirit coincided with the later camera work of Alfred Stieglitz and was the source of the thought that developed in his photographs during the 1920s, which he titled "Equivalents." From the pictures came the concept of equivalence, which at one level equates with the use of visual metaphor, and at another level equates with a metaphysic of photography. As the meaning grew, Stieglitz found that equivalence applied to all art, then to the grand recurrence of life, death, and resurrection.

The phenomenon having been named, equivalence was extended by way of Stieglitz to the photographic community. Thereafter, photography had a means to be free of the necessity to imitate painting in its attempts to emulate art. Any photographer with the wish and the *ability* might investigate the art of unique photography according to its specific characteristics. Equivalence applied gives the necessary bite to the uniquely photographic search for the deepest roots of art, which go back a long way, indeed.

Photography came of age during the 1920s, but the maturation that might have followed kept being diluted and postponed by the increasing hordes of beginners. This was not detrimental to the technology, but all other aspects still suffer. Nevertheless, in due time all the new forms of photographic manifestation were absorbed by the needs of those devoted to turning photography into art. All except the snapshot. Its position on the bottom of the critical totem pole assured the snapshot freedom enjoyed by no other form of photography. Snapshot remained free until in the seventies the "under-thirty" photographers employed it as protest and revolt against an establishment of any kind. Ironically, by so doing, they somehow or other gave rise to an "aesthetic of snapshot"! Just as the photogram suffered the fate of becoming an art form, so has the snapshot. Now the very foundations of photography are no longer safe from the critic.

As we approach the mid-1970s, technological sophistication, pictorial processes, and "spiritual" awareness have matured to various degrees. Equipment has become so complex and expensive that photographers are handicapped. Pictorial processes have multiplied, and in the hunger of ego-expression outmoded ones are being revived. Jerry Uelsmann has developed a mastery of "combination printing" never equaled before. Everything is photographed daily by millions of camera bearers. In the democratization that photography has thrust upon the world, potential "masters" have been absorbed in the mass effect of the media. The percentage of quality images that reaches display on walls or in books is dropping—as is the quality of those images. All this adds up to a growing dissatisfaction with the photograph (product). We are well into the impasse, "It's been done before and better."

This dilemma is causing a profound change in photography: Instead of product being of ultimate importance, the creative process looks more satisfying. Perhaps this is why the various pictorial processes are in such favor today. While thousands of photographers enjoy the therapy of making photographs outside in the sun, the more aesthetically oriented derive similar satisfactions working with the elaborate processes which take more time and less money.

When photographic process is directed toward seeing, when it assists in the opening up of seeing, the expansion of seeing into "Vision" may be more important than the photograph. When seeing is the aim, then the watching of "nature revealed" (Weston), the glimpsing of "spirit" through surfaces (Stieglitz), or the sensing of archetype (Jung), makes itself available to millions of camera bearers. The raising of seeing to the heights of Vision seems to be a possible way out of the "it's-been-done-before" impasse, because as individuals in each generation experience Vision, the clichés of Vision remain viable. It is not a matter of history or art, but the here-and-now experience of both.

The remedy just suggested may never be acceptable to photographers, because the art-hankering is thicker than blood. To me

it seems that the agonizing over photography-into-art is more than a seeking of status or financial reward, that it comes from a premonition that something at the roots of art is desirable and generally missing today in most media.

Photography is the only major art medium whose roots go back only so far as the materialistic up-swing of technology and science in the nineteenth century. All the rest of the art media reach back to a time when art and science were undifferentiated parts of sacred ritual. Something of this sacredness may be dimly felt by contemporary photographers living, as all of us do, in a profane world. The metaphysics of the term "equivalence" points toward deeper roots, or toward the profounder nature of the process of photography. Whenever photographic education diverts some of its attention to the photographer's audience and the human foibles of communication, audience as well as photographer can delight and benefit in the creative process. Among contemporary photographers we can name two whose work appears in this book—Walter Chappell and Paul Caponigro—who are conscious of "something" working through them and their photography.

Stieglitz was nearly alone in his drive to have "spirit" acknowledged in photography and art. Meanwhile, a crowd has gathered, though largely unconscious. Ralph Hattersley, in his book, *Discover Yourself Through Photography,* was not talking about ego, but a Self which is simultaneously exterior and interior. In reporting his observations that photography is evolving a sense of the sacred, he said that for thousands of unsuspecting people photographing is the closest they come to "religion." His observation that the working of a "photogeist" is hidden from most of us but is nonetheless surging, corresponds to observations that have found me. It makes no difference that I would prefer some other term than "religion"—for example, the word "Something"—and have it mean something that goes back to the time when art, science, and the sacred were one.

# Photography in America

The history of photography in America is strikingly similar to the history of the nation itself. Both are relatively young entities, and during their formative years both were dependent on European ideas and events. Initially, the medium was particularly suited to the national character. The problems of picture-making by a mechanical process were of a practical nature and readily comprehensible for Yankees who prized technical innovation and material proliferation. If, at first, America made no substantial changes in the intrinsic values of the medium, it did contribute substantially to the realization of its applications.

The first fifty years were a struggle between the photographer's visual aspirations and the physical limitations of his instrument. Native ability was more than equal to the import from abroad and it was stimulated, in all the visual arts, by a craving for European knowledge and heritage. By 1890, a strictly pragmatic approach began to give way to a yearning for emotional and intellectual content. At the same time, the medium's capacity for verity, already recognized as a singular value, was joined with a compassion for humanity. Later, the fidelity of the camera and a renewed concern for the pure beauty of the black-and-white tonal scale were re-emphasized as a reaction to the surfeit of reliance on pictorial modes taken from nineteenth-century painting. Although casual photography was made possible in England, the American Kodak made it truly democratic. The assimilation from Europe of technical improvements and new concepts in vision and content continued during the twentieth century, but the consequential contributions came from Americans who found in photography the means of creating images which were a manifestation of the intangible but basic spiritual forces of mankind.

From its inception, photography was recognized as an important means of visual communication, but, unlike the other visual media, it was considered as a rival rather than an aid to the artist. Before it became a work of art to be cherished and valued, the photograph needed the sanction of significant content and an apprehension of the unique properties of the medium. With the realization of these conditions through the authority of creative effort, photography in America became a vital art form, free of its European heritage.

The history of American photography begins in France. There, on August 19, 1839, before a joint meeting of the Academies of Sciences and Fine Arts, the director of the Paris Observatory, François Arago, described the first successful method for creating an image by mechanical means. Called the daguerreotype after its inventor, Louis Jacques Mandé Daguerre, a painter and proprietor of a theater called the Diorama, the process required that a silver-coated copper plate be made light-sensitive by contact with fumes of iodine and then be exposed in a camera obscura (a device used by artists and scientists to copy an image which was focused on a ground glass by a lens in the end of a box); the latent image was developed by placing the plate over heated mercury and was fixed by washing the plate with hyposulphite of soda. The public disclosure of this process meant that it was immediately available to all. Chemists, instrument makers, and opticians were quickly overwhelmed by demands for the necessary chemicals and equipment to make daguerreotypes. The desire to create pictures was intense, but a lack of dexterity and care was often the cause of failure. Daguerre gave a personal demonstration of his process in September, 1839, and wrote an instruction manual which was soon reproduced in several editions and languages. The popularity of the new invention spread as rapidly as newspapers and journals could carry the news. In the month following the announcement, the first daguerreotypes were made in America.

The painter and inventor Samuel F. B. Morse had visited Daguerre's studio in March, while visiting Paris in an attempt to interest the French government in his idea for the telegraph. He was immediately enthusiastic about the daguerreotype and reported his experience in a letter published by the *New York Observer* in April. He returned to the United States and continued to support Daguerre's efforts. In the fall, after sufficient instructions had reached America, Morse and his colleague John William Draper, a fellow professor at the University of the City of New York, tried to achieve a perfect daguerreotype. Moreover, they attempted to make portraits, a difficult task because the weak lenses and slow light-absorbing action of the plate held the sitter immobile for an uncomfortably long period of time. Despite such handicaps the number of daguerreotypists in America grew steadily, aided by the arrival of Daguerre's agent, François Gouraud, who sold apparatus and gave instruction. By the end of 1840, an improved lens was introduced and a method discovered for increasing the light-sensitivity of the plate. These improvements made portraiture a practicality rather than an ordeal.

Throughout the 1840s, the number of daguerreian galleries proliferated steadily. They appeared in every city and in villages as well. By far the greater number of daguerreotypes were portraits. It was the age of Jacksonian democracy, an era with new regard for the role of the common man. For many who placed themselves before the camera, the act was an affirmation of their existence. Some posed with family and friends, some with props or garments which specified a special interest, role, or trait of character. It was a time in which the nature of the image was more apt to be controlled by the subject than by the photographer, who was more involved with the mechanics of the process. An exception was the partnership formed in Boston by Albert Sands Southworth and Josiah Johnson Hawes. Both men had been entranced by the daguerreotypes exhibited by François Gouraud in Boston in 1840 and had immediately set out to become daguerreotypists; by 1841 they had joined forces. Most daguerreotypists rarely varied the practice of the seated or standing pose. Southworth and Hawes ignored the conventions of the trade and posed subjects in a manner they felt would bring out the character of the sitter: the dignity of a chief justice, the audacity of a popular actress, the modesty of an ex-president. Other daguerreotypists had taken their cameras from the studio and photographed the streets, structures, and scenes of America as it reached mid-century. Southworth and Hawes photographed ships in the harbor in wintertime, a class at a girls' school, and the interior of Boston's leading cultural institutions. At that time these were feats of skill and labor, the result of devotion to the medium above the traditional respect for craft excellence.

The daguerreotype was not the only photographic process in America at mid-century. An Englishman, William Henry Fox Talbot, invented a system for making images on light-sensitive paper, calling his process the calotype, or talbotype. He restricted the use of his discovery through patents, so it was never popular in America although widely used in France. Talbot had created the negative-positive process, the basis of most photography to come. The images he obtained were reversed—light areas becoming dark and solid objects becoming light—but he realized that this condition could be changed by using the original image to make a corrected version. In this way one negative would yield an indefinite number of copies, a tremendous advantage over the daguerreotype, which required a repetition of the entire process for each image.

During the next decade others sought to improve both processes. In March, 1851, Frederick Scott Archer published in England a description of a new method, the collodion, or "wet-plate," process. It called for glass plates to support a viscous substance—collodion—which formed a skin over the plate. A high degree of manual dexterity and skill was essential. The photographer had to clean and polish a sheet of glass, flow the liquid collodion over the plate, soak the coated plate in a bath of silver nitrate to make it light-sensitive, place it in a plate-holder, insert the plate-holder in the camera, make the exposure, remove the plate from the holder and treat it with pyrogallic acid or protosulphate of iron followed by hypo or potassium cyanide and a wash, dry the plate, and varnish it. The entire operation had to be carried out while the collodion was wet, and therefore a darkroom or its equivalent had to be at hand. Though unwieldy the wet-plate process had advantages: It produced a negative (which could be made positive when produced on an opaque support, the result being called an ambrotype or tintype); the materials involved were cheaper and easier to obtain than those required for a daguerreotype; larger plates were used and thus the photographer quite literally found his horizon expanding; there were no patent restrictions on the process itself, so it was available to any enterprising photographer. By 1855, it was well on the way to making the daguerreotype obsolete.

When the Civil War broke out, Mathew B. Brady was ready to seize a great opportunity. He was highly regarded as a photographer, the proprietor of several very successful galleries in New York and Washington, and the publisher of a series of portraits of prominent citizens called *The Gallery of Illustrious Americans*. Securing the necessary authorization from friends in the government, he dispatched cameramen in his employ to the front. Wagons were fitted as darkrooms and the photographers went out to record the conflict. Although they may have watched, and even photographed, from the edge of the battlefield, their wet-plate process was incapable of rendering movement, and scenes of actual combat were therefore impossible. Nonetheless, their photographs convey the horror and drudgery

11

of war through images of the human and material wreckage of the battlefields and the omnipresent objects of war—cannon, warships, shot and shell. For the most part, they aimed their cameras with the intention of obtaining as much information as possible; they adhered to a traditional perspective and the images they produced were unique for veracity but conventional in pictorial style. Only occasionally, by making the foreground more prominent, choosing structures with particular lines and geometry, or emphasizing the rhythms of stockpiled armaments, did the photographer indicate an awareness of aesthetic possibilities. More than three hundred men were engaged in photographing the war at one time or another. Brady employed many, but his practice of publishing all photographs under his own name angered some who worked for him, including Alexander Gardner. (When Gardner established his own studio, he made a practice, when publishing pictures of the war, to meticulously credit the maker of both negative and print.) Brady had hoped to make a profit from the sale of his war pictures, but the public wanted only to forget the conflict, and he emerged from the war badly in debt.

He had planned to market his pictures in the form of stereoscopic views. The stereograph and the stereoscopic viewer had become increasingly popular in America as a household pastime for a people eager to know more about their world. A stereograph is two images placed side by side. When seen through the lens of a viewer, an illusion of depth takes place. The camera was especially adept at making stereographs because it reproduced perspective automatically and it was only necessary to make an exposure, move the camera 2½ inches to the side, and expose again. Eventually, cameras were made with dual lenses, so that both exposures could be made simultaneously. The production of stereographs became a sizable industry in America, along with the business of making portraits. Many of the subjects were prominent or unusual buildings and landmarks, scenery and landscape, usually photographed with regard to their value as information only. But some photographers gave special attention and care to the stereograph. Often a photographer was able to seize the right combination of light, placement, and technique to achieve a unique image of time, place, and subject. They were produced by the millions and today form an incomparable record of life in America during its coming of age.

The growth of photography in America coincided almost exactly with the years of the westward movement. Daguerreotypists traveled in California to photograph the gold fields and the booming city of San Francisco, exploiting the veracity of the medium, its ability to record exactly and in detail everything that came before the camera. In 1853, an artist named John Mix Stanley carried and used a daguerreotype apparatus while accompanying a government expedition seeking a route for a railroad to the Pacific. A Baltimore artist and photographer, S. N. Carvalho, traveled with an expedition under the command of Colonel John C. Frémont and succeeded in making daguerreotypes under extremely difficult conditions. Carvalho reported that making one view usually took one to two hours, most of which was spent packing and unpacking the equipment. Finally, trapped by deep snow in the Rocky Mountains, he was forced to abandon his equipment but managed to save his plates. After the Civil War, the government began a systematic study of the western lands. Timothy H. O'Sullivan, a veteran of photography during the Civil War, accompanied the United States Geological Exploration of the Fortieth Parallel under the direction of Clarence King, a noted geologist. O'Sullivan spent many years photographing with various government expeditions to remote areas, enduring great physical hardship in order to photograph scenes few men had seen before. John K. Hillers joined Major John Wesley Powell's expedition to explore the Colorado River in 1871, and a year later found himself photographer-in-chief when the men he had been assisting became ill.

Landscape photography demanded a large expanse of image, but enlarging was not yet practical. Photographers were forced to pack and use big sheets of glass and bulky apparatus to accommodate them. By 1875, William Henry Jackson was using a camera which accepted 20 by 24-inch plates. A veteran of the Civil War, and a photographer since the age of twenty-five, Jackson devoted a lifetime to photographing the American West and Mexico. For many years, he worked with the government surveys under Dr. F. V. Hayden, and in 1872 his photographs were instrumental in passage of the bill which created Yellowstone National Park. To the eyes of the public accustomed only to graven images, the photograph contained an awesome sense of authenticity and unquestionable authority. It was indeed "the faithful witness."

While photographers were extending the role of the medium and demanding more from the process itself, others were working to make it better. In 1864, in England, a new dry coating for the plate was perfected, but it required very long exposures. In 1871, an English physician, Richard Leach Maddox, announced that he had achieved outstanding results with an emulsion based on gelatin. By the 1880s, the gelatin dry plate had been improved to the extent that perfect negatives were obtainable with relatively fast exposures. The new plates could be manufactured, packaged, stored, used, and developed at the convenience of the photographer; he was freed from the necessity of immediate processing. A tripod was no longer essential because the shorter exposure times permitted the camera to be held by hand and used quickly and easily. The era of the snapshot and amateur photographer was born. Their growing ranks became a multitude in 1888, when George Eastman brought out the Kodak, a small, sturdy camera equipped with a roll of film, a gelatin-bromide emulsion supported by paper. He also provided a service for developing and finishing the customer's pictures, and when—the following year—he substituted a clear plastic for the paper base of the film, he virtually completed the foundation of modern photography.

Now there was no limit to making pictures or to the choice of subject. The amateur, free from the conventions and fashions that dominated the work of the professional—whose chief industry was portraits—could allow his interests and imagination to direct his image-making. For most, this meant a simple act of recording family and friends in moments of pleasure and activity, but some realized that making pictures was a visual means of preserving and presenting concepts and ideas which occupied and inspired their lives. Kate Matthews photographed in her native Kentucky, making pictures of the characters and places in a series of books about life in the South, but her images of youth and its beauty transcend all sense of regionalism. Charles H. Currier was a professional photographer in Boston who sought escape from routine by recording the ostensible signs of an industrial nation—steam engines and railroad locomotives, building exteriors and interiors—with the camera placed in a manner calculated to reveal the inherent geometry of each subject. Adam Clark Vroman was a successful bookstore proprietor in Pasadena, California, who took up photography in 1892. Three years later, he witnessed a Hopi Snake Dance Ceremony and immediately became obsessed with the realization that he had the means to fulfill a mission. For the next ten years, he devoted his efforts to making a thorough record of life among the Indians of the Southwest. He used his pictures in his lectures, attempting to awaken others to the rapidly declining conditions that were destroying Indian civilizations.

He was not the first to use photography as an instrument for social reform. Police reporter Jacob Riis, an immigrant from Denmark, carried on a personal campaign for improvement of life among the poor in New York. He wrote constantly, producing a continuous series of eyewitness reports of atrocious conditions in the tenements, and in 1888 he persuaded two amateur photographers to accompany him and photograph in the slums. Eventually, Riis learned photography and produced his own pictures which he used to illustrate lectures and his books, especially *How the Other Half Lives;* he realized that the authenticity of the photograph was a greater weapon in the cause of social reform than the printed or spoken word.

Shortly after the turn of the century, a young school teacher named Lewis W. Hine began to photograph the immigrants pouring through Ellis Island. He followed them to their new homes in the slums and industrial cities. His photographs always affirmed the dignity of the individual, and they began to appear regularly in the new journals devoted to social reform. In 1908 he began a photographic indictment of child labor. He traveled constantly, often facing hostility and working with stealth in dank mills and factories. The extent and force of his photographs were a vital part of the effort that resulted in the passage of laws prohibiting child labor. In their time, the photographs of Riis and Hine were intended as no more than evidence, but the humanitarian nature of the content and the quality of the image have assured their place in history.

Photography required a mastery of technique and encouraged a pride in craftsmanship. Photographic societies and clubs were established to hold exhibitions which were organized by mechanical, scientific, and industrial classifications with little consideration given to the photograph as a fine picture. In England several photographers used the camera to record costumed and posed figures in scenes which echoed the heavily sentimental subject matter favored by many artists of the Victorian era.

By 1893, a group called the Linked Ring was able to present in London the first of a series of exhibitions devoted solely to photographs which were conceived as beautiful pictures. In America, recognition for the concept of photography as fine art became the passion and cause of Alfred Stieglitz. American by birth, he had studied the science and technique of photography in Berlin and traveled throughout Europe. Returning to America in 1890, he continued to study and experiment, using chemicals and papers that other photographers considered impractical or unsuitable to produce prints with salient tonal qualities and textures. He used a hand camera under the most difficult conditions; photographing in rain and snow, he pushed himself and the medium to the utmost. He was aware that photography was a means of releasing his personal feelings, and his pictures made in the city streets expressed the dynamics of urban life in a harmonious relationship of line and form. Stieglitz was not content to work alone; he shared his ideas with other photographers through writing and lectures, continually exhorting his colleagues to demand more from the medium and themselves.

In 1893, he joined the editorial staff of the magazine *American Amateur Photographer* and brought new criteria to the selection of pictures. He often refused photographs submitted to the magazine with the terse comment, "technically good, pictorially rotten." In 1897, he became editor of *Camera Notes*, the publication of the Camera Club of New York, and made it the finest photographic journal of its time. He was determined to find and publish only those photographs which showed "...the development of an organic idea, the evolution of an inward principle; a picture rather than a photograph, though photography must be the method of graphic representation." Such ideals brought to the exhibitions of the Camera Club and the pages of *Camera Notes* the most talented photographers of America. Gertrude Käsebier studied in Paris to become a painter and later applied her knowledge of the old masters to create photographs illustrating allegorical themes. She was also a successful portrait photographer and maintained a studio on Fifth Avenue in New York. Joseph Keiley was a lawyer by profession, as well as a photographer, author, and critic. F. Holland Day, a wealthy Boston dilettante who loved to dress in Arabic costumes, was one of the first photographers to work with the nude male figure and sparked a bitter controversy by making a series of photographs depicting the head of Christ. Stieglitz filled the pages of *Camera Notes* with the work of these and other photographers who were consistently striving to make the photograph a work of art. Clarence White was a clerk in a Newark, Ohio, grocery company, much against his own wishes, for he wanted a career in the arts. Purchasing a Kodak to use in trips about the countryside, he progressed to portraits of women and children in graceful poses. Edward J. Steichen was completely self-taught in photography, his only guide the reproductions he saw in *Camera Notes*. His ambition was to be a painter, and by 1900 he had saved enough money to go to Paris. He paused in New York only long enough to see Stieglitz, who extracted from him the promise that "he would never give up photography."

But such support and devotion was rare. More often, Stieglitz encountered bitter opposition to his goals for photography. Late in 1901, he was invited to organize an exhibition of artistic photography at the National Arts Club in New York. Stieglitz seized the opportunity and shortly before the exhibition opened announced the formation of a new group, the Photo-Secession. It was not a formal organization so much as a gesture, a breaking away from the established photographic organizations by those who believed that photography was indeed a fine art. The unifying force was allegiance to Stieglitz, who defined the aims of the Photo-Secession: "...to hold together those Americans devoted to pictorial photography in their endeavor to compel its recognition, not as the handmaiden of art, but as a distinctive medium of individual expression."

The prints displayed on the walls of the National Arts Club by the members of the Photo-Secession did show some individuality in choice of subject and composition, but at the turn of the century any photograph made with aesthetic intent was classified as "pictorial photography," a vague term which generally referred to a style of image made in the fashion of the popular painters, especially Whistler, Corot, and the French Barbizon School. Subject matter ran to landscapes, mist-covered fields or forest; figure studies of attractive women, heads bowed, draped in flowing robes; and genre subjects which depicted rural folk engaged in domestic chores or carefree pastimes. Tonal quality was based on a diffused light which softened line and form and suppressed detail to create an "impression." Pictorial photography was in effect a quite deliberate emulation of the current vogue in painting. In fact, some photographers practiced techniques

14

which gave the appearance of being worked by hand. Frank Eugene took extraordinary license with the photographic process, reworking and drawing on the emulsion of his negatives so that when printed they resembled a drawing or etching. The gum-bichromate process, perfected by the Frenchman Robert Demachy in the 1890s, was popular because the photographer could produce a print which resembled a painting. The process replaced the thin, hard, smooth emulsion of the standard photographic papers with a thick, malleable coating which simulated the viscous substance of oil painting. Working in a medium with no tradition as an art form, the photographer turned to the established art media for precedents. During the twentieth century, pictorial photography lived on in camera-club exhibitions, but it suffered a steady decline and became a sterile formula for making pictures of little interest.

A record of the Secessionists and their achievements appears in the pages of *Camera Work,* a quarterly first issued in January, 1903. It was illustrated with photogravures printed on Japanese tissue paper and tipped into each copy by hand. Photogravure was a printing process of such fidelity that each print was an exact copy in tone and texture of the original. To see those reproductions today is to experience a portfolio of original prints by such photographers as Gertrude Käsebier, Clarence White, or Edward Steichen. Often unknown photographers had their first showing in the pages of *Camera Work.* The articles discussed various aspects of all the arts and were written by such important authors as George Bernard Shaw and Gertrude Stein. In this handsome format, the work of the Photo-Secession was given a permanent record of its place in art history. *Camera Work* was edited and produced by Stieglitz, who was winning vindication for his idea of the recognition of all forms of artistic endeavor by placing exhibitions of work by the Photo-Secession in several American museums.

During the early years of the Photo-Secession, Stieglitz was beset by the difficulties of exhibiting work by members. Too many exhibitions still admitted photographs solely for their value as technical examples and many lacked the dignified presentation which Stieglitz demanded. His friend and colleague Edward Steichen found the solution. Persuading Stieglitz to rent rooms at 291 Fifth Avenue, adjacent to his own apartment, Steichen transformed them into a gallery. On November 24, 1905, the

''Little Galleries of the Photo-Secession'' were formally opened. A group show by members of the Secession led off and was followed by one-man exhibitions of leading Secessionists, alternating with surveys of photographs by French, British, and German photographers. The last show of the first season was a one-man exhibition of work by Edward Steichen, planned to coincide with an exhibition of his paintings at another New York gallery. Each exhibition was carefully planned and timed. In the case of the dual exhibitions by Steichen, it was a method of drawing attention to the fact that an artist could successfully work in both painting and photography. The catalogue of the first exhibition stated that there would also be ''other exhibitions of Modern Art not necessarily photographic.'' Both Steichen and Stieglitz believed that photography should be shown with painting and sculpture to demonstrate its validity as an art form in its own right, and the gallery was a place for the affirmation of their beliefs on life and art, not a commercial enterprise.

Steichen returned to Europe and selected a show of drawings by the French sculptor Auguste Rodin, which Stieglitz presented in January, 1908. The mixed critical reaction was calm compared to the furor which erupted in April as the Little Galleries showed prints and drawings by Henri Matisse. His bold renderings of the female nude were considered an affront by the public and press. Stieglitz was delighted with the controversy, which challenged the complacency of the art world. During the next decade, the Little Galleries, or ''291'' as the place was better known, became the agent for introducing modern art to America. There, for the first time, the public could see paintings by Henri Rousseau, prints by Henri de Toulouse-Lautrec, watercolors by Paul Cézanne, drawings by Pablo Picasso, sculpture by Matisse and Constantin Brancusi, as well as the first exhibition of African tribal art anywhere in the world. Stieglitz supported and exhibited the work of young American artists who stopped making representational images of the world around them in favor of abstract studies of color and form. Arthur G. Dove, John Marin, Marsden Hartley, Alfred Maurer, Georgia O'Keeffe, and others who shaped the course of twentieth-century art in America had their first showings at 291. Stieglitz watched and encouraged the emergence of modern art, realizing as he did so that photography would also take new directions.

The turning point was chronicled in *Camera Work*: "...photography in order to assert its aesthetic possibilities strenuously strove to become 'pictorial'; and this endeavor produced in recent years the singular coincidence that, while men of the lens busied themselves with endowing their new and most pliable medium with the beauties of former art expressions, those of the brush were seeking but for the accuracy of the camera plus a technique that was novel and unphotographic."

Once again an opportunity presented itself. Invited to organize a major exhibition for the Albright Art Gallery of Buffalo, New York, in 1910, Stieglitz summarized the progress of pictorial photography with all the Secessionist work, a foreign section, and a selection of calotypes by the Scottish firm of Hill and Adamson. The installation was designed by the young American painter Max Weber and the exhibition drew large crowds, but it was the last effort in the name of the Photo-Secession. *Camera Work* and 291 went on, though now devoted exclusively to new ideas in painting and sculpture. It was Stieglitz's method of demonstrating that photography could no longer emulate the other plastic arts and that for the time being there were no photographs worthy of being brought to the attention of the public.

Among the people who came to 291 was a young high-school student named Paul Strand. The prints he saw there inspired him to master photography. Stieglitz showed the young photographer his own prints, images of the new metropolis made with a strict regard for the technical characteristics and properties of the medium which allowed him to depict the facts of form and substance cloaked by the tonal values of light. In 1915, Strand brought to Stieglitz a series of photographs revealing a startling new approach to the medium. In the streets of New York, he had made a series of portraits: a blind woman, a fat man, elderly human derelicts unaware of the camera, playing out the tragedy of their existence, while in another scene figures move beneath the vast forms of the buildings they inhabit. Strand had used his camera to portray the terror of the urban environment. He saw beauty in the forms and patterns made by an arrangement of bowls or a picket fence. Stieglitz immediately showed Strand's prints at 291 and wrote in *Camera Work*: "...his work is rooted in the best tradition of photography. His vision is potential. His work is pure. It is direct. It does not rely upon tricks of process...." In a gesture of finality, Stieglitz devoted

the last two issues of *Camera Work* to Strand's work, describing him as "...the man who has actually done something from within. The photographer who has added something to what has gone before. The work is brutally direct. Devoid of flim-flam, devoid of trickery and any 'ism,' devoid of any attempt to mystify an ignorant public, including the photographers themselves. These photographs are the direct expression of today."

The outbreak of World War I caused dislocations which led to the closing of 291 and the end of *Camera Work*. It also changed the life of Edward Steichen. He had established a household in Voulangis, France, but returned to America with his family when France was overrun by the Germans. Enlisting in the Signal Corps as a photographer, he was sent back to Europe, where he transferred to the Air Service. After the war he returned to Voulangis, gave up painting, and concentrated on photography. His experience with aerial photography had awakened a new interest in the problem of making a print with maximum tonal clarity and an image that was as visually acute as possible. He set himself the task of learning, as he recalls, "all that could be expected from photography." For many months he photographed the same cup and saucer again and again simply as an exercise. To find a method of representing volume, scale, and weight, he photographed fruit from his garden. By re-examining all he knew and repudiating a reliance on light to screen the subject, he achieved a rapport with pure photography, prints of the utmost brilliance, definition, and detail. In 1922 he returned to New York and a brilliant career which saw him employ his sense of the dramatic to become preeminent in portraiture and pictorial journalism.

Many photographers have risen to prominence from the ranks of the amateur. At the age of six, Edward Weston received his first camera as a gift from his father. By 1911, he had opened his own commercial studio at Tropico, California. He followed the customary practices of such places, using a soft-focus lens to control the light and obscure details, posing the subjects in pleasing arrangements and retouching the print with pencil and brush. He loathed these deceits, which he felt compelled to practice for the benefit of his customers, and preferred to work for his own satisfaction when he could make new attempts at composition with subjects such as the form of a shadow on a woman's breast. In 1922, his friend Tina Modotti took some of

Weston's prints to Mexico where they were enthusiastically received by her friends and other artists. Encouraged by such response and eager for an opportunity to change his life and work, Weston moved to Mexico City and opened a studio with Tina Modotti.

Life was hard, customers few, but there was time to work and the circumstances forced him to consider the possibilities of every object and moment. He photographed gourds and jugs, the clouds overhead, the faces of friends, Tina lying nude on the patio in the bright sun. Every moment, every exposure in the camera were vital. Nothing was unimportant. He sought form and found it in the glistening curves of a toilet bowl as readily as he did when photographing the monumental Aztec pyramids. There was endless variety in the textures of the land and its buildings, the shapes of artifacts, the emotions registered on the human face, the smoothness of skin and the roughness of rock. To record such sensations, he perfected his technique until he could record limitless detail and continuous tone, the infinite range of gradation from white to black.

By 1926, he had returned to California; in 1929, he settled in Carmel. It was his habit to record his thoughts from day to day in a diary which he called the "daybook." On March 15, 1930, he wrote: "It is but a logical step, this printing on glossy paper, in my desire for photographic beauty. Such prints retain most of the original negative quality. Subterfuge becomes impossible; every defect is expressed, all weakness equally with strength. I want the stark beauty that a lens can so exactly render, presented without interference of 'artistic effect.' Now all reactions on every plane must come directly from the original seeing of the thing, no second hand emotion from exquisite paper surfaces or color; only rhythm, form and perfect detail to consider...." A month later he wrote: "I start with no preconceived idea—final form of presentation seen on the ground glass, the finished print pre-visioned complete in every detail of texture, movement, proportion, before exposure—the shutter's release automatically and finally fixes my conception, allowing no after manipulation—the ultimate end, the print, is but a duplication of all that I saw and felt through my camera."

Weston used a view camera which held an 8 by 10-inch film size. The negative was contact-printed to every edge and was never altered in any way from the original image seen through the ground glass of the camera. Other photographers in the Bay Area of the West Coast formed a great respect for Weston's methods and his consistent regard for reality as the approach to subject matter. For a few years they organized their efforts under the name f/64 Group, a reference to the smallest lens opening which provided the greatest resolution in the negative and the sharply defined image which all the members sought.

One of them was Imogen Cunningham, whose lifetime devotion to photography brought her through a pictorial phase to the study of forms enhanced by light and seen as fragments of reality. People were also a constant concern and she photographed them in a manner which described the ideas and environments that shaped their lives. Another member was Ansel Adams, a musician who brought to photography the pursuit of excellence he had experienced in training to play the piano. Adams set himself the goal of making the perfect photograph through absolute control of process and thus definition and tonal quality. No aspect of technique was neglected, no tool of the craft ignored. In 1935, he published his research on the techniques of photography in the book *Making a Photograph*. By 1941, he was able to codify his work under the title "the zone system of planned photography," a method for controlling the process through analysis of exposure and development, and thus realizing the final print itself before the exposure is made in the camera. The publication of these and subsequent texts provided both amateur and professional with a source for the means to achieve pure photography. Adams' own photographs are interpretations of light, texture, place, and mood, always produced with the ultimate clarity of detail and tonal values. An ardent conservationist, he finds a blade of grass, a charred stump, the movement of water as consequential as the lofty grandeur of a mountain range or the vast space of valleys and lakes. His images are an affirmation of the enduring relationship of man and nature.

During the twentieth century, human interests became increasingly significant subject matter for the photographer. Alfred Stieglitz believed that only by observing an individual during a lifetime could a true portrait emerge. Therefore, he constantly photographed his wife, Georgia O'Keeffe, revealing the changes in her emotions, body, and spirit. It was a deeply personal relationship expressed through the camera and in its cumulative aspect a record which transcends private references to become representative of the value in all human relationships. He had always been fascinated by the effect of light in the sky and so he began to photograph clouds, finding in the infinite variations of light and form a means of visualizing his thoughts and emotions. He called these photographs "equivalents," because they were symbols of his life experience and he endorsed them with the efforts of a career spent reconciling the confrontations of art and life. By 1937, failing health forced him to give up photography. In 1921, he had written: "...my teachers have been life—work—continuous experiment... every print I make, even from one negative, is a new experience, a new problem.... Photography is my passion. The search for truth my obsession."

Paul Strand shared these ideals and added to them a belief in art as a service to social progress. He continued to amplify his earlier concerns with the object itself, photographing in close-up plant and rock forms with careful attention to shapes and textures. While working in the Gaspé Peninsula in 1929, he became aware of a problem, "...trying to unify the complexity of the broad landscape," and inevitably his affinity for the people whose lives were shaped by their relation to the land and each other led to a continuing series of portraits of the people. Over the years he photographed Mexican peons, New England farmers, Italian and French peasants, Hebrides fishermen, and Egyptian fellahin. Each subject was seen and photographed directly, with the result that the image was not only an individual portrait but also a symbol of human dignity. Because of this grand passion for humanity, Strand's photographs became a testament to the heroic condition of mankind.

Walker Evans was also deeply involved with human consciousness. In 1936, he traveled in the American South with the author James Agee to do a study of tenant farmers. The result was published as the book *Let Us Now Praise Famous Men*, in which prose and photographs share equally the burden of conveying the stark reality of rural life and the ways of human destiny. Evans used his camera for a dispassionate recording of material things, revealing form, line, and usage, and seeking spiritual and social meanings. His vision encompassed shifts of culture and tradition. He photographed a crushed Doric capital made of tin, a slender Ionic column adorned with a "for

sale" sign, a stone cross outlined against a vast industrial complex. He saw these fragments of heritage as icons of contemporary civilization, a testament to the growing supremacy of the machine and the gradual extinction of craftsmanship. He saw the American experience expressed in the artifacts of the people.

The equipment and materials available to the photographer continued to improve. Lenses with greater light-passing power, flashbulbs, and electronic flash made night work easier and permitted the recording of movement within a split second. Roll film was so perfected that a number of frames could be made on a strip of small width. The first Leica camera was introduced in 1924 and became the standard for small cameras using film of 35 millimeters. They were soon referred to as "candid cameras" because their ease and rapidity of operation permitted the photographer to seize instantaneously moments of human activity which might otherwise be hidden by dignity and decorum. The importance of the camera as a tool for reportage increased significantly, since the photographer could quickly travel anywhere unencumbered by his equipment.

The Depression and a severe drought in America during the 1930s were events which led to an extensive and comprehensive attempt to chronicle the life of the nation. In 1935, Rexford Guy Tugwell, Assistant Secretary of Agriculture, appointed Roy Stryker head of the historical section of the Rural Resettlement Administration, later and better known as the Farm Security Administration. Stryker's experience as a teacher and his interest in using pictures for instruction made him ideally suited for the job of arousing city dwellers to the plight of the depressed rural population. To provide illustrations for newspapers, reports, and exhibits, Stryker engaged Carl Mydans, Walker Evans, and Ben Shahn. Each photographer was made thoroughly familiar with the social and economic history of the area in which they were to travel, but once in the field they were free to select their subjects. The tragedies of the land—drought, floods, wind storms, and worn-out fields—demanded and got immediate attention. But the photographers also recorded the faces, the structures, the activities of America. More were hired; Dorothea Lange had already begun to photograph the distress of the unemployed in California and the migrants forced to flee from their destitute farms to the fields of California. Her photographs, as well as those of other FSA photographers, were dramatic evidence of the tragedy of displacement but they included moments of hope, laughter, and tranquility as well. All who photographed for the FSA maintained an abiding respect for human nature and constant consideration for the feelings of the people they portrayed. When the office was closed in 1943, the FSA photographers had created a mirror of America and established definitive procedures for implementing the attitudes and intentions that were now known as documentary photography. The value of the medium as a means of communication was demonstrated by the introduction of picture magazines and the rapid growth of photographic publishing. Assignments and stories created for the printed page were often the means of presenting memorable images, such as those of W. Eugene Smith, whose photography has been a crusade for better human relations and a record of all that is noble in man.

The possibilities inherent in the manipulation of the photographic process have always stimulated the imagination of those who sought new ways to create an image. The control of light and experimentation with light-sensitive materials suggested the possibility of discoveries of abstraction, images of design elements rather than a segment of finite detail. A young American living in London named Alvin Langdon Coburn was well aware of the new movements in the arts, particularly ''Vorticism,'' a worship of motion and the machine founded by the English painter, Percy Wyndham Lewis. Coburn resolved to make an abstract picture by photographic means. In 1917, he exhibited eighteen ''vortographs'' in London. To make them he constructed an instrument of three mirrors joined in the form of a triangle. The mirrors acted as a prism and the bits of wood and crystal photographed through a glass were split into segments. They were praised by the poet Ezra Pound, who admitted that viewing them required an eye for form and pattern.

A few years later, another American living abroad began to reconsider certain effects of the photographic process. Man Ray was both a painter and photographer. Arriving in Paris in 1921, he became affiliated with the Dada painters and poets, who scorned all conventions and relished ephemeral material such as debris, and ironic concepts such as chance and simultaneity. Man Ray courted improvisation in his work by a deliberately casual approach to technique. Almost by chance he found a

means of reversing the black-and-white tones of the photograph. Usually called solarization, the process of rearranging tonal values is also known as the Sabattier effect, after a French scientist who also discovered it fortuitously. Man Ray was delighted by his discovery and pushed on, deliberately trying to provoke accidents in the darkroom. One day he placed some handy objects on a sheet of light-sensitive paper, turned on the light and watched a distorted image of the objects form on the paper. He went on, using all sorts of implements, varying the effect with translucent or opaque objects and stationary or moving light. He called these images ''Rayographs,'' delighting in the beauty which was obtained by such undisciplined means.

Meanwhile, a Hungarian painter living in Berlin named Laszló Moholy-Nagy was also experimenting with the effect of light striking sensitized material to produce what he called ''photograms.'' He was drawn to photography out of a deep belief in the relationship of art and technology, and considered it ''the self-sufficient vehicle for direct, visual impact based upon the properties of the light-sensitive emulsion....'' Eventually his researches in photography encompassed not only the gradations of light values obtained by the photogram, but also reportage, instantaneous photography, movement spread over a period of time, microphotography, radiography, extremities of viewpoint, distortion, and simultaneity by superimposition. He developed these ideas while an instructor at the Bauhaus, an influential German art school which taught a thorough curriculum of basic design. In 1937, he was appointed director of the New Bauhaus (later the Institute of Design) in Chicago. There he was joined by Arthur Siegel, a versatile photographer whose career included both documentary photography with the historical section of the Farm Security Administration and his own experimentation with the photogram. As a teacher, Siegel emphasized awareness of tone, texture, and light, which—through knowledge of sophisticated techniques such as multiple exposure and solarization—provided the means of expressive ability; he taught this program with Harry Callahan, whom he brought to the Institute in 1946.

Callahan was already engaged in making by means of photography a catalogue of his feelings about everything with which he had contact. From the profusion of images available in nature, he selected delicate linear compositions of grass in the snow or reeds in the water. Chicago awakened his sensitivity to the urban environment, the patterns and forms of buildings, the complexity and rapid tempo of the streets, the movement of people, their virtual isolation, and the tension which controls public behavior. Photographs of his wife and daughter reveal a veneration for woman as the source and sustenance of life.

In 1951, Callahan met Aaron Siskind and invited him to join the faculty of the Institute of Design. Siskind had been involved with documentary photography since the early 1930s and had been active with the Photo League, a group of New York photographers dedicated to making pictures of humanity. But the primary importance of subject matter ceased to interest Siskind in 1943, and by the following year he had found a new approach. From the chaos of the real world, he retrieved images of order and balance. The source of his imagery is the planes and surfaces of the world, walls, signs, and rocks, which afford a rich variety of forms, shapes, figures, and totems, all scrupulously composed on the flat plane of the picture within the confines of the rectangle. Thus, by isolating a minute segment of the world and objectifying its existence, he was able to extend an awareness and description of reality. His photographs became icons for free association.

Several years before, a young poet named Minor White considered his work in photography and wrote: "Surfaces reveal inner states—cameras record surfaces. Confronted with the world of surfaces in nature, man, and photographs, I must somehow be a kind of microscope by which the underlying forces of spirit are observed and extended to others." Like Stieglitz and Edward Weston, whose work he venerated, White worked with the straight, unmanipulated photograph, and commanded a consummate technique which courted the ultimate in photographic sensuality. The content of his pictures are real fragments of all that his eye sees but their subject is the experience of "what else they might be." White's intention is to set up a transaction between himself and his audience with his photographs acting as the visible agent for eliciting feelings and thoughts of a very personal kind. To aid the viewer's response, he devised the use of sequencing to allow single images to reinforce one another within a contextual concept. Through his teaching in both private and institutional situations, and as editor of the journal *Aperture,* White has exerted a profound influence on the

art of photography. Both Paul Caponigro and Walter Chappell have worked with White and share his awareness of the metaphorical and motivational potential in the medium. But Caponigro is also interested in the scope of the land and has widely photographed the landscape of Ireland and the Druidic monuments. Chappell abstracts natural phenomena and the human form, working with a highly personal style of chiaroscuro which takes the fullest advantage of the tonal qualities of the photograph. All three photographers are committed to a belief in their medium as a means of both achieving and encouraging spiritual growth and realization.

Before World War II, compassion was the keynote for the photographers who used their cameras to reveal the problems of mankind, but there were those who saw the foibles as well. Arthur Fellig, who preferred to call himself Weegee, delighted in recording the tribal rites of urban life in places like dance halls and movie houses. He preferred the human comedy and his pictures often had a high quotient of satire. In 1958, the publication in France of a book entitled *Les Américains* signaled a harsher, more ironic consideration of mankind. The pictures in the book were made by Robert Frank, a Swiss-born photographer who had traveled throughout America. He photographed a country transformed by the dominance of the automobile, a new urban landscape which was often grotesque, and people who lived their own lives more conscious of possessions than relationships. Diane Arbus photographed the backwaters and eddies of humanity—freaks, transvestites, nudists—searching beyond the masks and façades, sharing the secrets she saw all around her. Richard Avedon plumbs the psyche, creating incisive portraits of the personalities from the panorama of public life.

Like many visual and literary artists before him, the photographer in the decades after the war had discovered the lure of the banal and commonplace. It was not a matter of questioning or even ridiculing the nobility of man, but rather reveling in a new source of subject matter that existed on every hand and was as omniprevalent as man himself. It is rich and readily available visual material, the product of a society both accustomed and dependent on the power of advertising goods and services, conditioned to accept and desire the physical object as a goal and value in its own right. To reflect the transient, impermanent nature of society, the photographer adopted a more spontane-

20

ous, intuitive manner of observation. Strange juxtapositions, awkward poses, unintentional revelations of self, disregard for balanced compositions were photographed in a mode similar to that of the "snapshot." The desire to find a new reality is a matter of penetration, using the camera like a scalpel to cut out segments of American life. The photographer often allows re-action to govern his compulsion for making pictures, but he never relinquishes the responsibility for finding meanings and significance beyond reality.

In recent years the visual arts were affected by a more expansive, a more adventurous attitude. In part this was the result of a desire to accommodate and utilize the knowledge, materials, and equipment made available through advanced technology, and in part to a highly conscious rejection of preconceived patterns of thought, particularly in regard to the choice of subject matter. It was another assertion that the authority and value of the work of art was found as much in the intentions of its creator as in the work itself. To his repertoire of multiple imagery, collage, photograms, and variations in negative and positive images, the photographer added holography and xerography, printing by blueprint, cyanotype, silk-screen, and metal plate. Old techniques were restudied, especially the gum-bichromate process and the Sabattier effect. Fabric, wood, glass, metal, and ceramic were coated with light-sensitive emulsion so that the support became a prominent part of the work itself. Robert Heinecken uses standard photographic materials which he integrates with paint, chalk, real objects, and a variety of reproductive processes including lithography, offset printing, etching, and image transfer. His interests and purpose lie "in the relationship and play between an unfamiliar picture/object content and the familiar photographic image." For Jerry Uelsmann, the dark-room is a laboratory for visual research where postvisualization takes advantage of changes and innovations in the creative process. Within his laboratory, he selects and combines image fragments to make pictures which suggest the world of the subconscious and defy reason and logic. Lucas Samaras also works with an awareness of the emotional forces and pressures within the self. Preferring the immediacy of the Polaroid process, Samaras has created a cumulative self-portrait of images which combine the opulence of an artistic sensibility and the impartial attitude of rigorous observation. The mingling of media and methods has made categorical distinctions obsolete. The artist continues to use a variety of methods to create a single work of art. The photographer now has a greater selection of means and opportunities for creativity than ever before. It remains to be seen how the options will be realized.

Every artist, in every medium, creates a personal record of his social experience. Attitudes, ambitions, and intentions are tempered by myths and ideologies which are themselves affected by current events. The continual change in the forces and ideals which dominate society effects a perpetual redefinition and search for significant content and conceptions of aesthetic concern. The process is expedited by development and accumulation of knowledge about technique, styles, and subject matter.

On the level of individual experience, the creative process is controlled by such factors as intuition, association, and education. Seen through the perspective of time, the history of photography is perceived as a coherent and rational development, with technical and pictorial ideas and achievements appearing and continuing in an interrelated sequence. But a theory of inevitability obscures the fact that many decisions had to be made along the way, many concepts formed and discarded, many choices made and rejected. In photography, the options are far greater than in any other visual art. Each image, no matter how casual or complex, is wrested from the chaos and bewildering complexity of all that the eye sees. Every exposure is a discovery, both in the revelation of subject and the thoughts and emotions of the photographer himself. The ultimate achievement is reached when all the elements of craft, content, and intention are so perfectly balanced that the image is an entity in spirit and form.

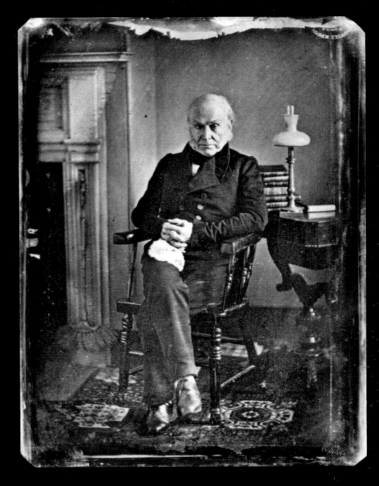

Albert Sands Southworth 1811–1894 and
Josiah Johnson Hawes 1808–1901
JOHN QUINCY ADAMS
*The Metropolitan Museum of Art, New York, gift of I. N. Phelps Stokes,*
*Edward S. Hawes, Alice Mary Hawes, Marion Augusta Hawes*

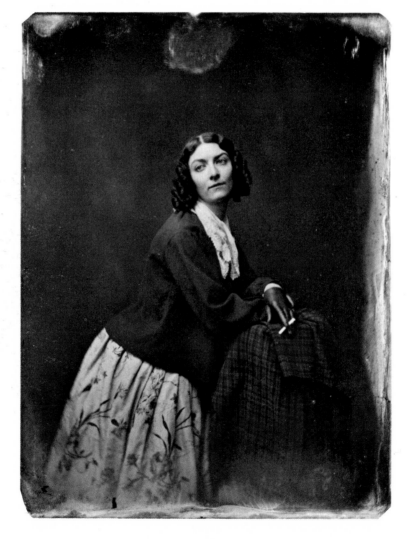

Albert Sands Southworth 1811–1894 and
Josiah Johnson Hawes 1808–1901

LOLA MONTEZ

*ca. 1851. The Metropolitan Museum of Art, New York, gift of I. N. Phelps Stokes,
Edward S. Hawes, Alice Mary Hawes, Marion Augusta Hawes*

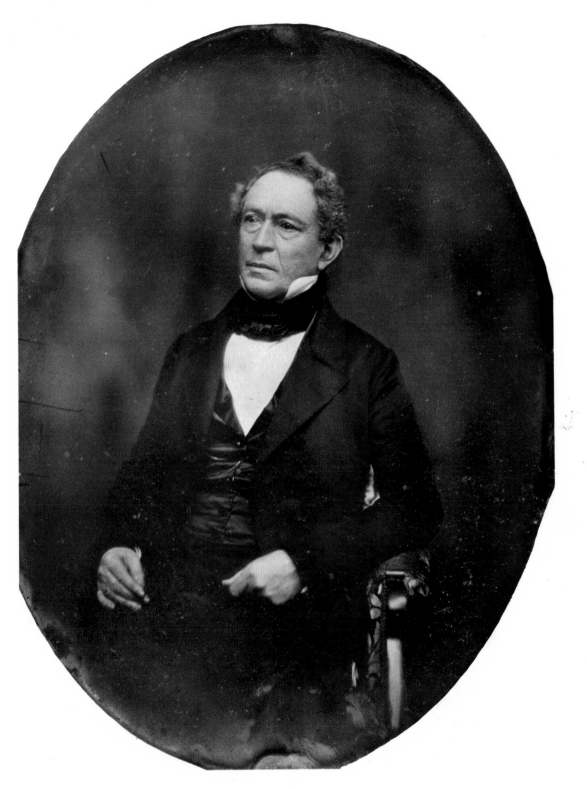

## Albert Sands Southworth 1811–1894 and
## Josiah Johnson Hawes 1808–1901

EDWARD EVERETT

*ca. 1848. The Metropolitan Museum of Art, New York, gift of I. N. Phelps Stokes,*
*Edward S. Hawes, Alice Mary Hawes, Marion Augusta Hawes*

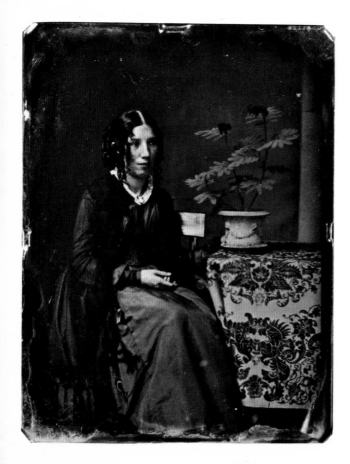

## Albert Sands Southworth 1811–1894 and
## Josiah Johnson Hawes 1808–1901
HARRIET BEECHER STOWE
*The Metropolitan Museum of Art, New York, gift of I. N. Phelps Stokes,*
*Edward S. Hawes, Alice Mary Hawes, Marion Augusta Hawes*

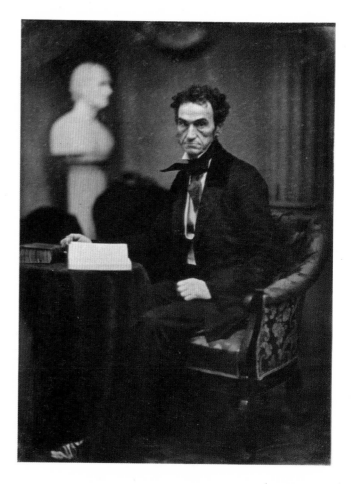

## Albert Sands Southworth 1811–1894 and
## Josiah Johnson Hawes 1808–1901
RUFUS CHOATE
*The Metropolitan Museum of Art, New York, gift of I. N. Phelps Stokes, Edward S. Hawes,*
*Alice Mary Hawes, Marion Augusta Hawes*

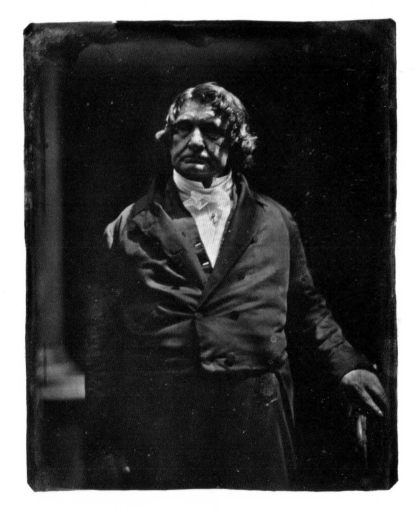

**Albert Sands Southworth** 1811–1894 and
**Josiah Johnson Hawes** 1808–1901
LEMUEL SHAW
*The Metropolitan Museum of Art, New York, Anonymous Gift*

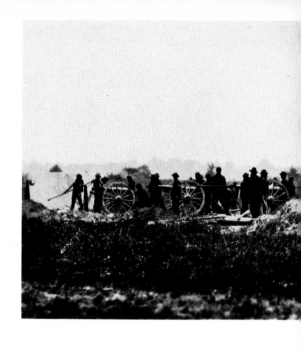

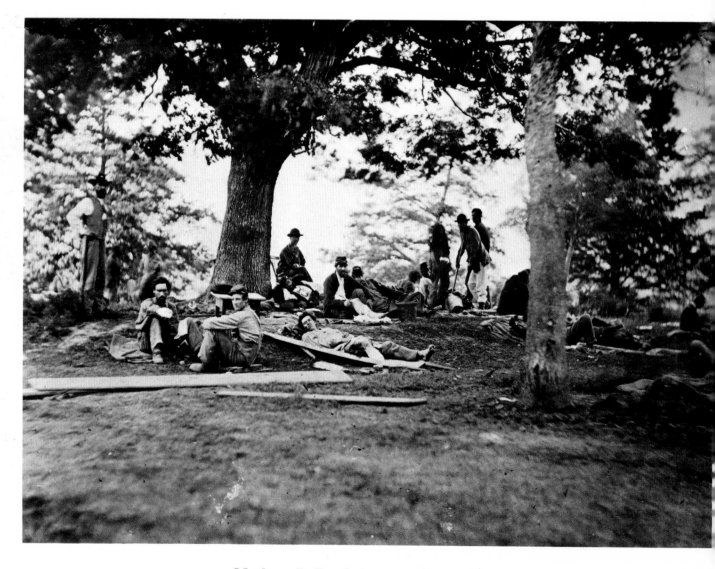

**Mathew B. Brady** (attributed to) 1823–1896
WOUNDED SOLDIERS AT FREDERICKSBURG
*ca. 1862. The Metropolitan Museum of Art, New York, Harris Brisbane Dick Fund*

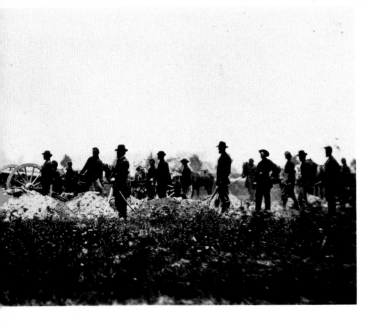

**Mathew B. Brady** (attributed to) 1823–1896
BATTERY B. PENNSYLVANIA LIGHT ARTILLERY IN FRONT OF PETERSBURG
*ca. 1862. The Metropolitan Museum of Art, New York, Harris Brisbane Dick Fund*

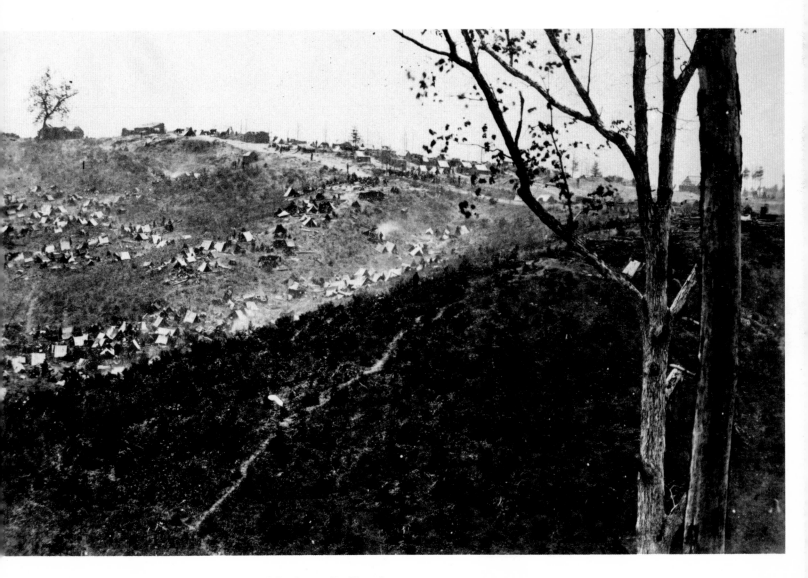

**Mathew B. Brady** (attributed to) 1823–1896
CAMP OF CONFEDERATE PRISONERS, BELLE PLAIN, VIRGINIA
*ca. 1862. The Metropolitan Museum of Art, New York, Harris Brisbane Dick Fund*

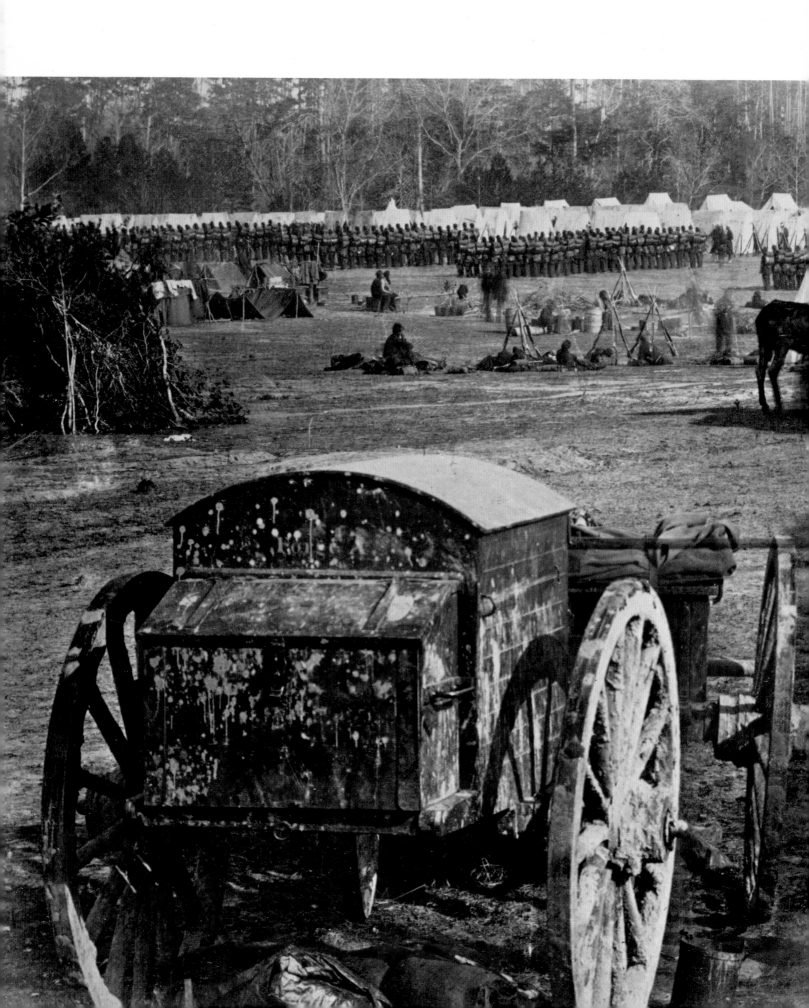

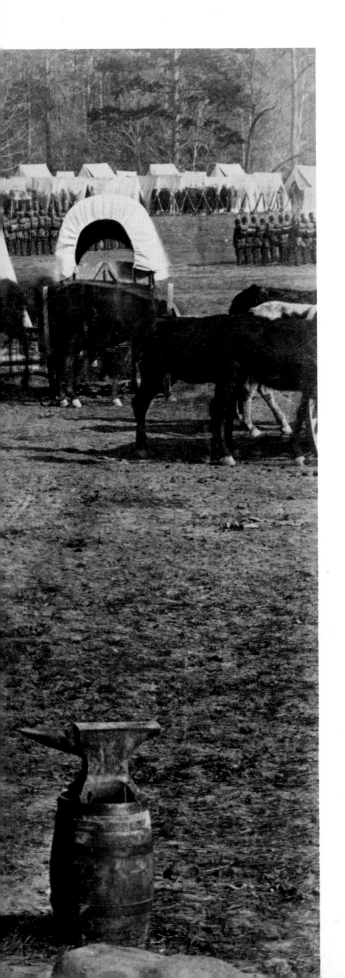

Wood and Gibson (active 1862–1865)
INSPECTION OF TROOPS AT CUMBERLANDING, PAMUNKEY, VIRGINIA
*1862. The Art Institute of Chicago*

(overleaf)
George N. Barnard 1819–1902
CITY OF ATLANTA, GEORGIA, NUMBER 1
*1864. International Museum of Photography at George Eastman House, Rochester, N.Y.*

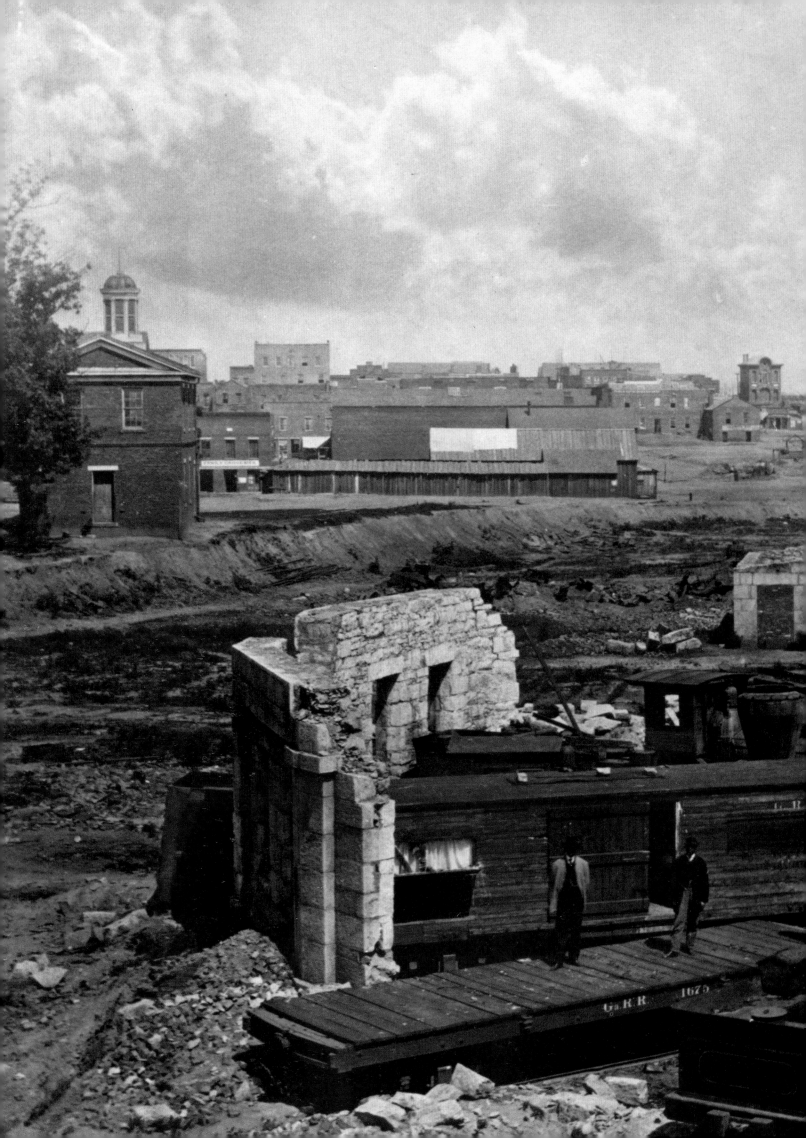

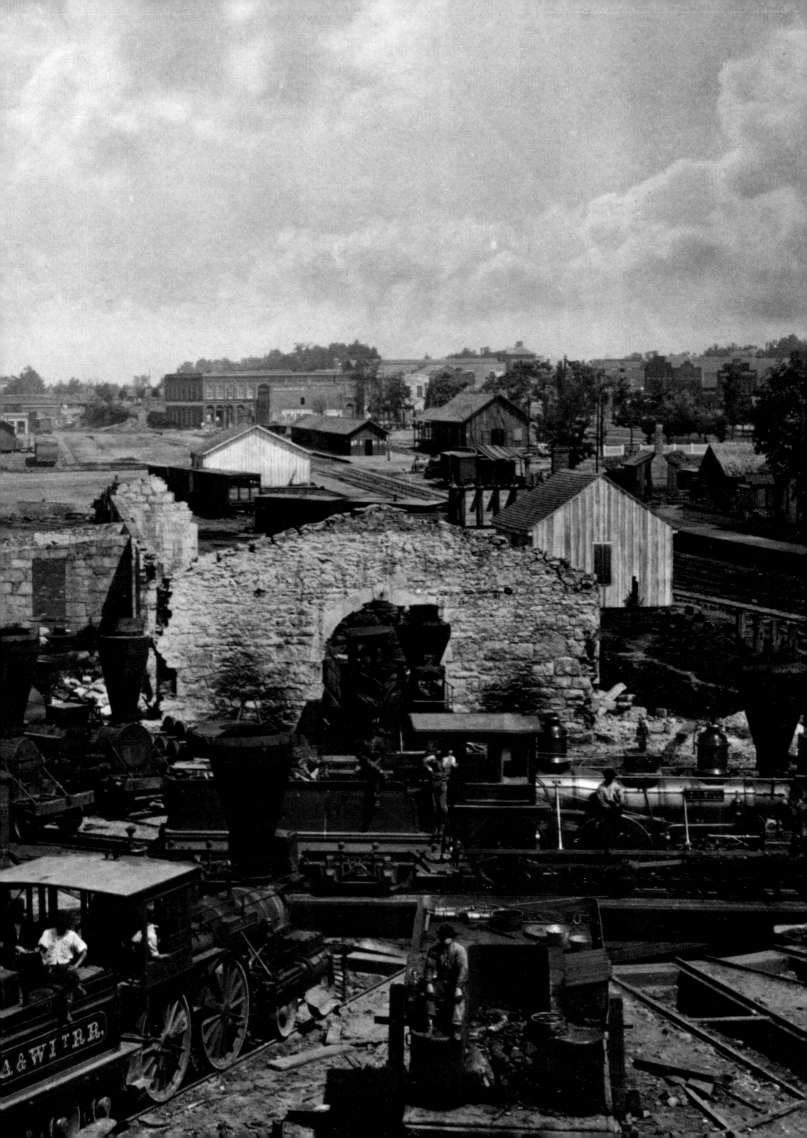

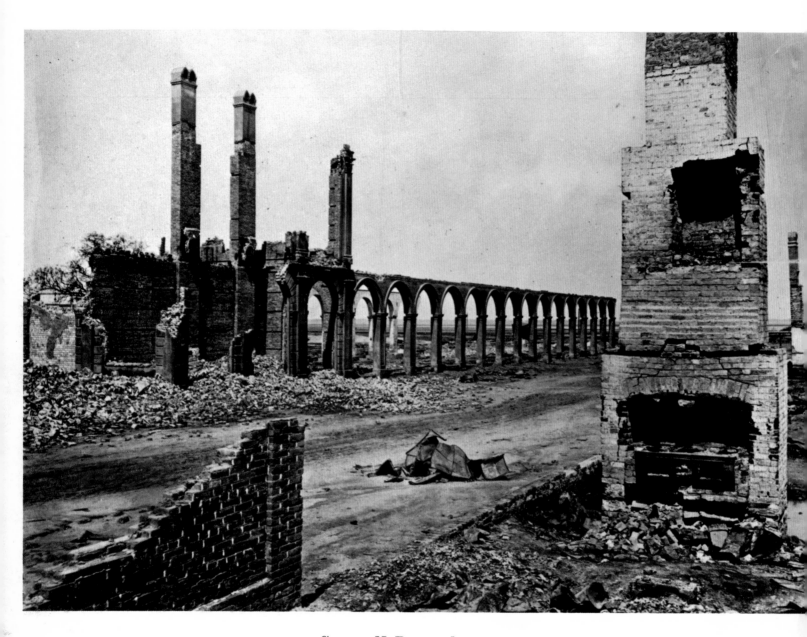

**George N. Barnard** 1819–1902
RUINS OF THE RAILROAD DEPOT, CHARLESTON, SOUTH CAROLINA
*1865. International Museum of Photography at George Eastman House, Rochester, N.Y.*

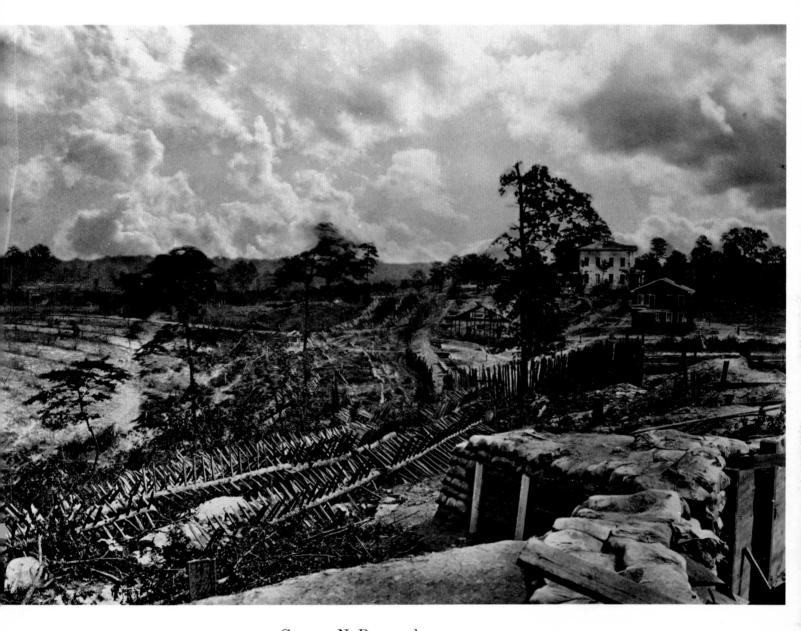

George N. Barnard 1819–1902
REBEL WORKS IN FRONT OF ATLANTA, GEORGIA, NUMBER 1
*1864. International Museum of Photography at George Eastman House, Rochester, N.Y.*

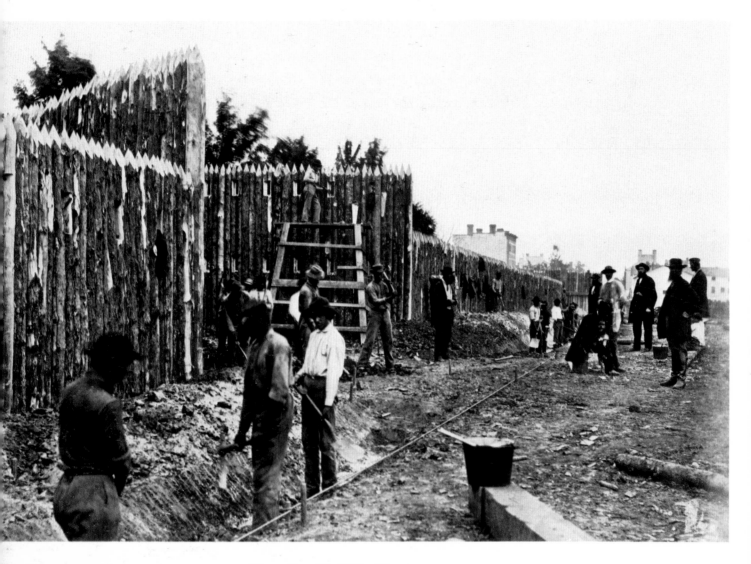

Timothy H. O'Sullivan 1840–1882
STOCKADE BUILT BY GENERAL HAUPT
*ca. 1863. Collection of Lee Witkin, New York*

Timothy H. O'Sullivan 1840–1882
FACILE DECENSUS (CLARENCE C. KING IN ROCK CLEFT)
*ca. 1868. International Museum of Photography at George Eastman House, Rochester, N.Y.*

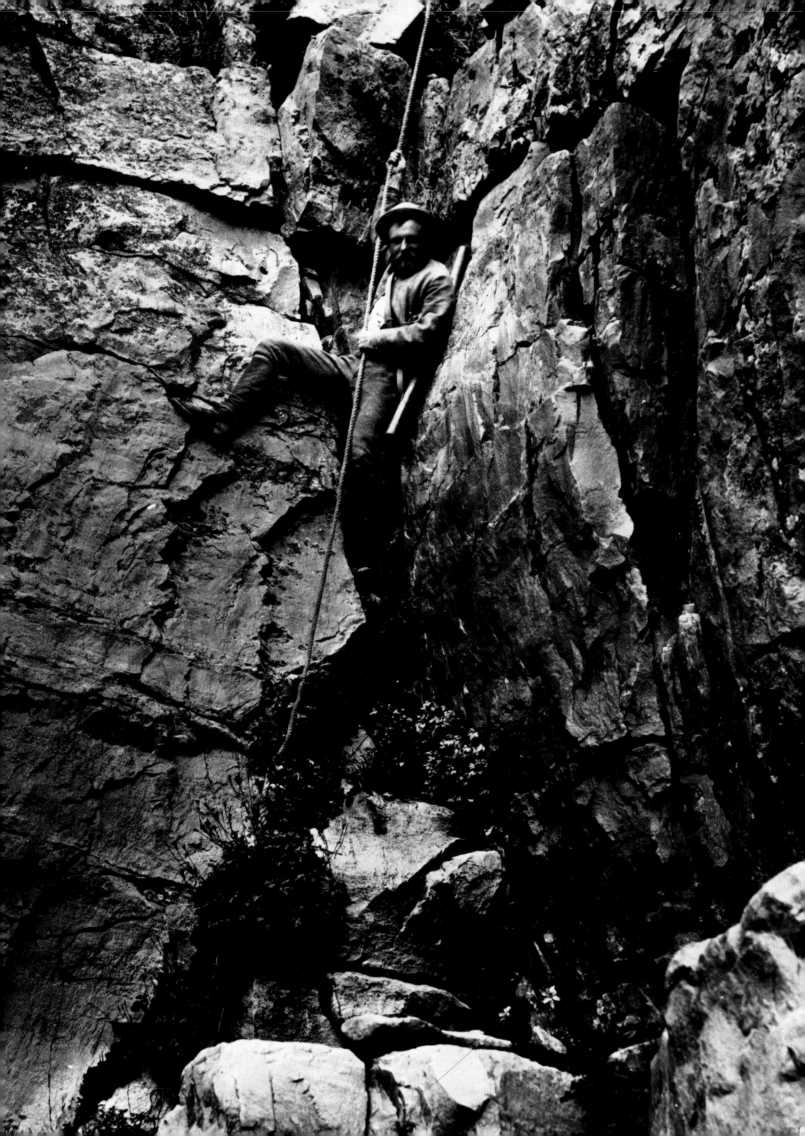

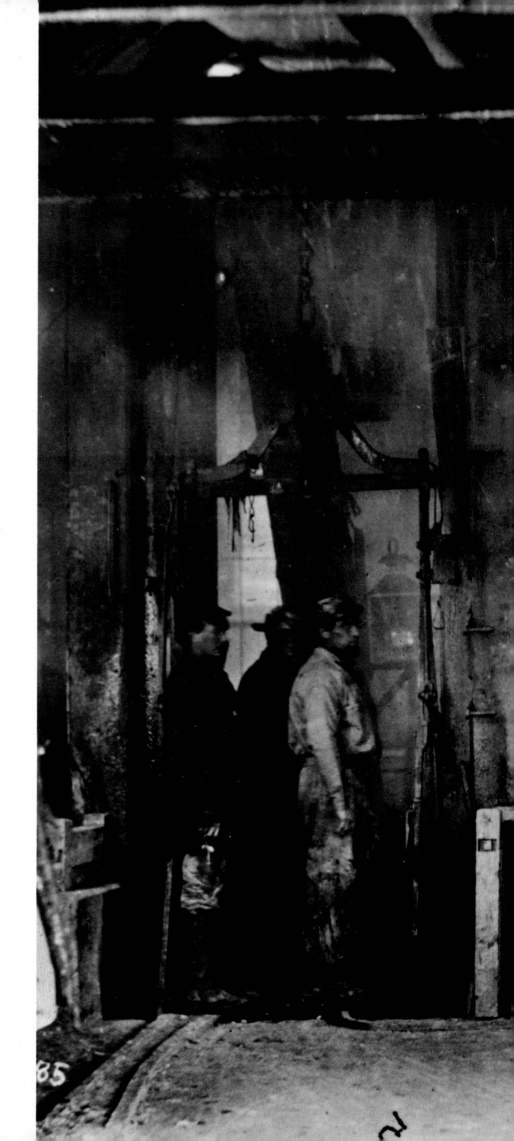

Timothy H. O'Sullivan 1840–1882
MOUTH OF CURTIS SHAFT—SAVAGE MINE
*1868. International Museum of Photography at
George Eastman House, Rochester, N.Y.*

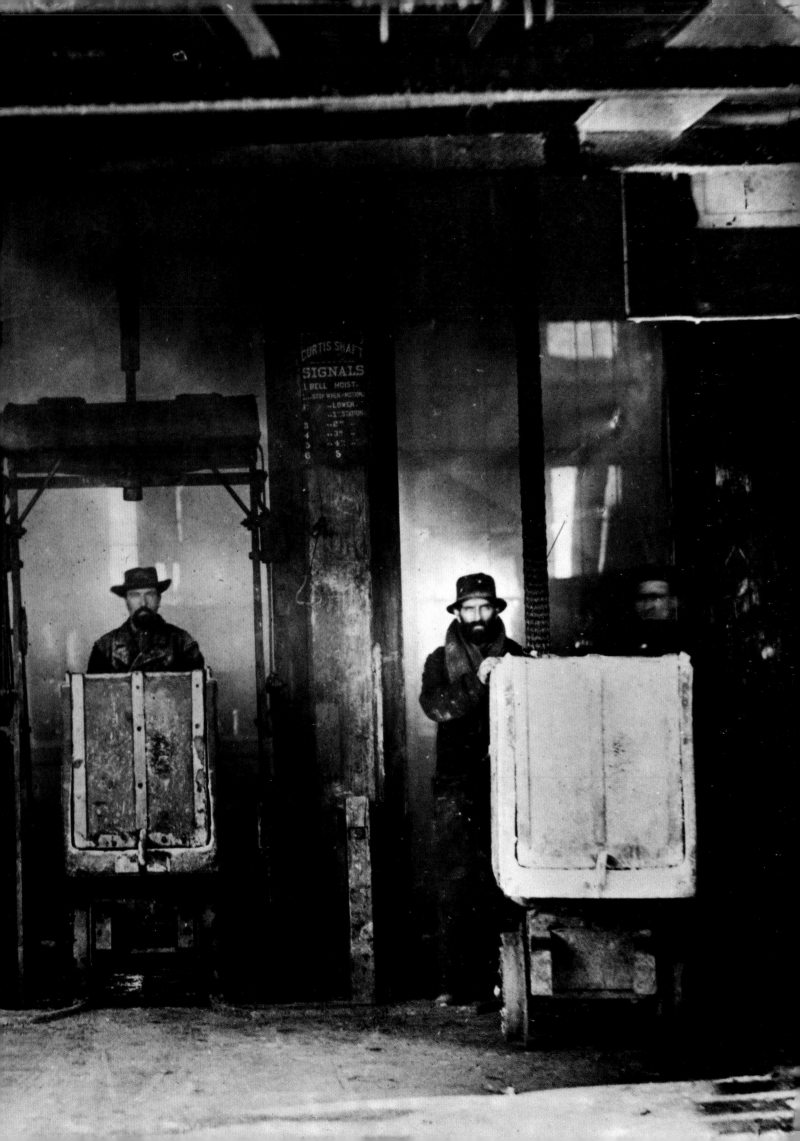

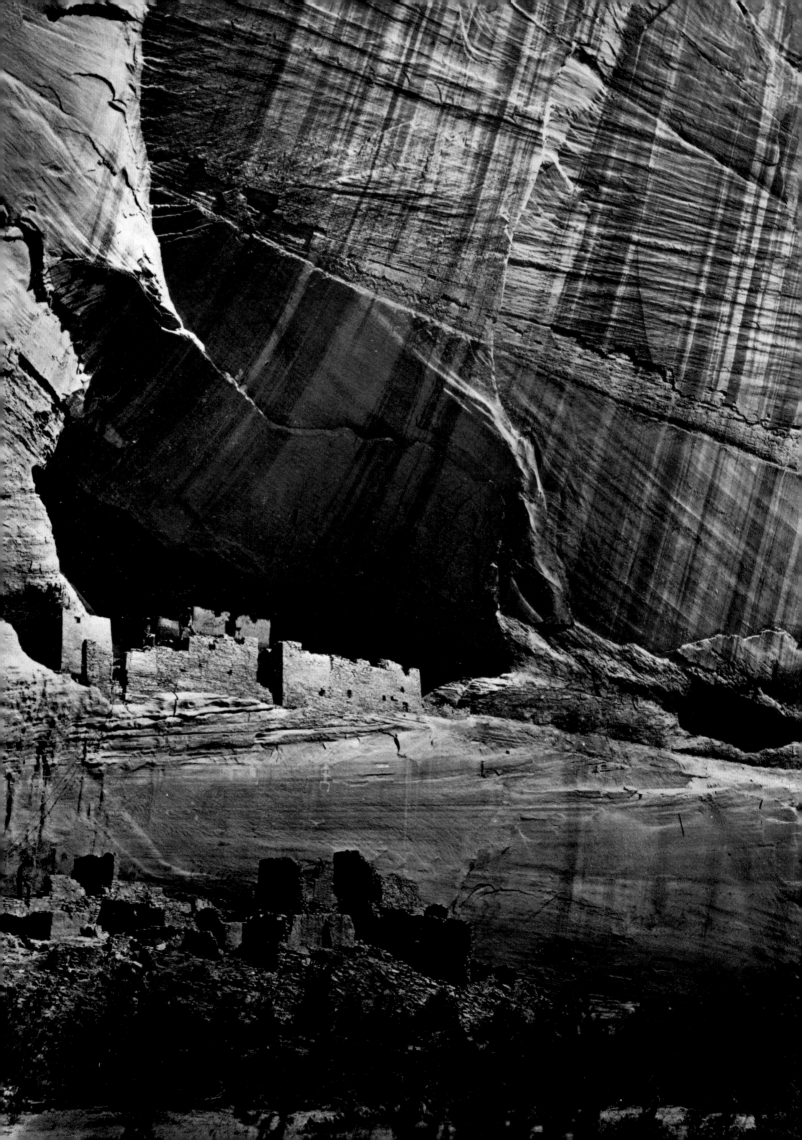

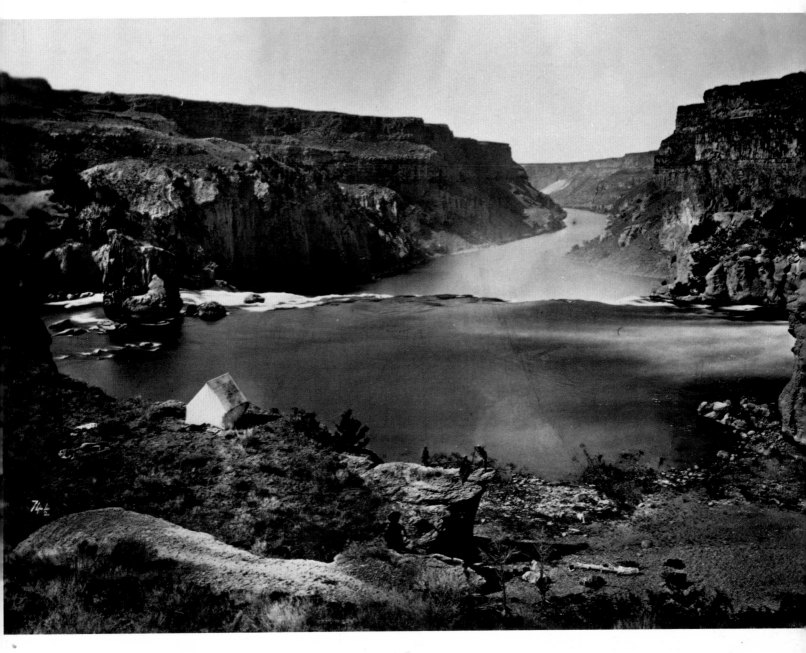

Timothy H. O'Sullivan 1840–1882
SHOSHONE FALLS, IDAHO
1868. International Museum of Photography at George Eastman House, Rochester, N.Y.

Timothy H. O'Sullivan 1840–1882
ANCIENT RUINS IN THE CAÑON DE CHELLE, NEW MEXICO
1873. The Witkin Gallery, Inc., New York

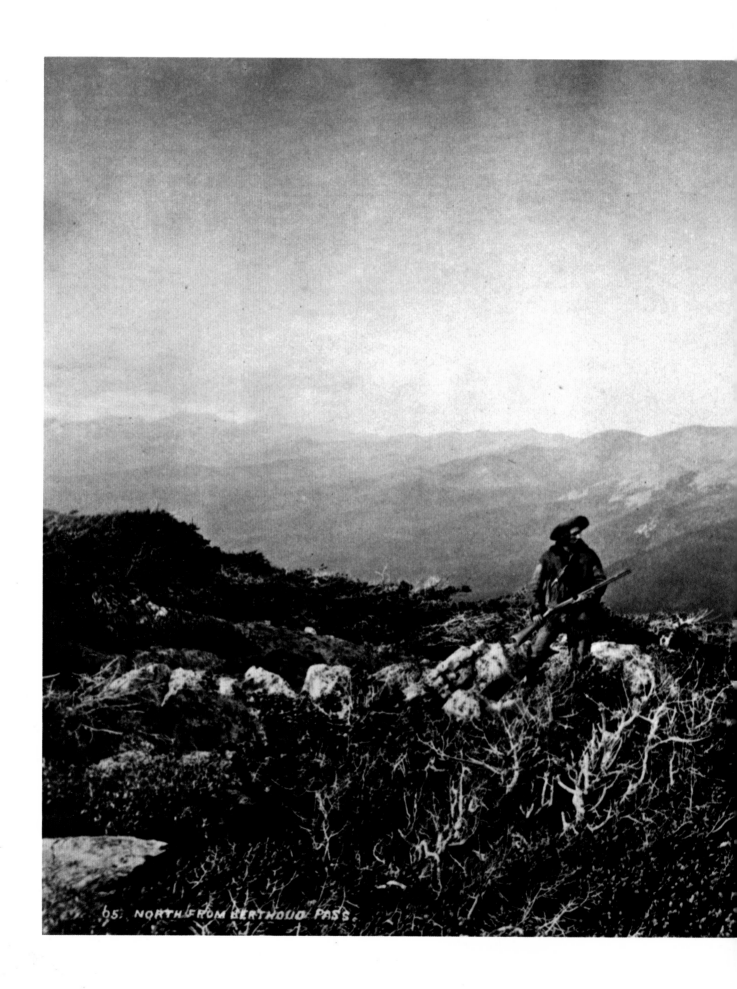

65. NORTH FROM BERTHOUD PASS

42

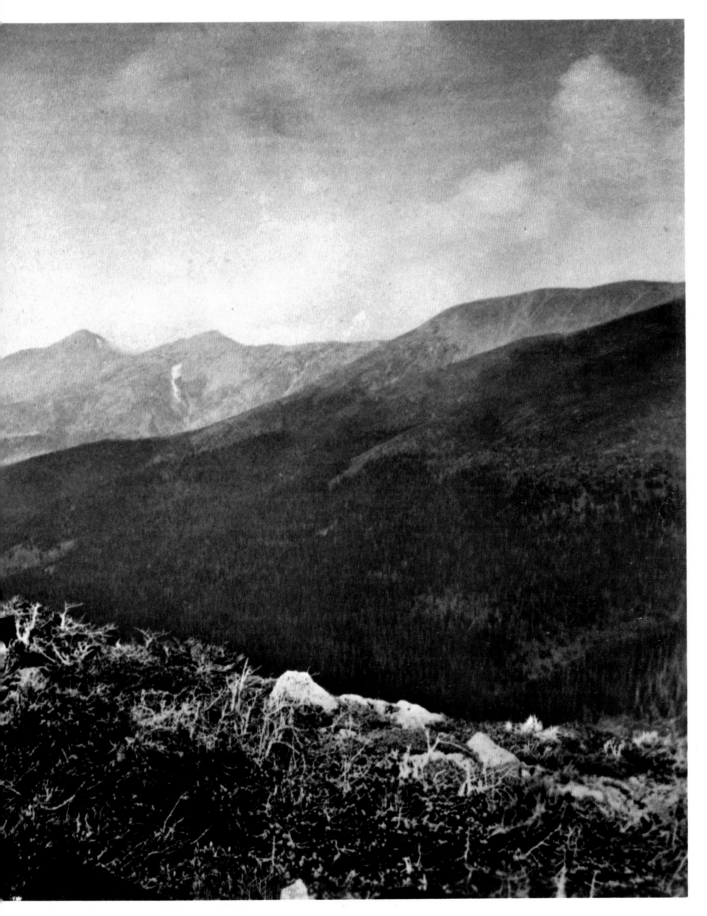

43

**William Henry Jackson** 1843–1942
NORTH FROM BERTHOUD PASS
*1874. International Museum of Photography at George Eastman House, Rochester, N.Y.*

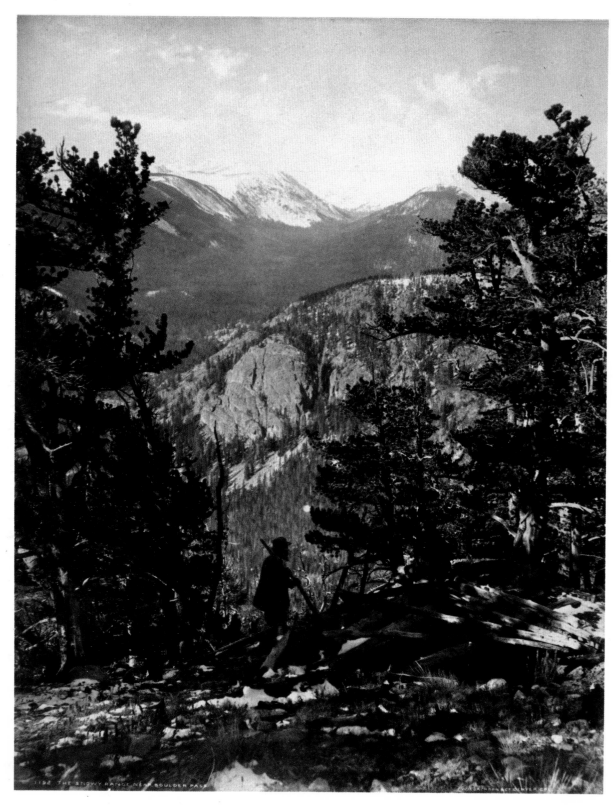

**William Henry Jackson** 1843–1942
THE SNOWY RANGE NEAR BOULDER PASS, COLORADO
*ca. 1875. International Museum of Photography at George Eastman House, Rochester, N.Y.*

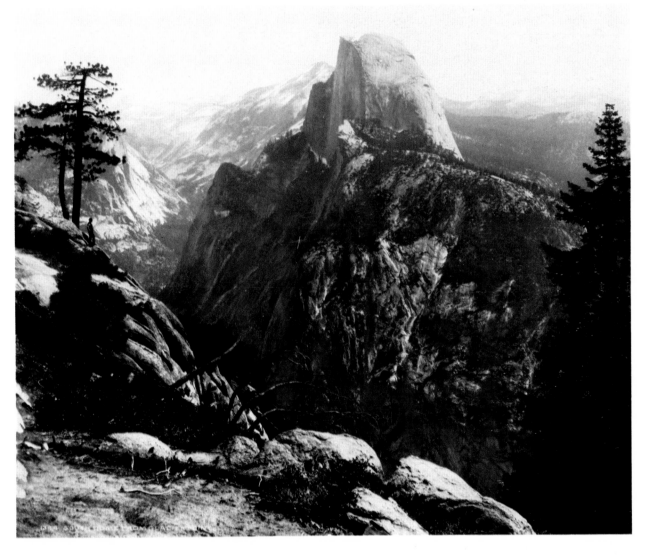

**William Henry Jackson** 1843–1942
SOUTH DOME FROM GLACIER POINT, CALIFORNIA
*ca. 1875. International Museum of Photography at George Eastman House, Rochester, N.Y.*

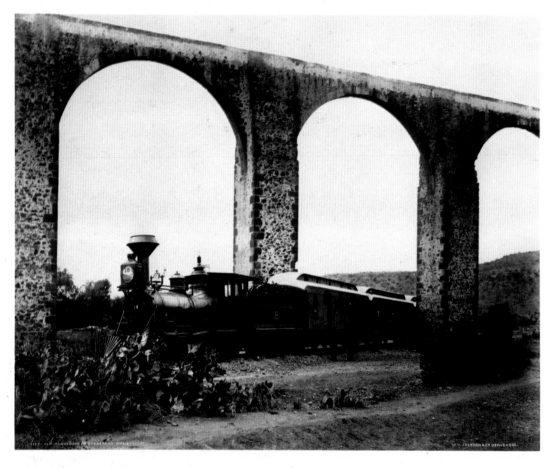

**William Henry Jackson** 1843–1942
OLD AQUEDUCT AT QUERETARO, MEXICO
*ca. 1880. The Witkin Gallery, Inc., New York*

**William Henry Jackson** 1843–1942
FALLS OF THE SAN MIGUEL, COLORADO
*ca. 1875. International Museum of Photography at George Eastman House, Rochester, N.Y.*

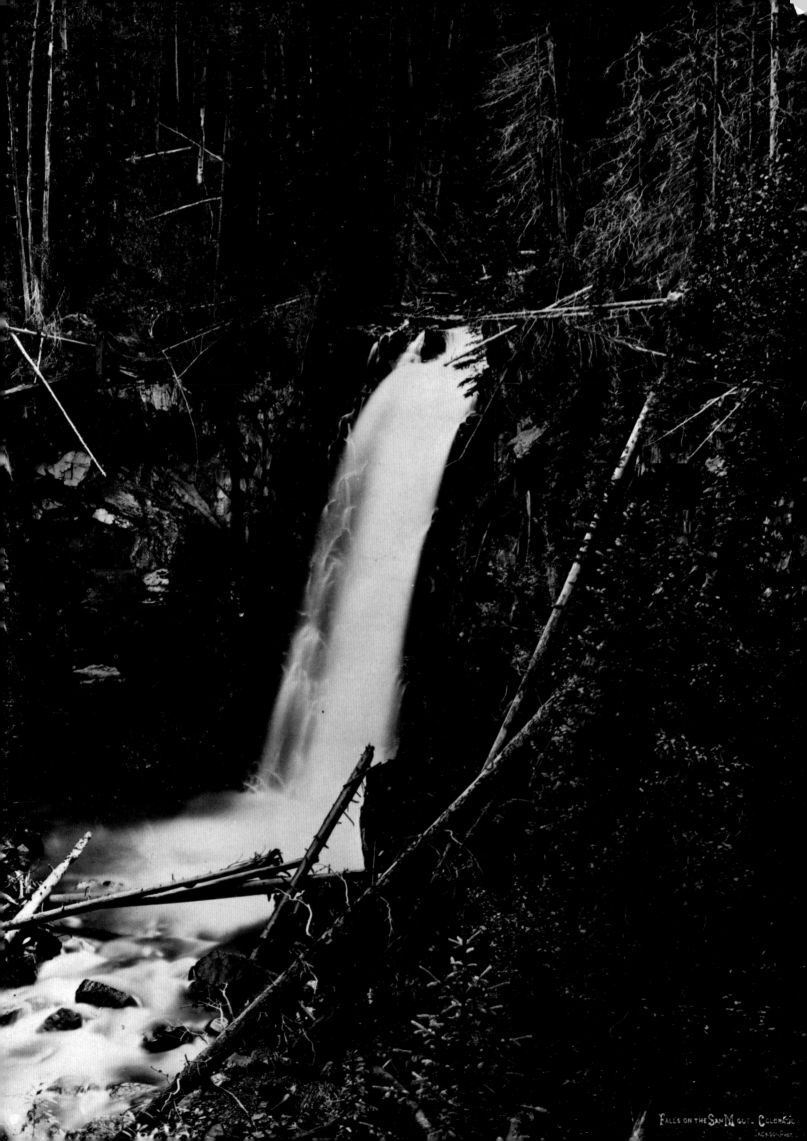

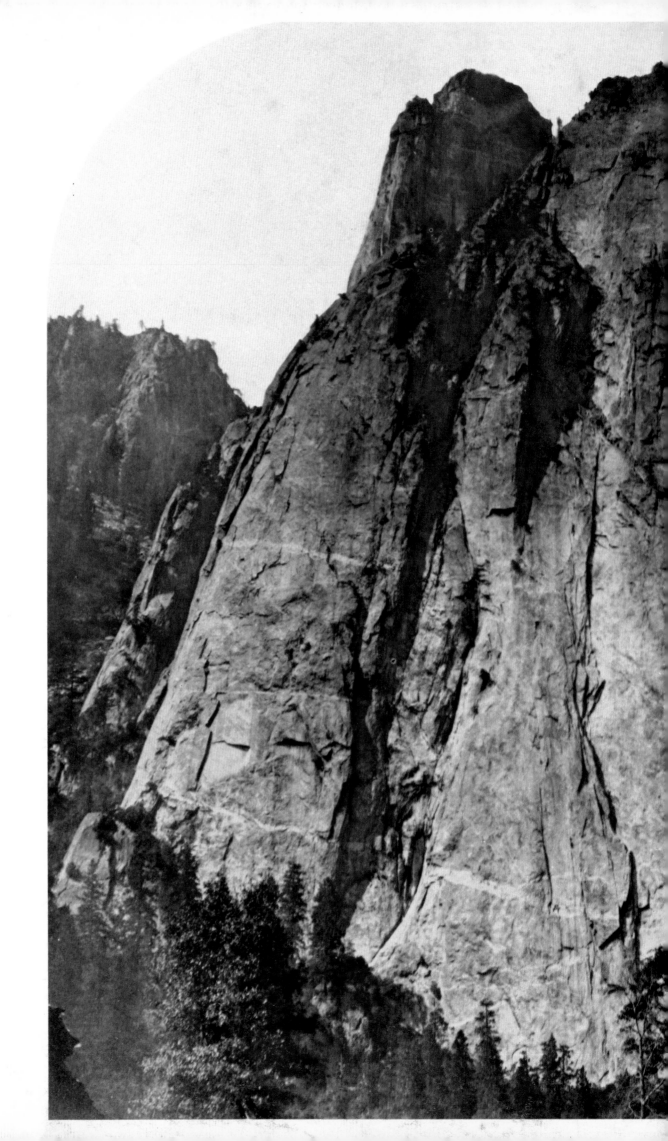

48

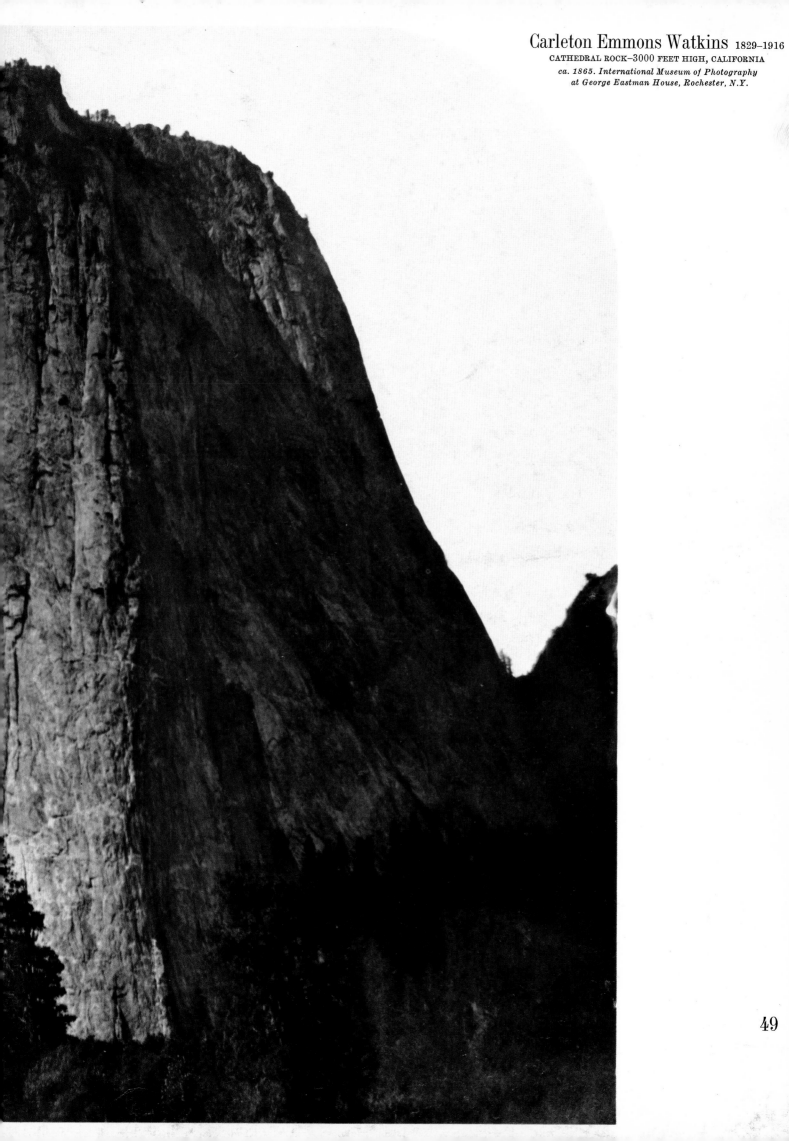

Carleton Emmons Watkins 1829–1916

CATHEDRAL ROCK—3000 FEET HIGH, CALIFORNIA

ca. 1865. International Museum of Photography
at George Eastman House, Rochester, N.Y.

49

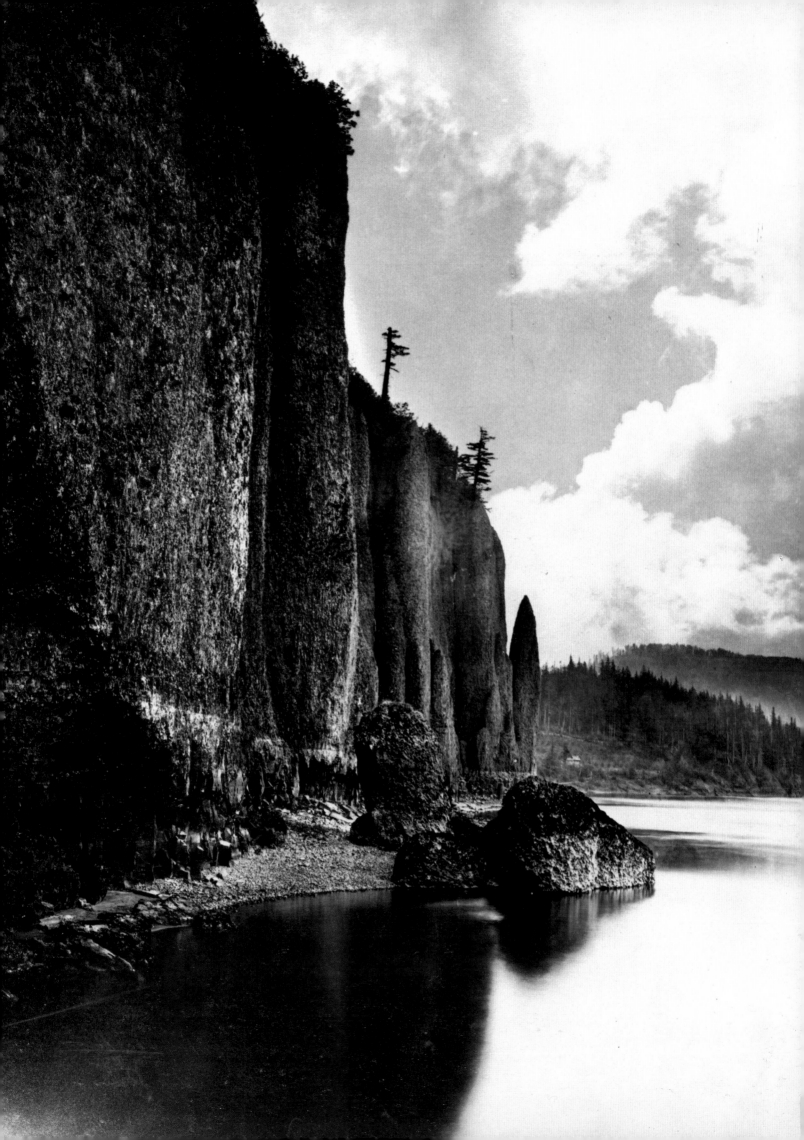

**Carleton Emmons Watkins** 1829–1916
CAPE HORN, COLUMBIA RIVER, OREGON
*ca. 1870. International Museum of Photography at George Eastman House, Rochester, N.Y.*

**Carleton Emmons Watkins** 1829–1916
PI-WY-AC OR VERNAL FALLS, CALIFORNIA
*ca. 1865. International Museum of Photography at George Eastman House, Rochester, N.Y.*

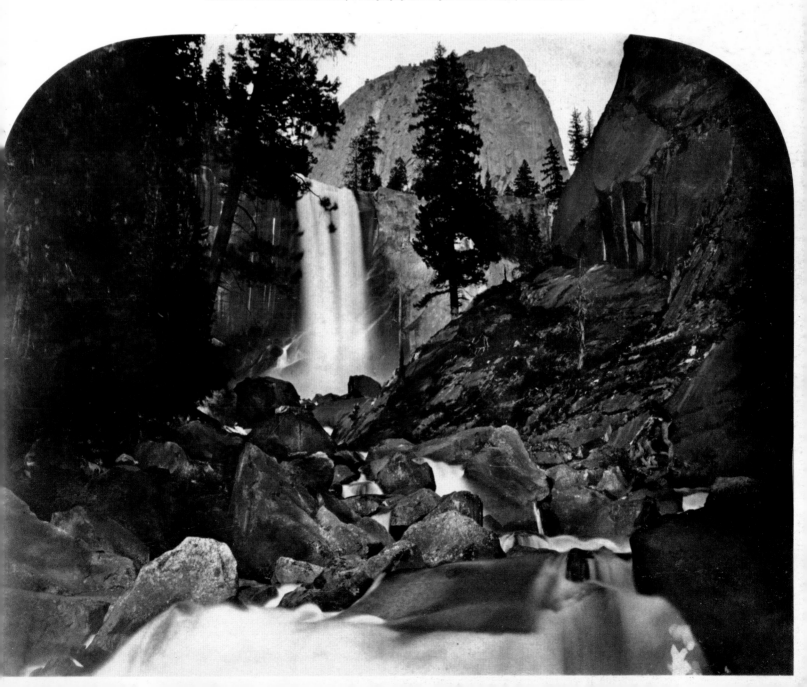

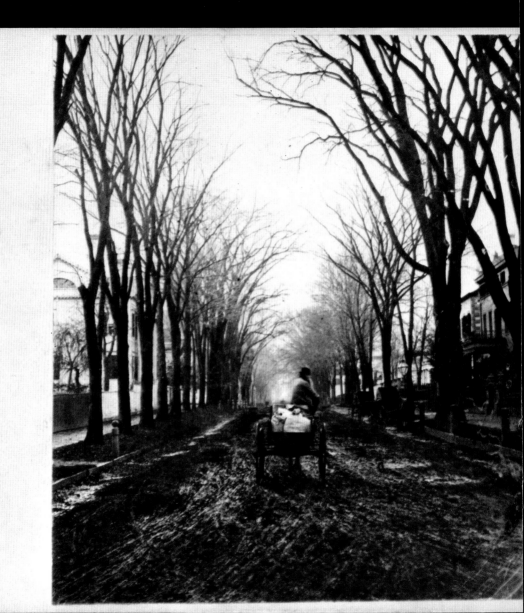

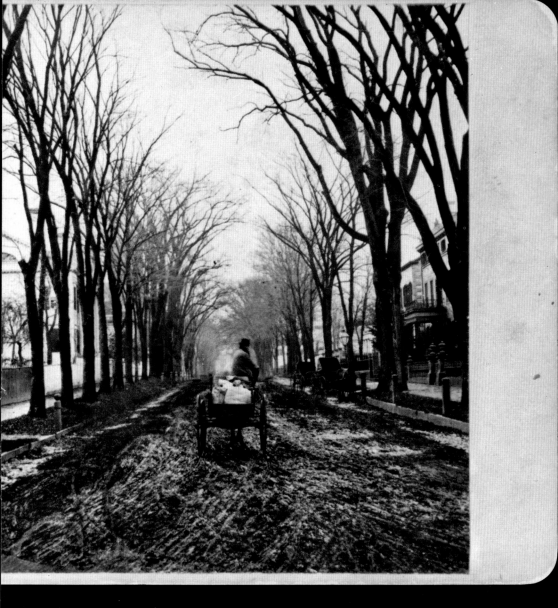

# Henry S. Peck (active 1864–1870)

VIEW OF NEW HAVEN, CONNECTICUT

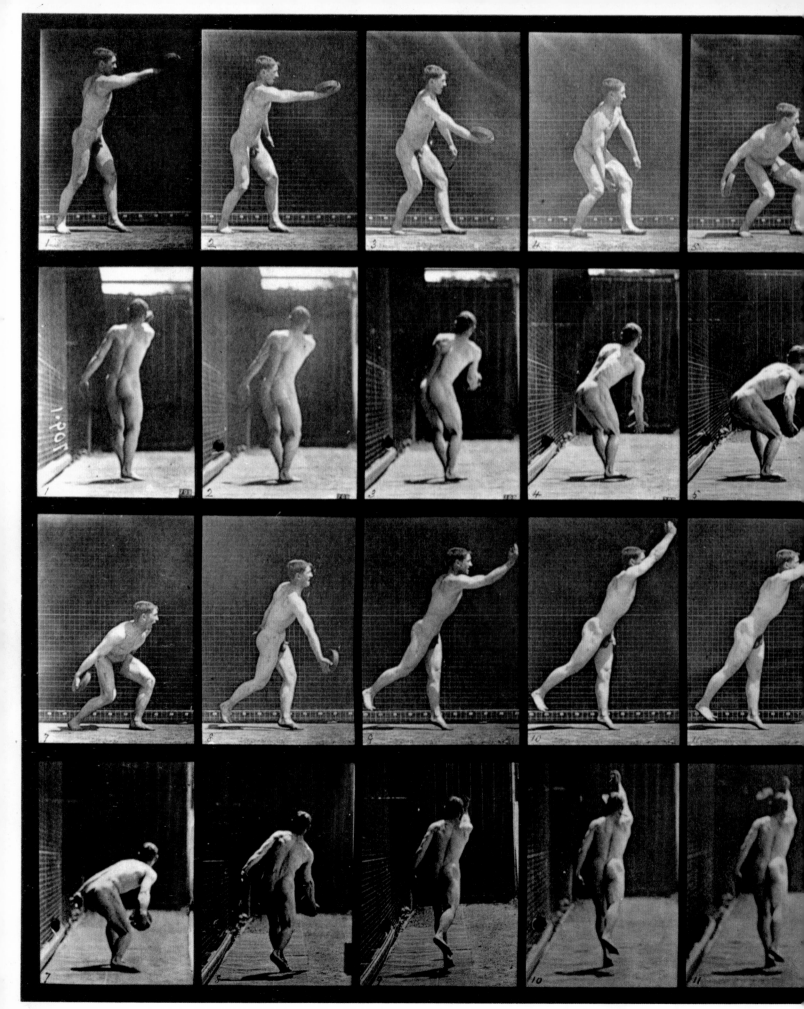

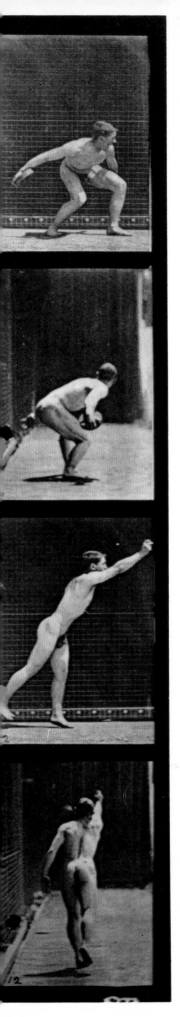

Eadweard Muybridge 1830–1904
ANIMAL LOCOMOTION : PLATE 307
*1887. The Metropolitan Museum of Art, New York, gift of the Philadelphia Commercial Museum*

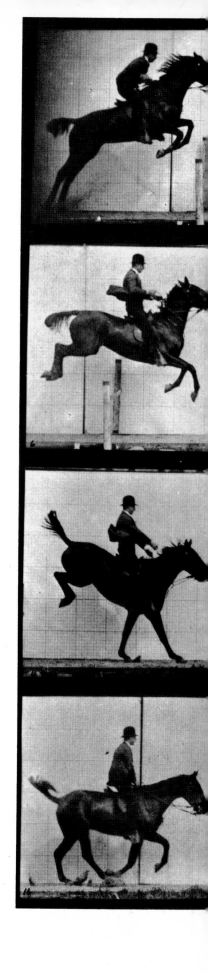

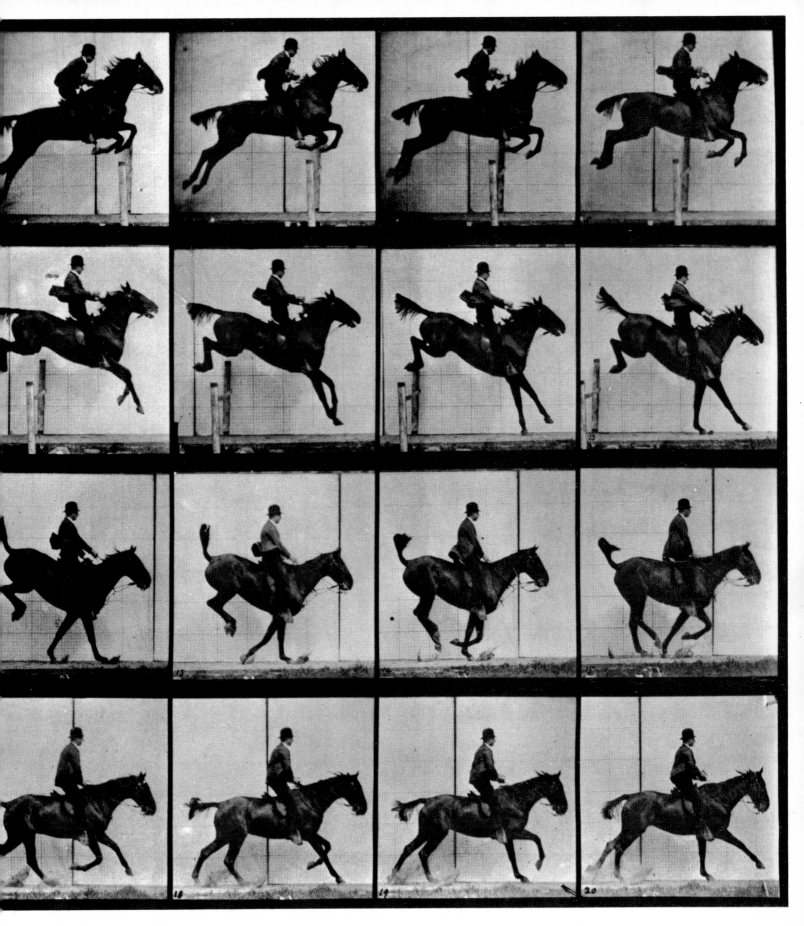

## Eadweard Muybridge 1830–1904
ANIMAL LOCOMOTION : PLATE 637

*1887. The Metropolitan Museum of Art, New York, gift of the Philadelphia Commercial Museum*

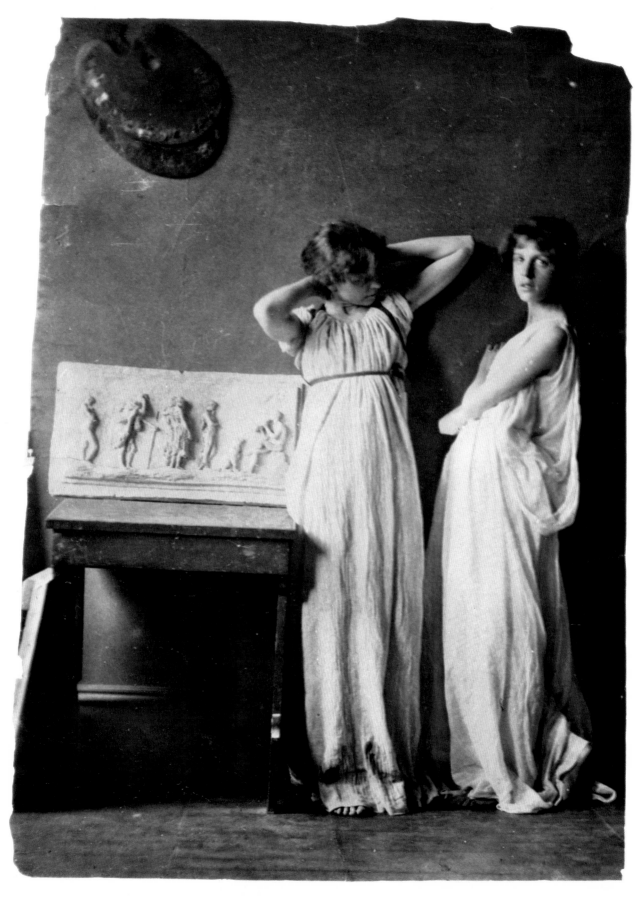

**Thomas Eakins** 1844–1916
TWO PUPILS IN GREEK DRESS BESIDE PLASTER CAST OF EAKINS' "ARCADIA"
*ca. 1880. The Metropolitan Museum of Art, New York, David Hunter McAlpin Fund*

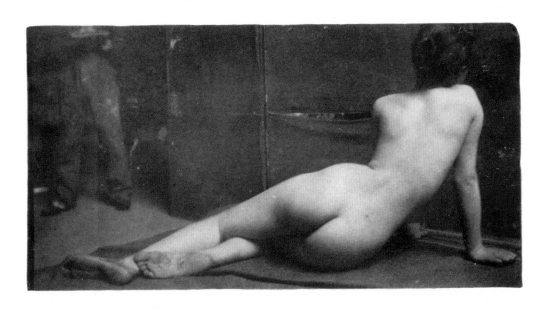

## Thomas Eakins 1844–1916
### TWO NUDE STUDIES
*ca. 1880. The Metropolitan Museum of Art, New York, David Hunter McAlpin Fund*

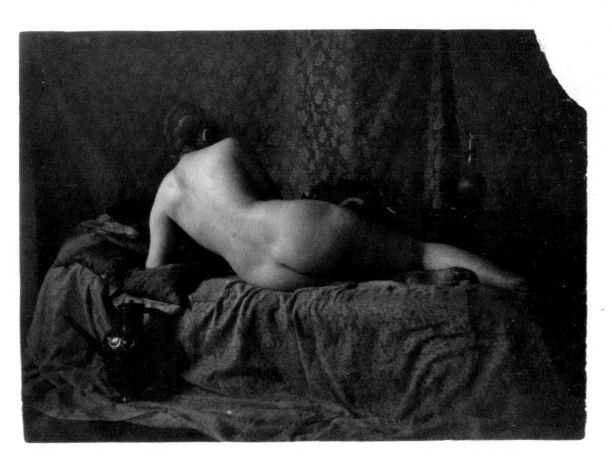

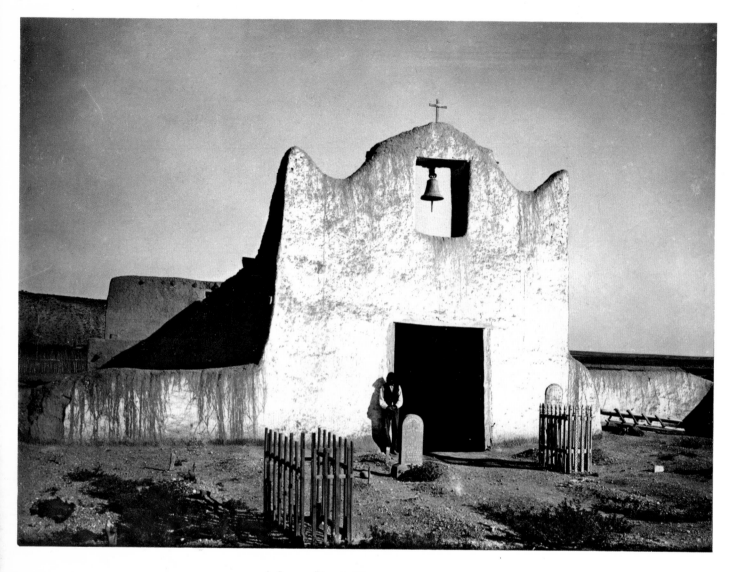

### Adam Clark Vroman 1856–1916
MISSION–SANTA CLARA PUEBLO, NEW MEXICO

*1899. Collection of the Friends of Photography, Carmel, California, courtesy History Division,*
*Natural History Museum of Los Angeles County*

### Adam Clark Vroman 1856–1916
NAVAJO MAN–"COYOTE"

*1901. Collection of the Friends of Photography, Carmel, California, courtesy History Division,*
*Natural History Museum of Los Angeles County*

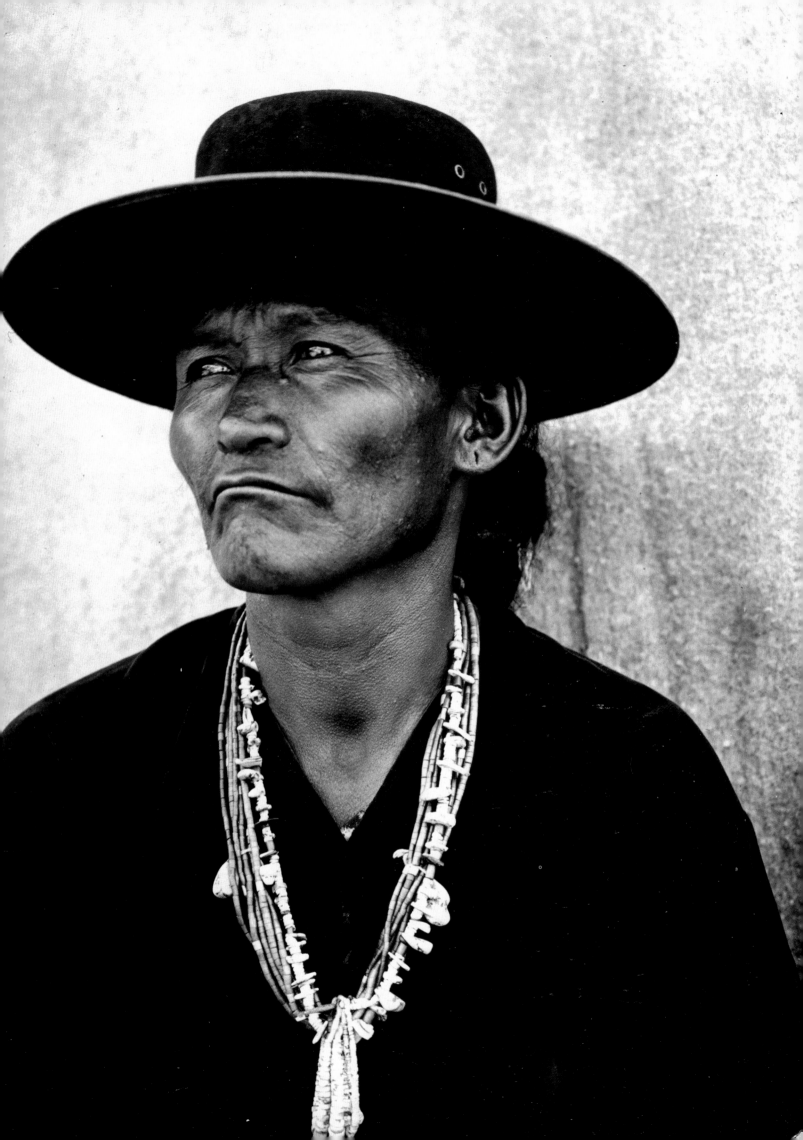

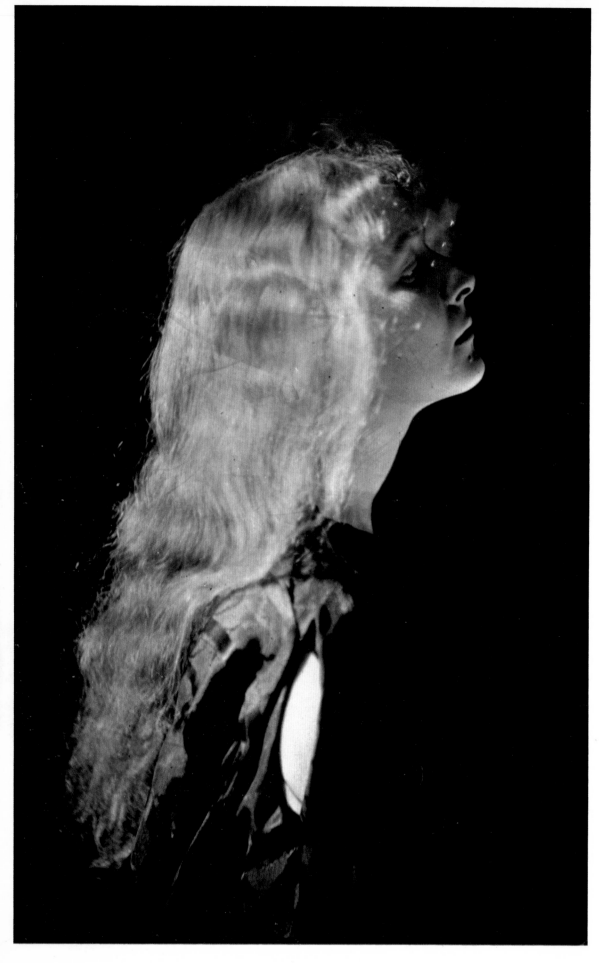

## Kate Matthews 1870–1956
### MARY JOHNSON
*ca. 1900. University of Louisville, Louisville, Ky., Photographic Archives*

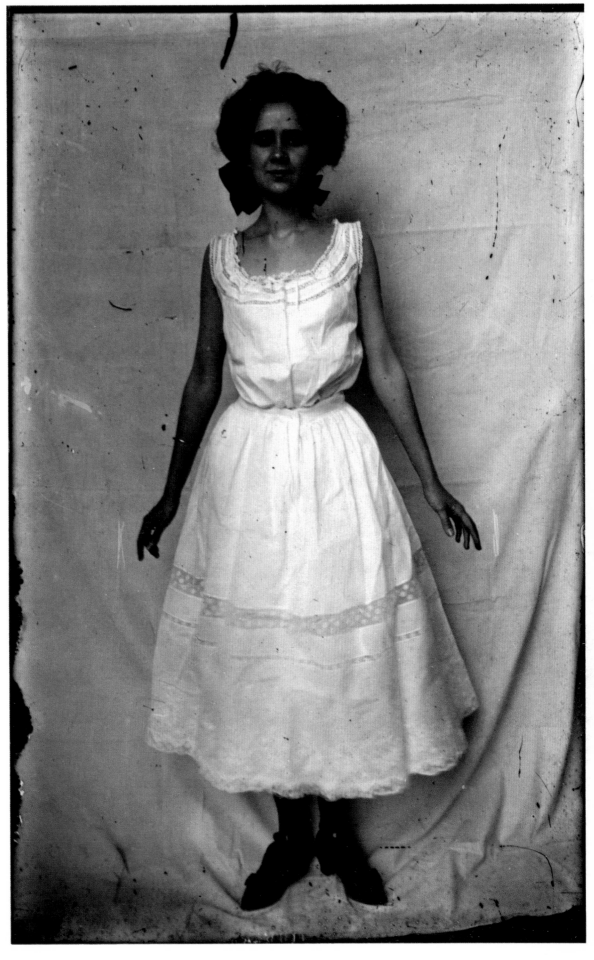

**Kate Matthews** 1870–1956
THE LITTLE COLONEL
*1898. University of Louisville, Louisville, Ky., Photographic Archives*

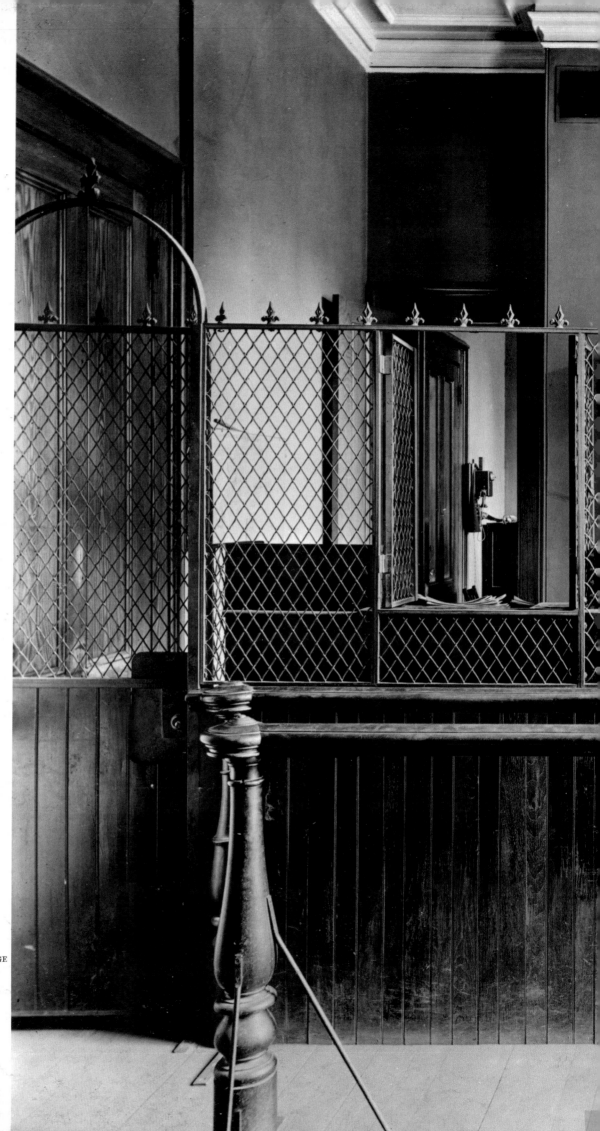

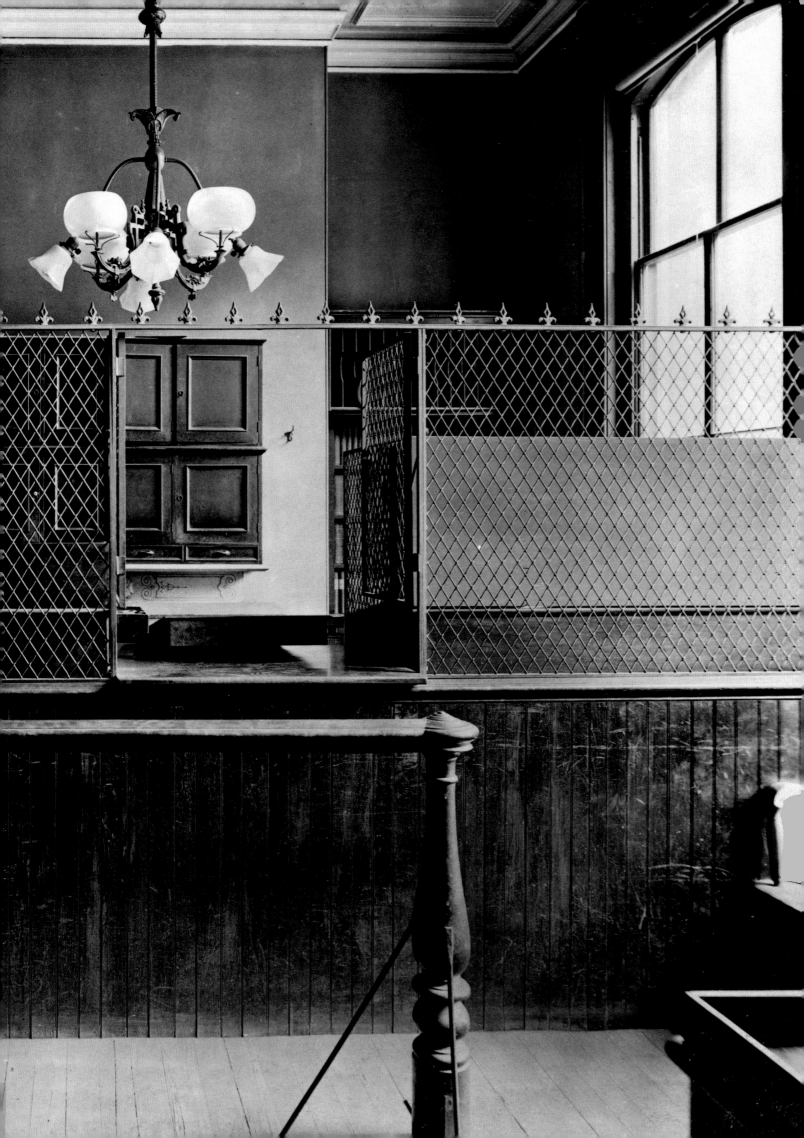

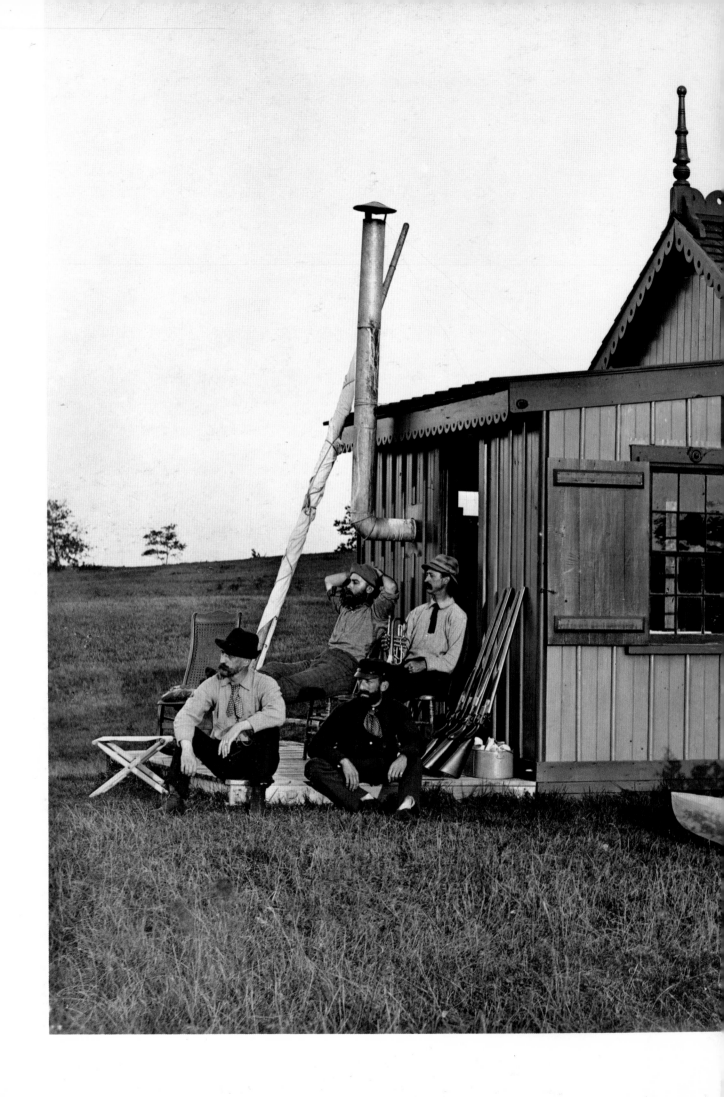

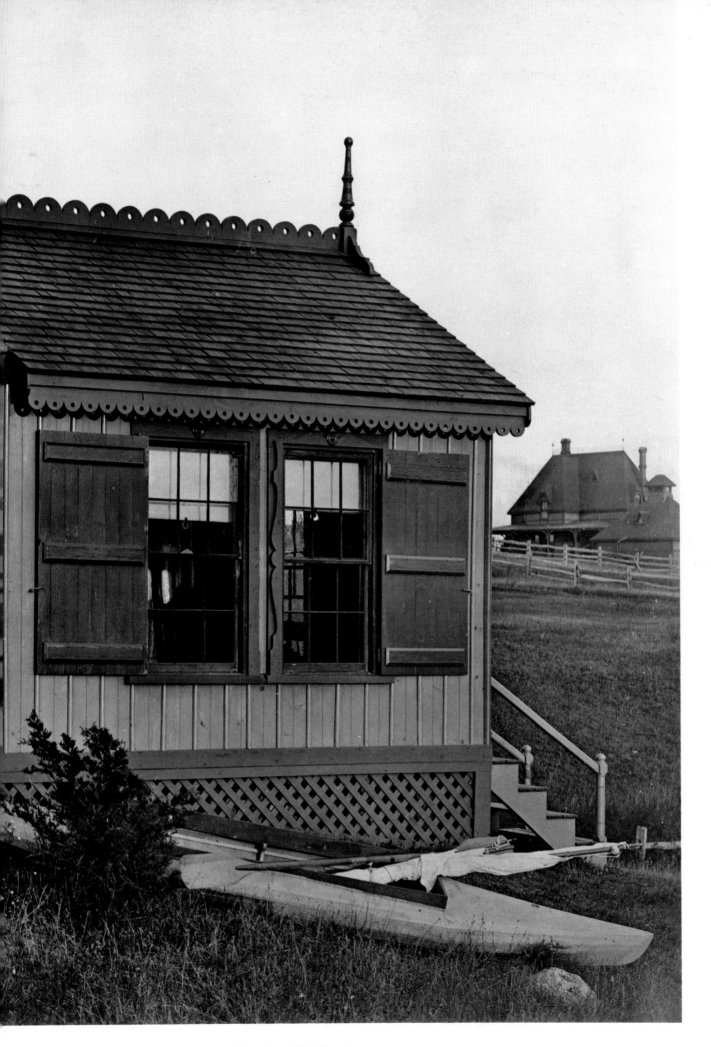

## Charles H. Currier 1851–1938
FOUR HUNTERS AND THEIR CABIN
*ca. 1900. The Library of Congress, Prints and Photographs Division, Washington, D.C.*

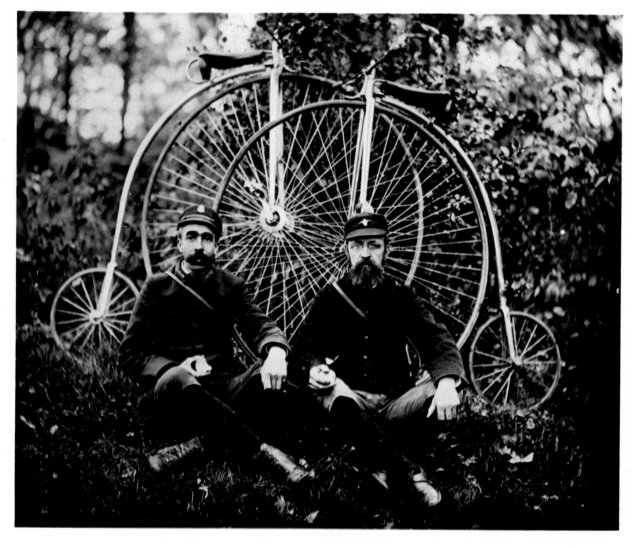

**Charles H. Currier** 1851–1938
THE BICYCLE MESSENGERS SEATED
*ca. 1900. The Library of Congress, Prints and Photographs Division, Washington, D.C.*

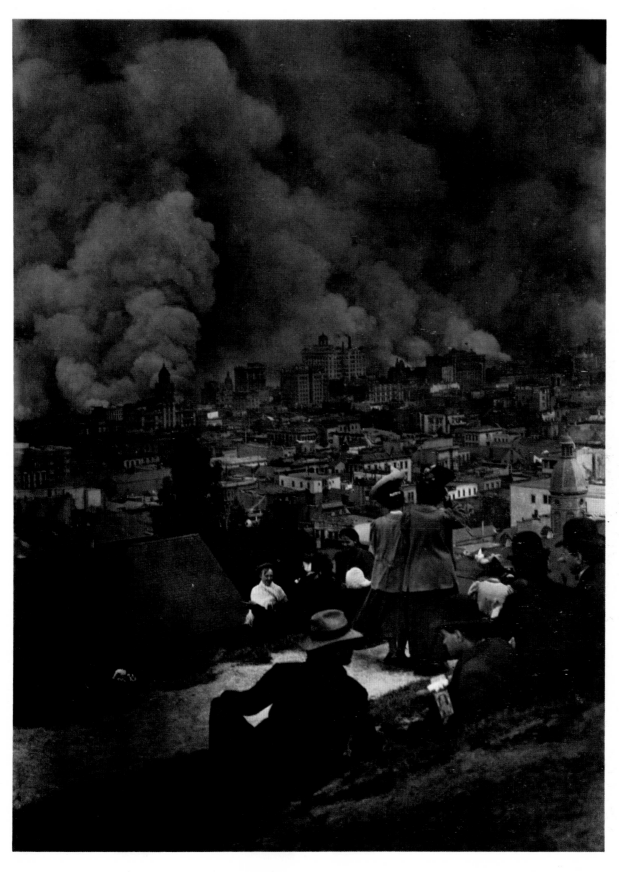

**Arnold Genthe** 1869–1942
WATCHING THE APPROACH OF THE FIRE
*1906. The Museum of Modern Art, New York, gift of the Photographer*

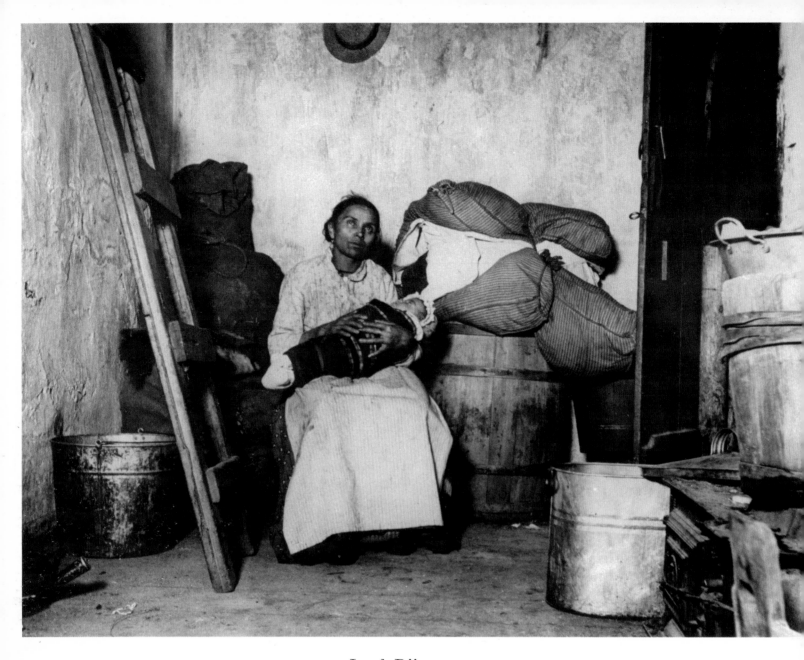

Jacob Riis 1849–1914
ITALIAN MOTHER AND HER BABY IN JERSEY STREET
*ca. 1889. The Museum of the City of New York, The Jacob A. Riis Collection*

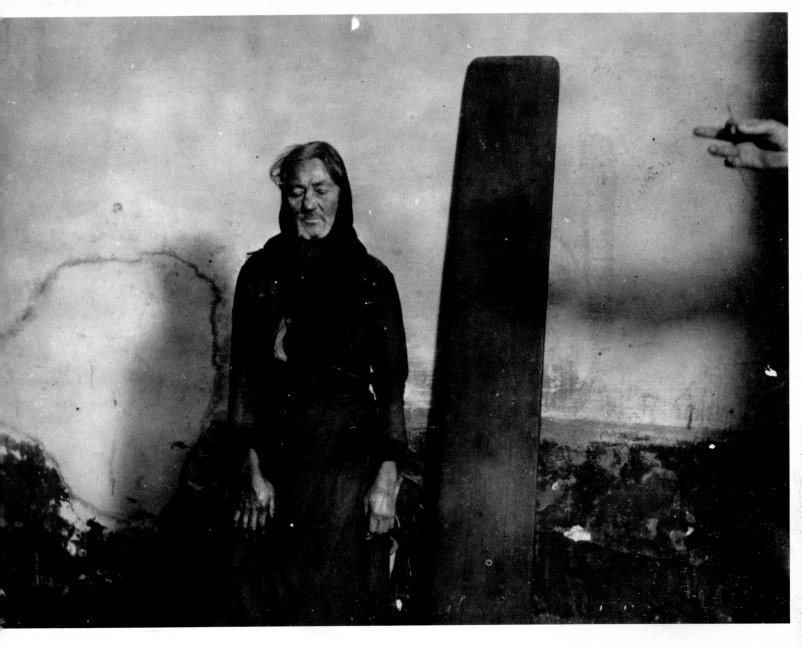

**Jacob Riis** 1849–1914

POLICE STATION LODGER

*ca. 1890. The Museum of the City of New York, The Jacob A. Riis Collection*

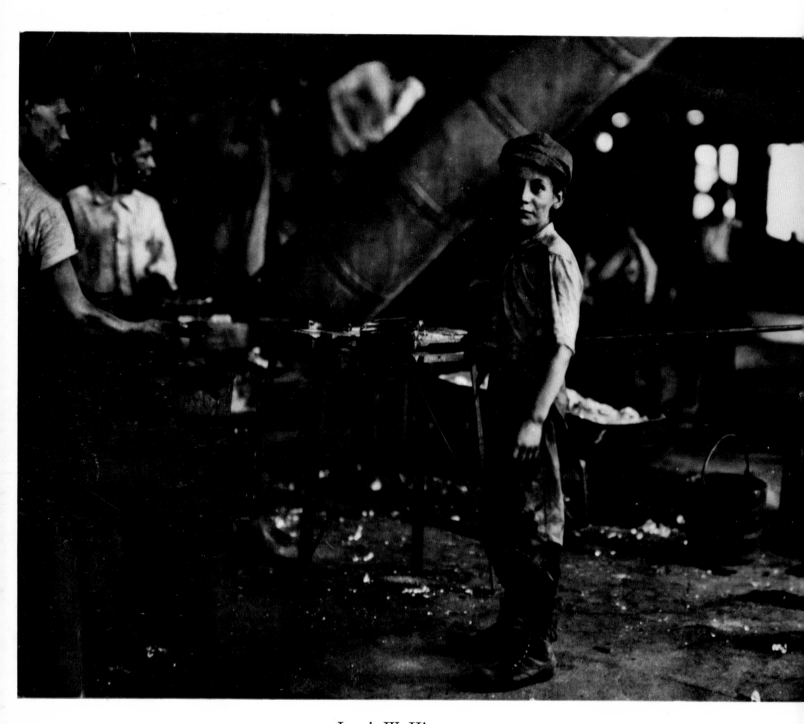

**Lewis W. Hine** 1874–1940
CARRYING-IN BOY IN A GLASS FACTORY, ALEXANDRIA, VIRGINIA
*1909. International Museum of Photography at George Eastman House, Rochester, N.Y.*

## Lewis W. Hine 1874–1940
STEELWORKER.  FROM THE "PITTSBURGH SURVEY"
*ca. 1908. International Museum of Photography at George Eastman House, Rochester, N.Y.*

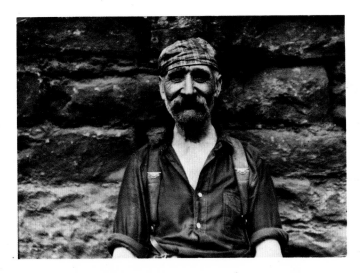

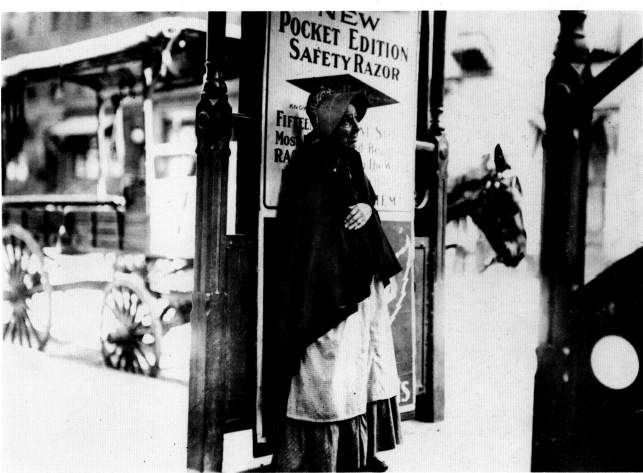

## Lewis W. Hine 1874–1940
BEGGAR, NEW YORK
*1910. International Museum of Photography at George Eastman House, Rochester, N.Y.*

73

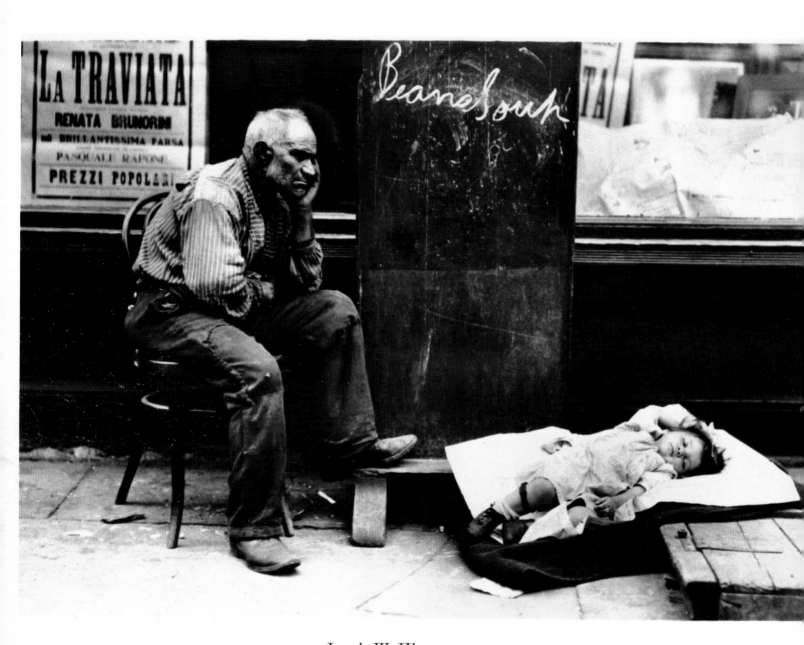

**Lewis W. Hine** 1874–1940
FRESH AIR FOR THE BABY, NEW YORK EASTSIDE
*1907. International Museum of Photography at George Eastman House, Rochester, N.Y.*

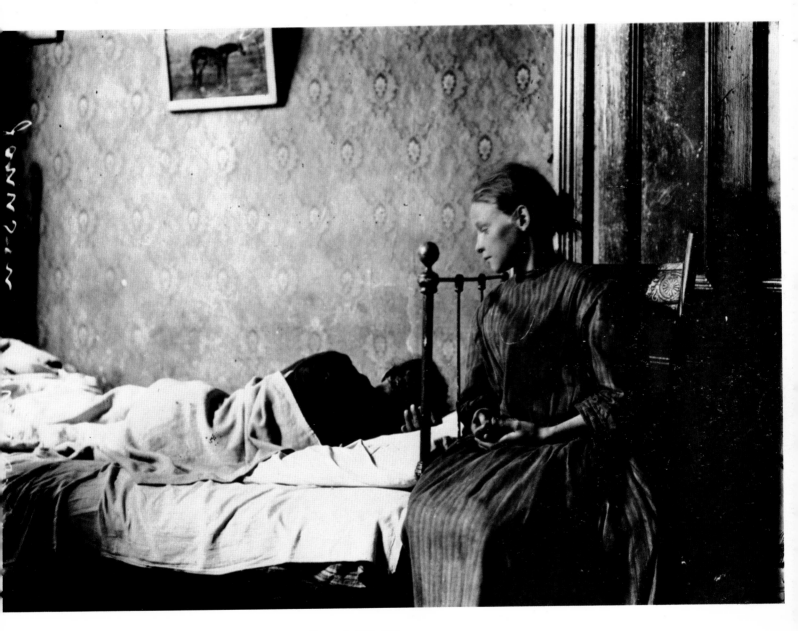

**Lewis W. Hine** 1874–1940

GIRL AND FATHER

*ca. 1908. International Museum of Photography at George Eastman House, Rochester, N.Y.*

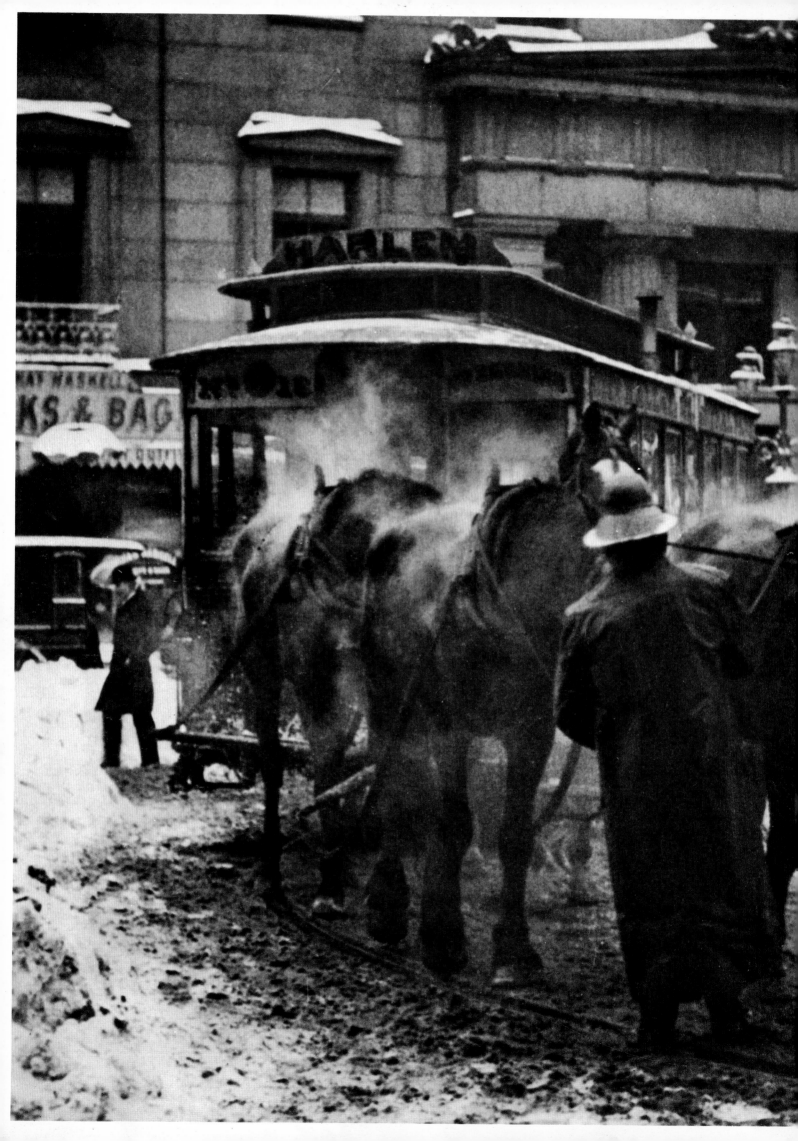

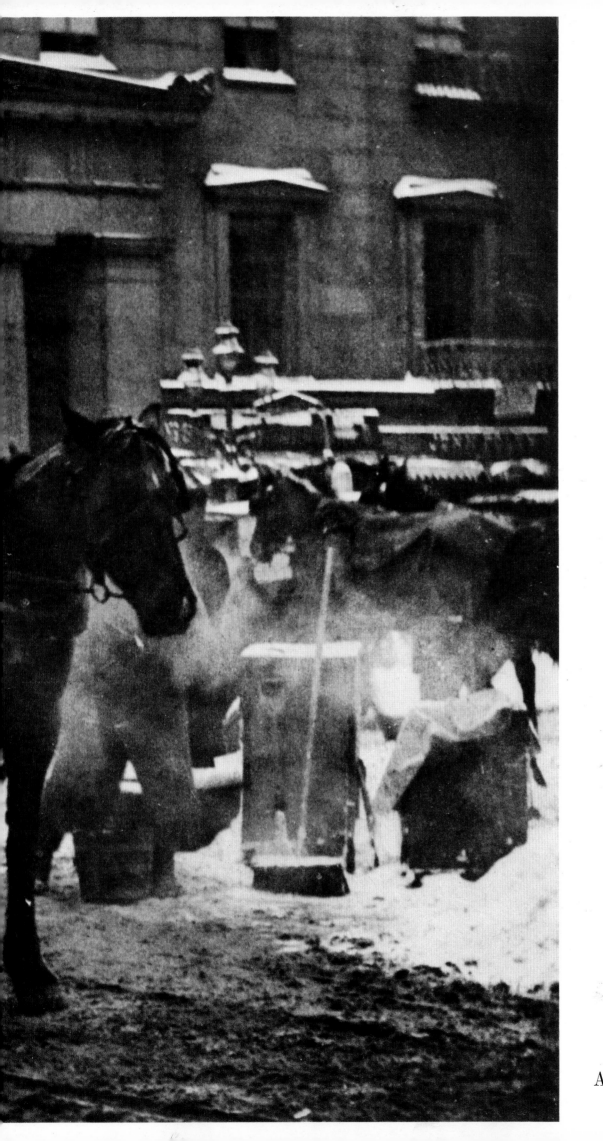

77

**Alfred Stieglitz** 1864–1946
THE TERMINAL
*1893. The Art Institute of Chicago,*
*The Alfred Stieglitz Collection*

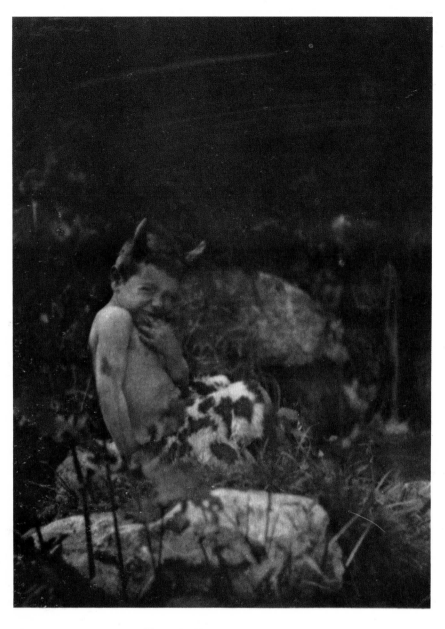

Frank Eugene 1865–1936
SMALL BOY DRESSED AS A FAUN
*ca. 1908. The Art Institute of Chicago, The Alfred Stieglitz Collection*

Frank Eugene 1865–1936
MOSAIC
*ca. 1908. The Metropolitan Museum of Art, New York, gift of Alfred Stieglitz*

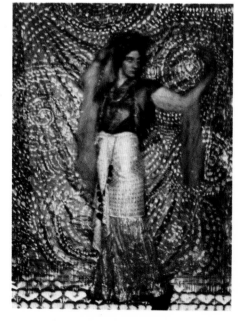

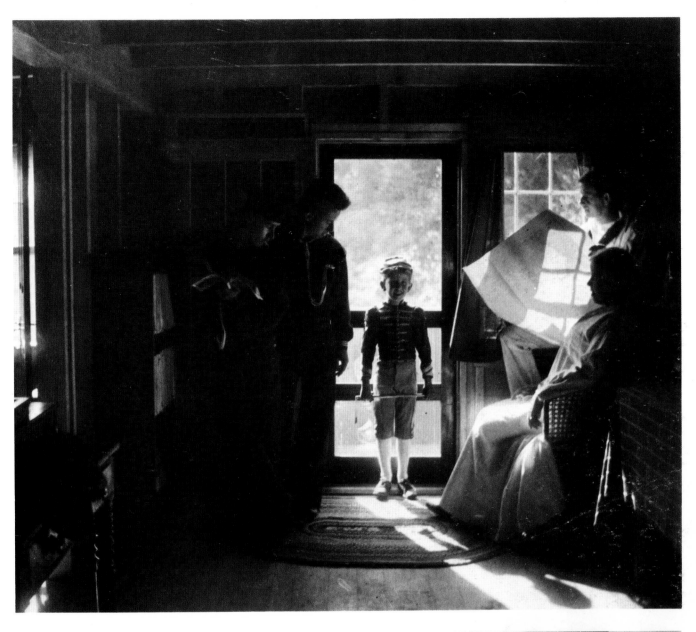

Gertrude Käsebier 1852–1934
CLARENCE H. WHITE AND FAMILY
*ca. 1910. International Museum of Photography at George Eastman House, Rochester, N.Y.*

Gertrude Käsebier 1852–1934
EVELYN NESBIT
*ca. 1903. International Museum of Photography at George Eastman House, Rochester, N.Y.*

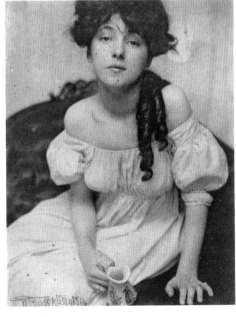

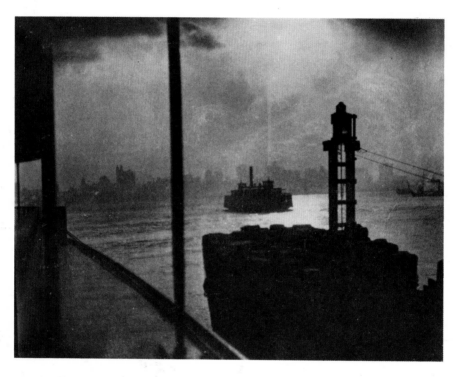

**Joseph T. Keiley** 1869-1914
NEW YORK FERRY
*1907. The Metropolitan Museum of Art, New York, gift of Alfred Stieglitz*

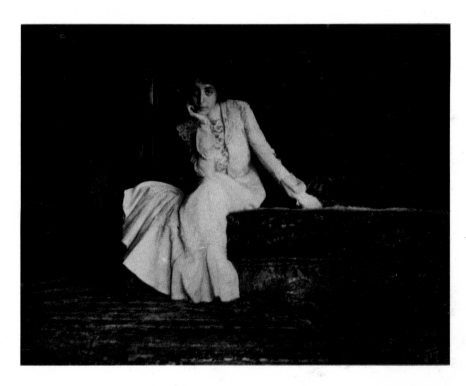

**Joseph T. Keiley** 1869–1914
PORTRAIT: MISS DE C
*ca. 1908. The Metropolitan Museum of Art, New York, gift of Alfred Stieglitz*

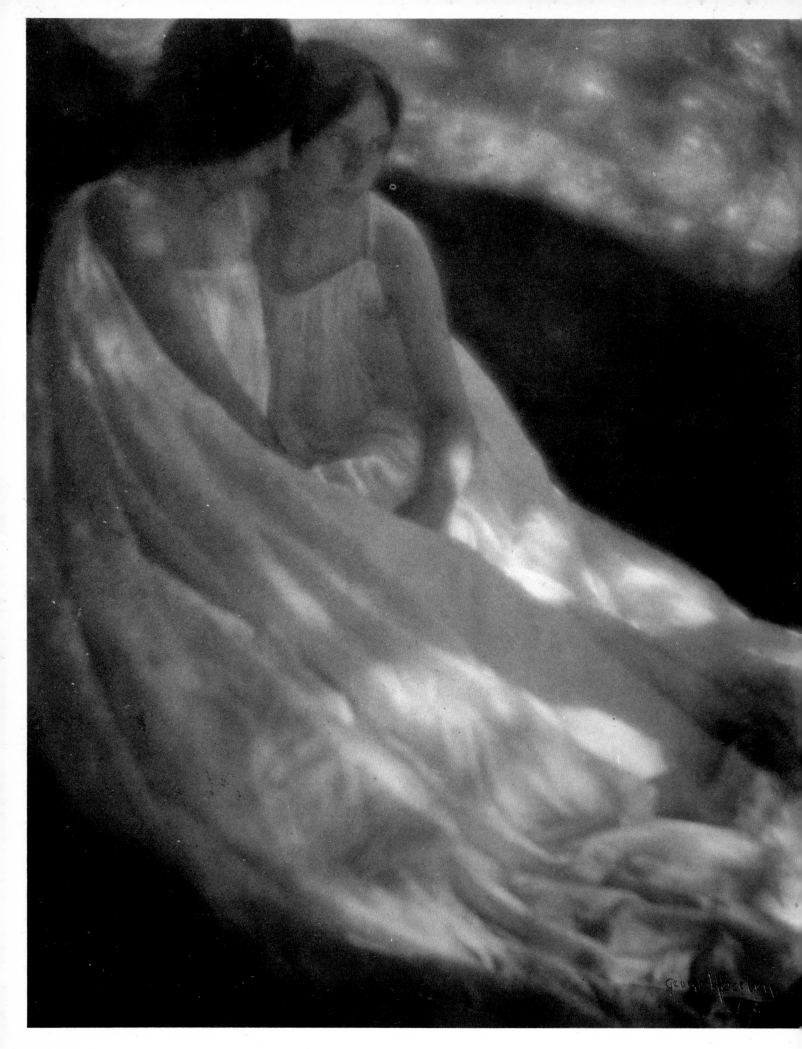

## George H. Seeley 1880–1955
THE BURNING OF ROME
*1906. The Metropolitan Museum of Art, New York, gift of Alfred Stieglitz*

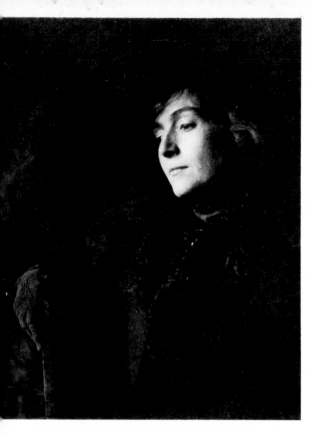

**F. Holland Day** 1864–1933
PORTRAIT OF MRS. POTTER PALMER
*890. The Metropolitan Museum of Art, New York, gift of Alfred Stieglitz*

**F. Holland Day** 1864–1933
PORTRAIT OF ZAIDA BEN YUSUF
*890. The Metropolitan Museum of Art, New York, gift of Alfred Stieglitz*

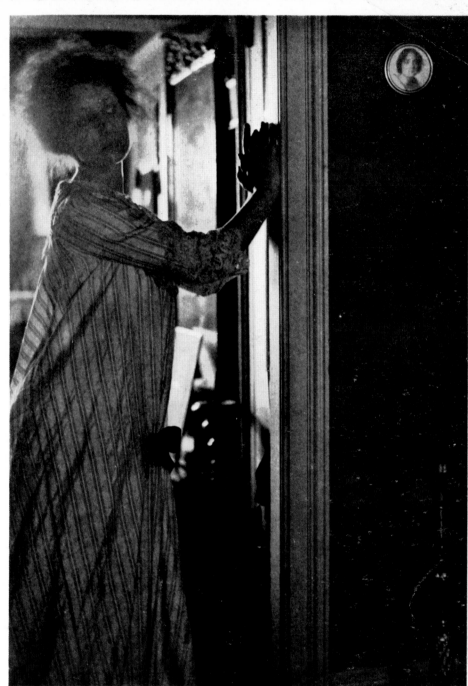

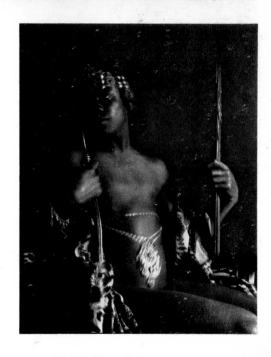

**F. Holland Day** 1864–1933
SEATED NEGRO BOY HOLDING SPEARS
*ca. 1890. The Art Institute of Chicago,*
*The Alfred Stieglitz Collection*

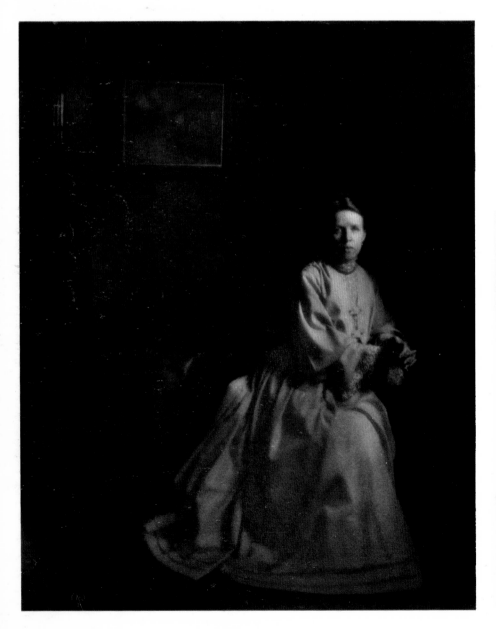

84

**Clarence H. White** 1871–1925
PORTRAIT OF MRS. CLARENCE H. WHITE
*ca. 1905. The Metropolitan Museum of Art, New York, gift of Alfred Stieglitz*

**Clarence H. White** 1871–1925
MISS BEATTY WITH FAN
*1909. International Museum of Photography at
George Eastman House, Rochester, N.Y.*

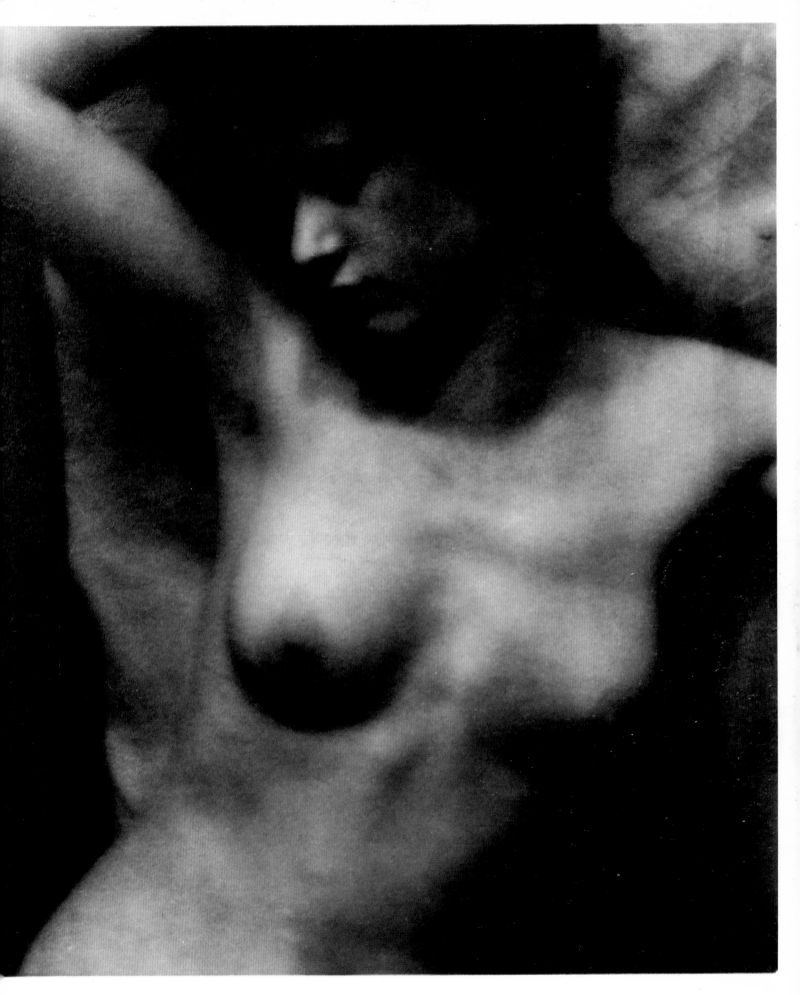

Clarence H. White 1871-1925 and
Alfred Stieglitz 1864–1946
TORSO
*The Metropolitan Museum of Art, New York, gift of Alfred Stieglitz*

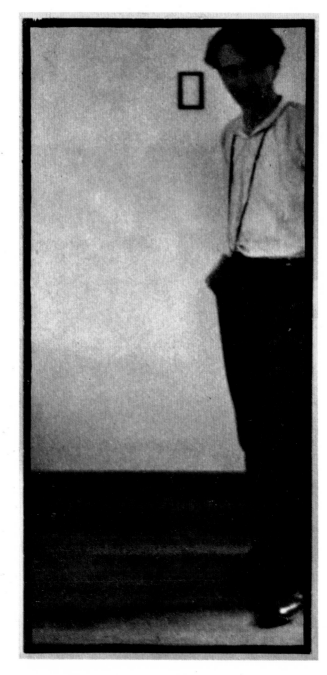

Edward J. Steichen 1879–1973
SELF-PORTRAIT
*1898. The Metropolitan Museum of Art, New York, gift of Alfred Stieglitz*

# Edward J. Steichen 1879–1973

WOOD-LOT, FALLEN LEAVES

*1898. The Museum of Modern Art, New York, gift of the Photographer*

Edward J. Steichen 1879–1973
WINTER LANDSCAPE
*1903. The Museum of Modern Art, New York, gift of the Photographer*

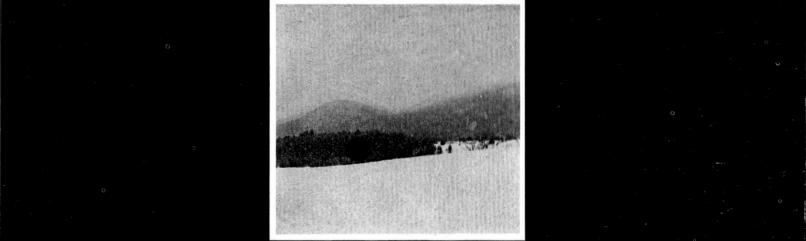

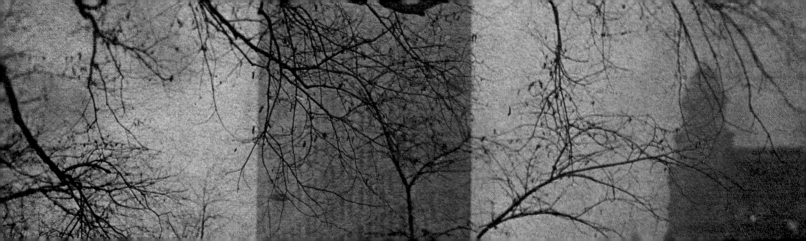

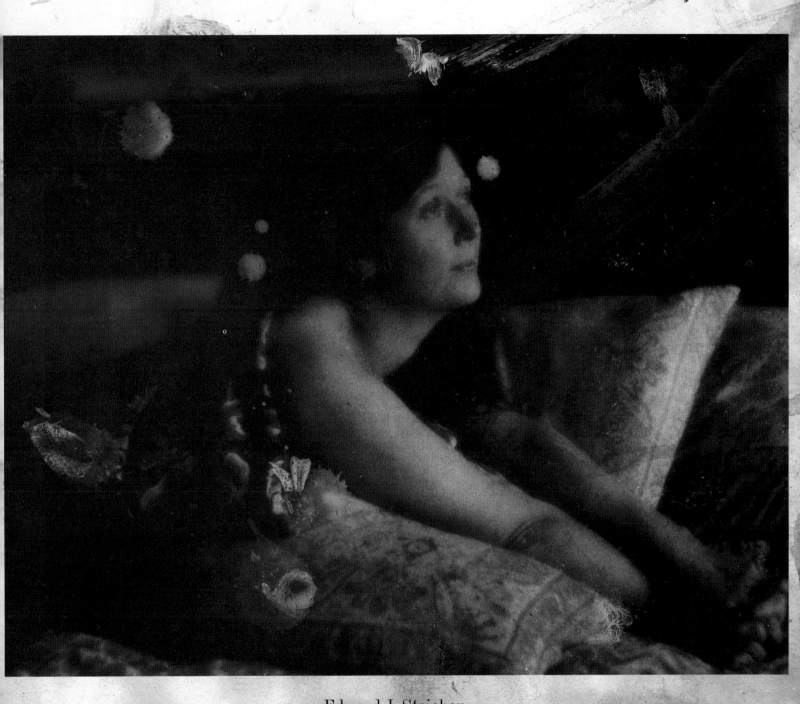

### Edward J. Steichen 1879–1973
ISADORA DUNCAN
*ca. 1910. The Museum of Modern Art, New York, gift of the Photographer*

### Edward J. Steichen 1879–1973
THE FLATIRON BUILDING—EVENING
*1905. The Metropolitan Museum of Art, New York, gift of Alfred Stieglitz*

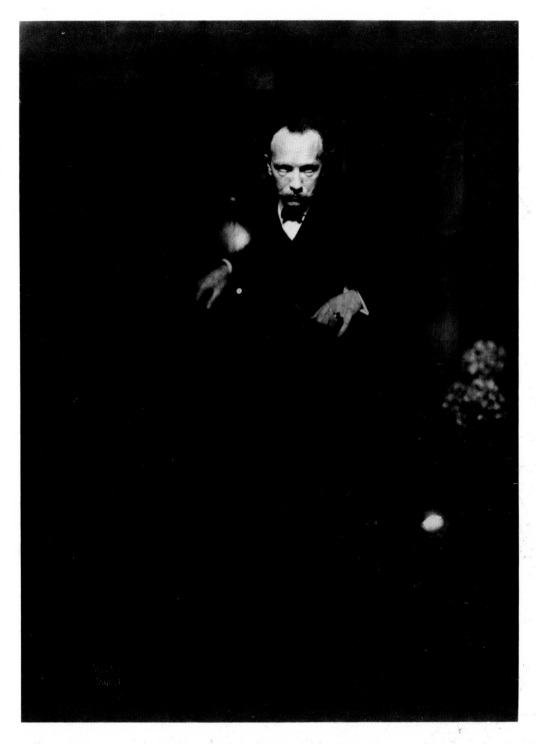

**Edward J. Steichen** 1879–1973
RICHARD STRAUSS
*1906. The Metropolitan Museum of Art, New York, The Alfred Stieglitz Collection*

**Edward J. Steichen** 1879–1973
J. PIERPONT MORGAN
*1903. The Metropolitan Museum of Art, New York, The Alfred Stieglitz Collection*

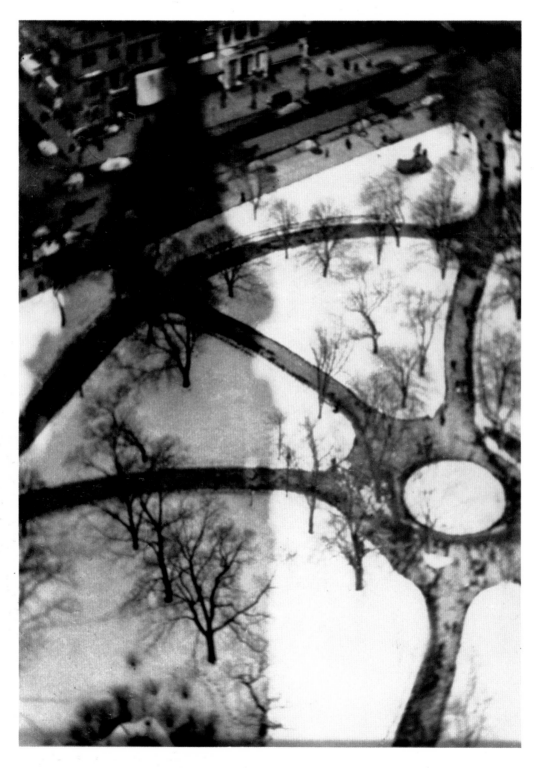

**Alvin Langdon Coburn** 1882–1966
THE OCTOPUS, NEW YORK
*1912. International Museum of Photography at George Eastman House, Rochester, N.Y.*

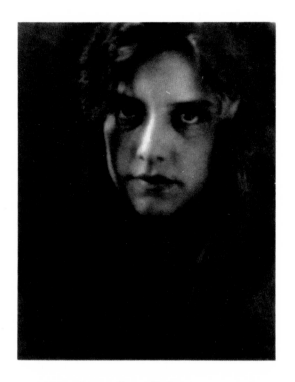

**Alvin Langdon Coburn** 1882–1966
LANDON RIVES
*1904. The Metropolitan Museum of Art, New York, gift of Alfred Stieglitz*

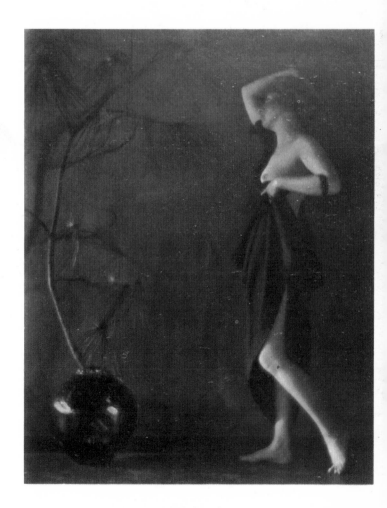

**Edward Weston** 1886–1958
UNTITLED
*ca. 1920. The Art Institute of Chicago*

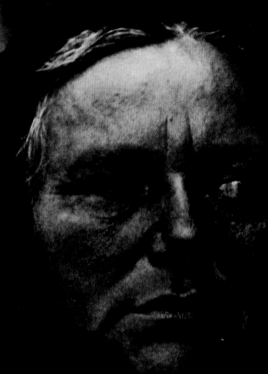
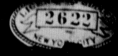

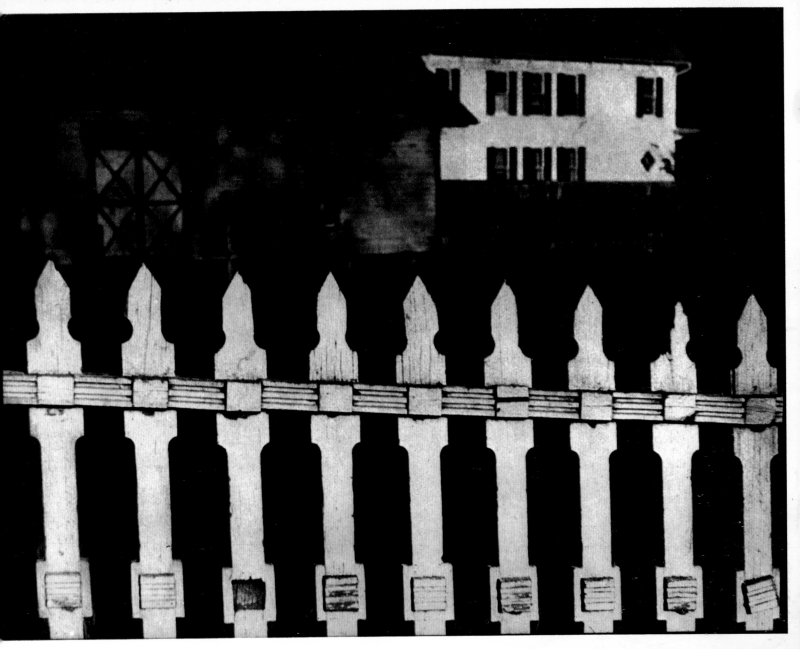

Paul Strand b. 1890
THE WHITE FENCE
*1916. International Museum of Photography at George Eastman House, Rochester, N.Y.*

Paul Strand b. 1890
BLIND
*1916. The Metropolitan Museum of Art, New York, gift of Alfred Stieglitz*

Paul Strand b. 1890
BOWLS
*1916. The Metropolitan Museum of Art, New York, The Alfred Stieglitz Collection*

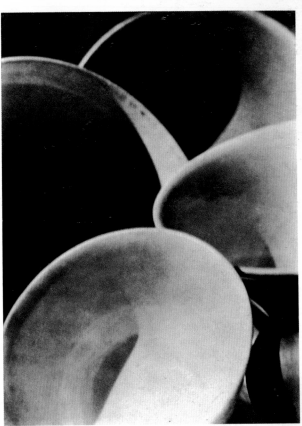

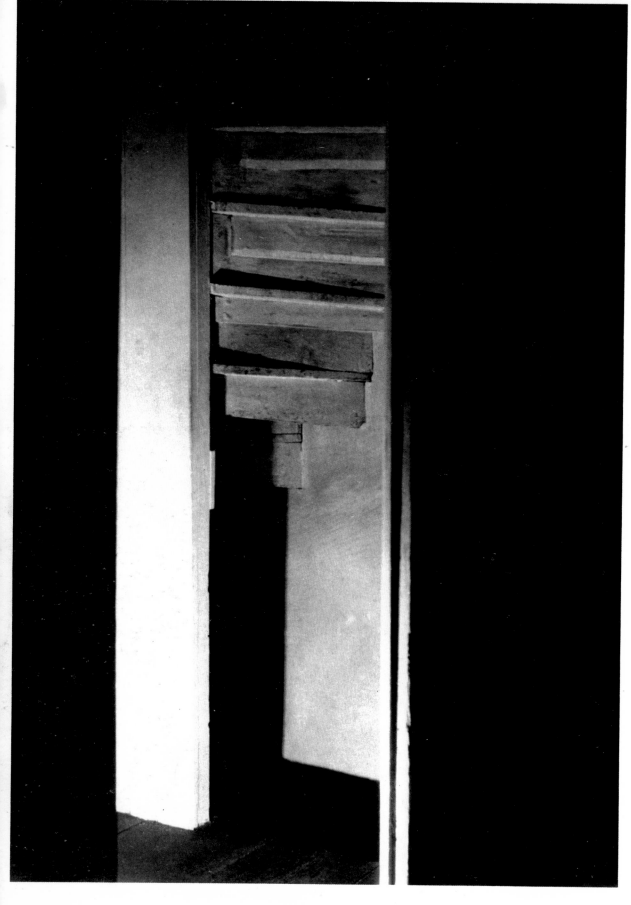

**Charles Sheeler** 1883–1965
THE STAIRWELL
*1914. The Metropolitan Museum of Art, New York, gift of Alfred Stieglitz*

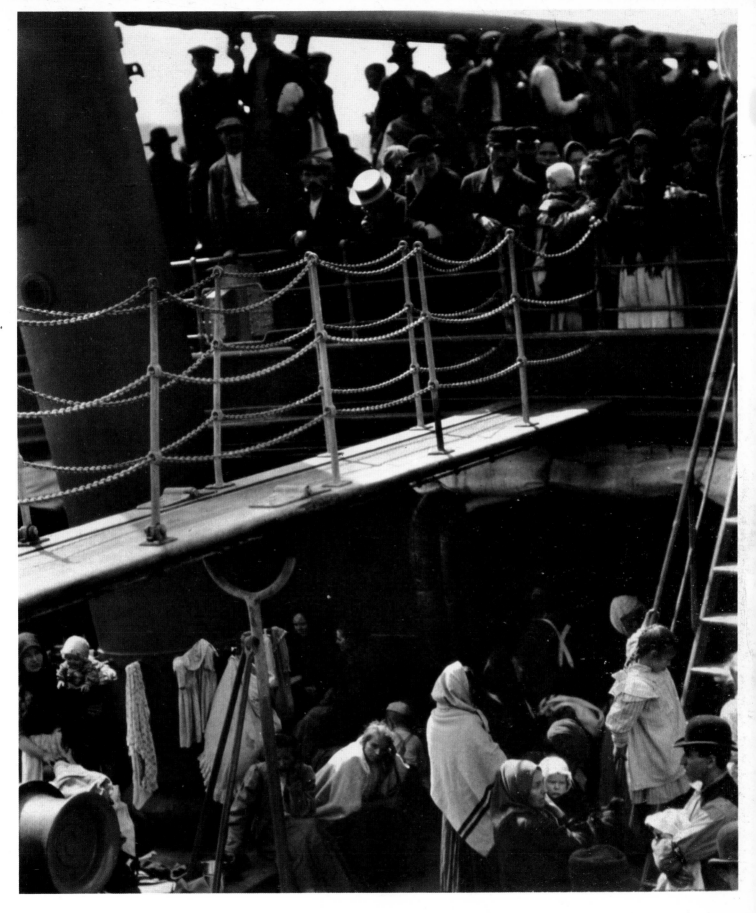

**Alfred Stieglitz** 1864–1946
THE STEERAGE
*1907. The Art Institute of Chicago, The Alfred Stieglitz Collection*

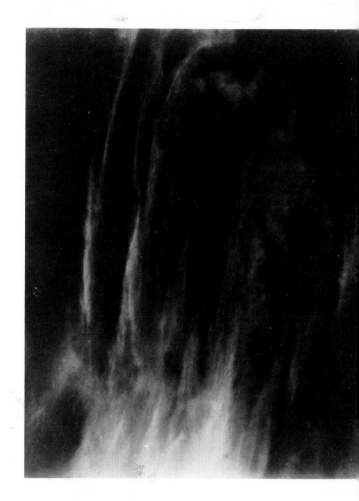

Alfred Stieglitz 1864–1946
EQUIVALENT, SET E
*1925. The Art Institute of Chicago, The Alfred Stieglitz Collection*

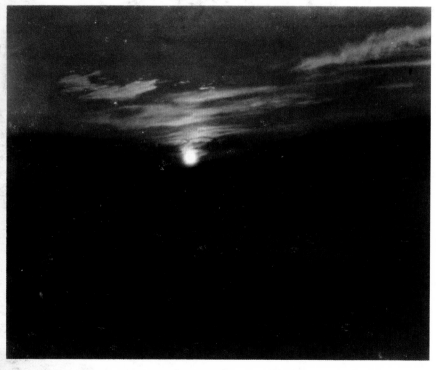

Alfred Stieglitz 1864–1946
EQUIVALENT, SET E
*ca. 1925. The Art Institute of Chicago, The Alfred Stieglitz Collection*

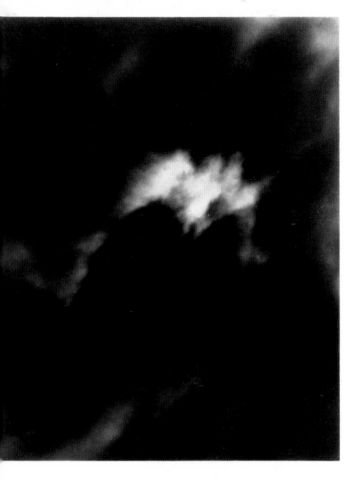

**Alfred Stieglitz** 1864–1946
EQUIVALENT, SET E
*ca. 1926. The Art Institute of Chicago, The Alfred Stieglitz Collection*

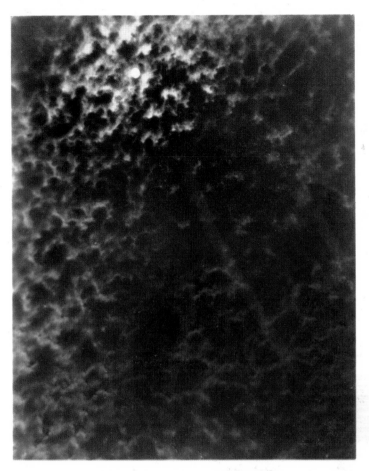

**Alfred Stieglitz** 1864–1946
EQUIVALENT, SET E
*1929. The Art Institute of Chicago, The Alfred Stieglitz Collection*

## Alfred Stieglitz 1864–1946
DOROTHY NORMAN
*1932. The Art Institute of Chicago, The Alfred Stieglitz Collection*

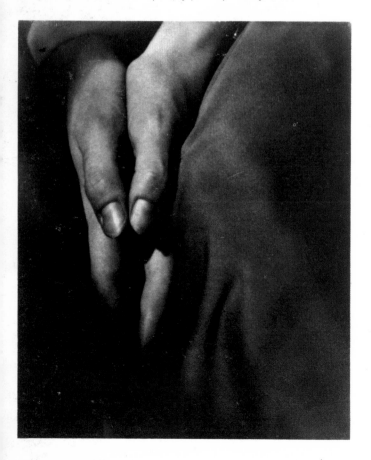

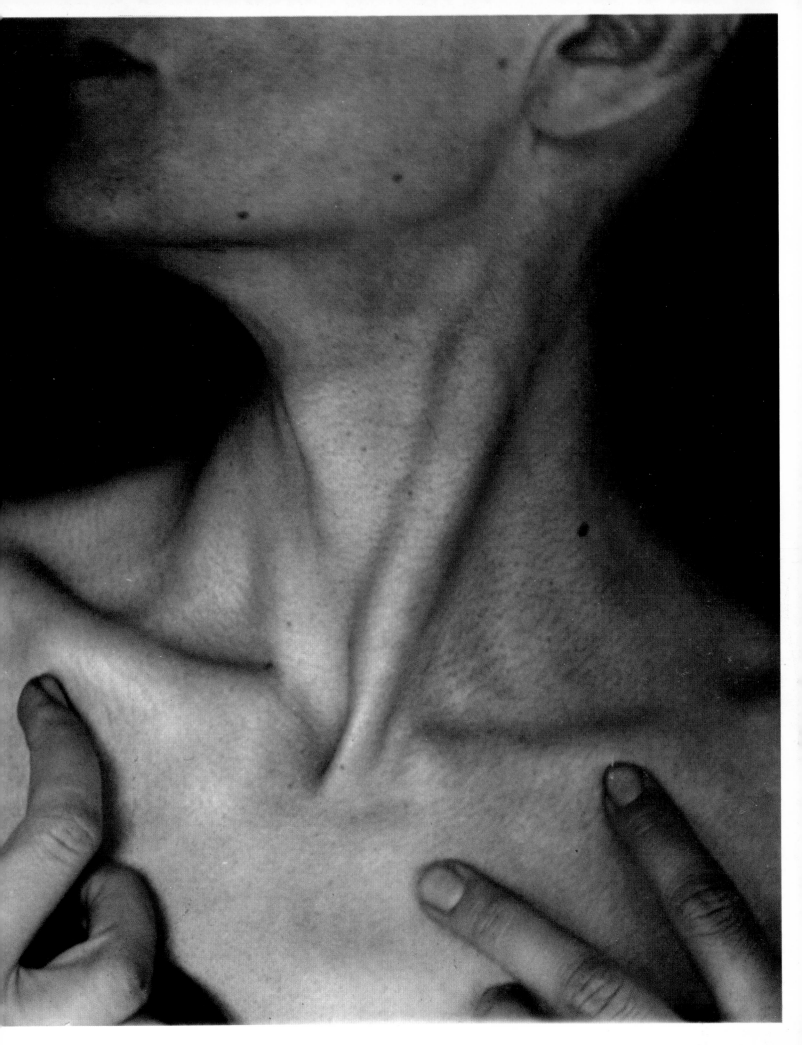

**Alfred Stieglitz** 1864–1946
GEORGIA O'KEEFFE
*1921. The Art Institute of Chicago, The Alfred Stieglitz Collection*

# Alfred Stieglitz 1864–1946

WALDO FRANK

*1922. The Art Institute of Chicago, The Alfred Stieglitz Collection*

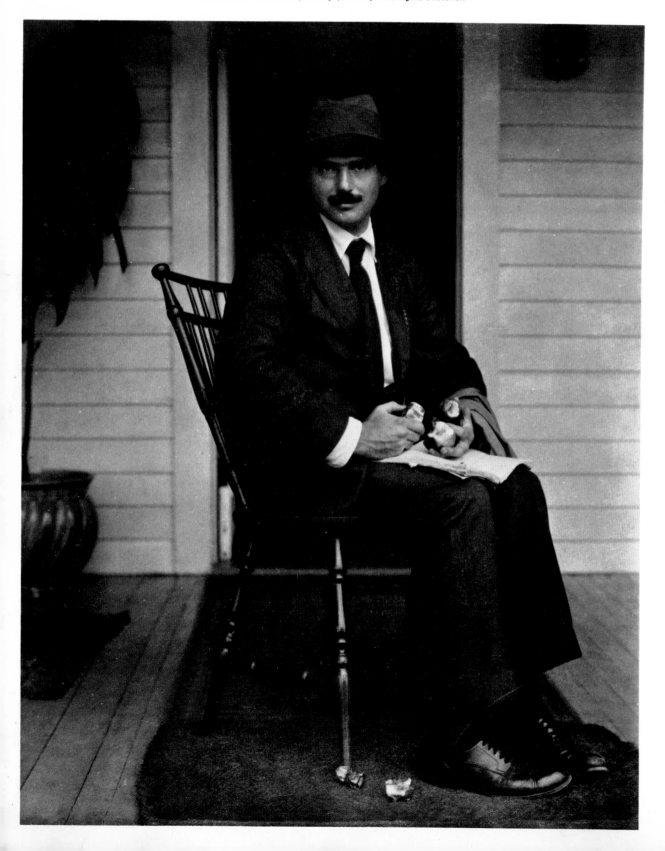

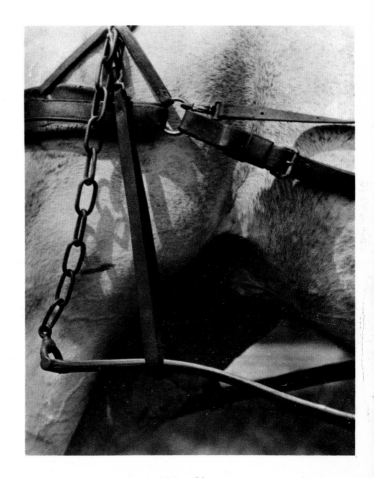

**Alfred Stieglitz** 1864–1946
SPIRITUAL AMERICA
*1923. The Art Institute of Chicago, The Alfred Stieglitz Collection*

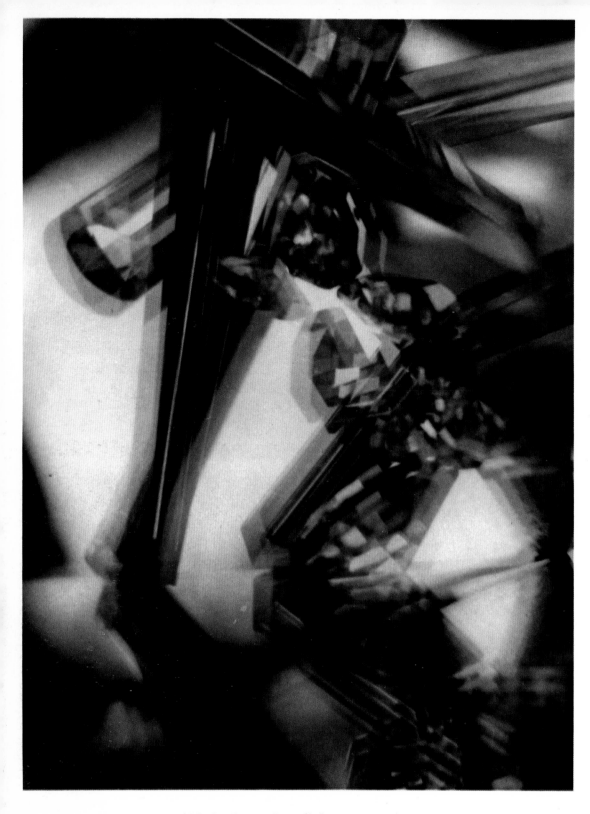

**Alvin Langdon Coburn** 1882–1966
VORTOGRAPH
*1917. The Museum of Modern Art, New York, gift of the Photographer*

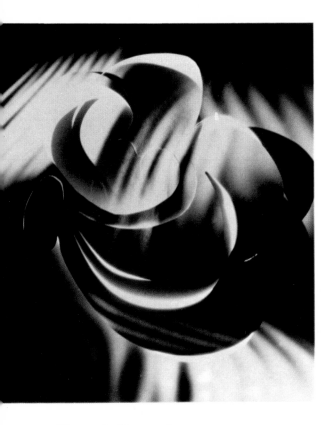

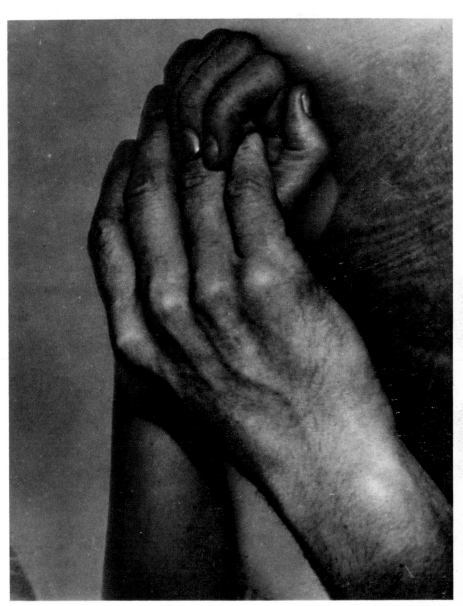

Francis Bruguiere 1880–1945
THE HEART REJOICES AT RELEASE
ca. 1925. International Museum of Photography
at George Eastman House, Rochester, N.Y.

Francis Bruguiere 1880–1945
HANDS
ca. 1930. International Museum of Photography at George Eastman House, Rochester, N.Y.

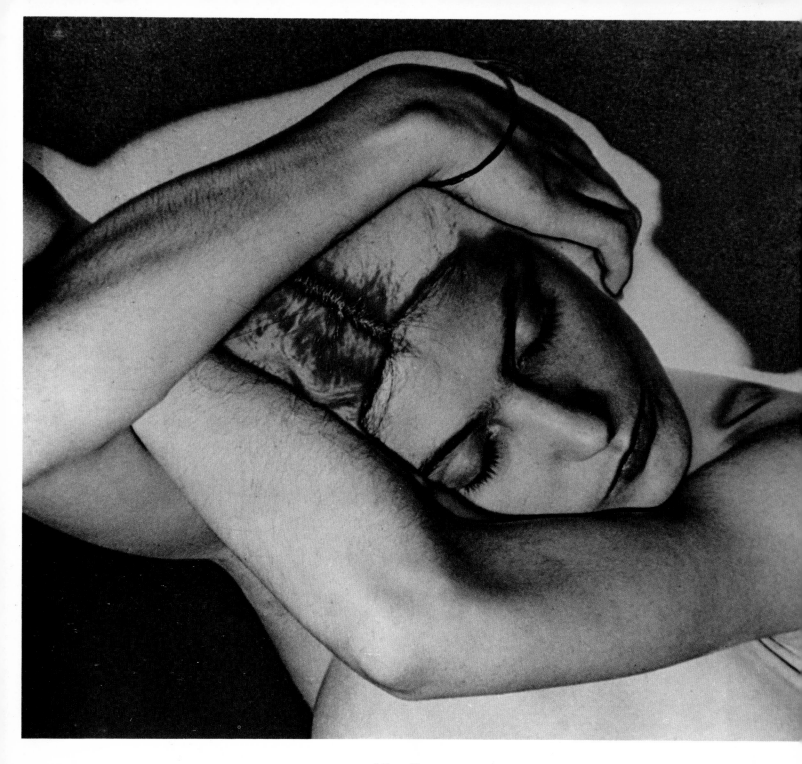

**Man Ray** b. 1890
SOLARIZATION
*1929. International Museum of Photography at George Eastman House, Rochester, N.Y.*

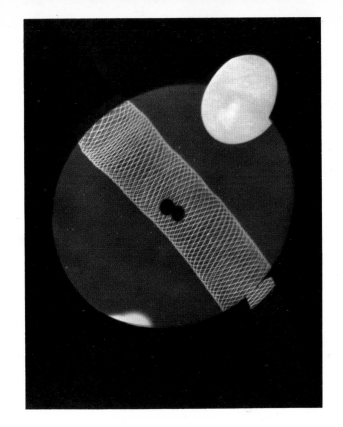

## Man Ray b. 1890
### RAYOGRAPH
*1923. Whitney Museum of American Art, New York, gift of the Simon Foundation*

## Man Ray b. 1890
### RAYOGRAPH
*1922. Whitney Museum of American Art, New York, gift of the Simon Foundation*

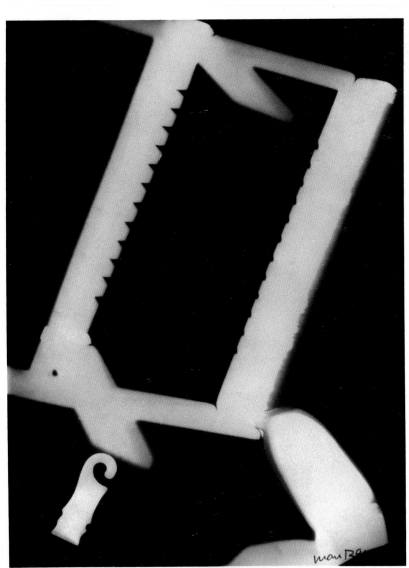

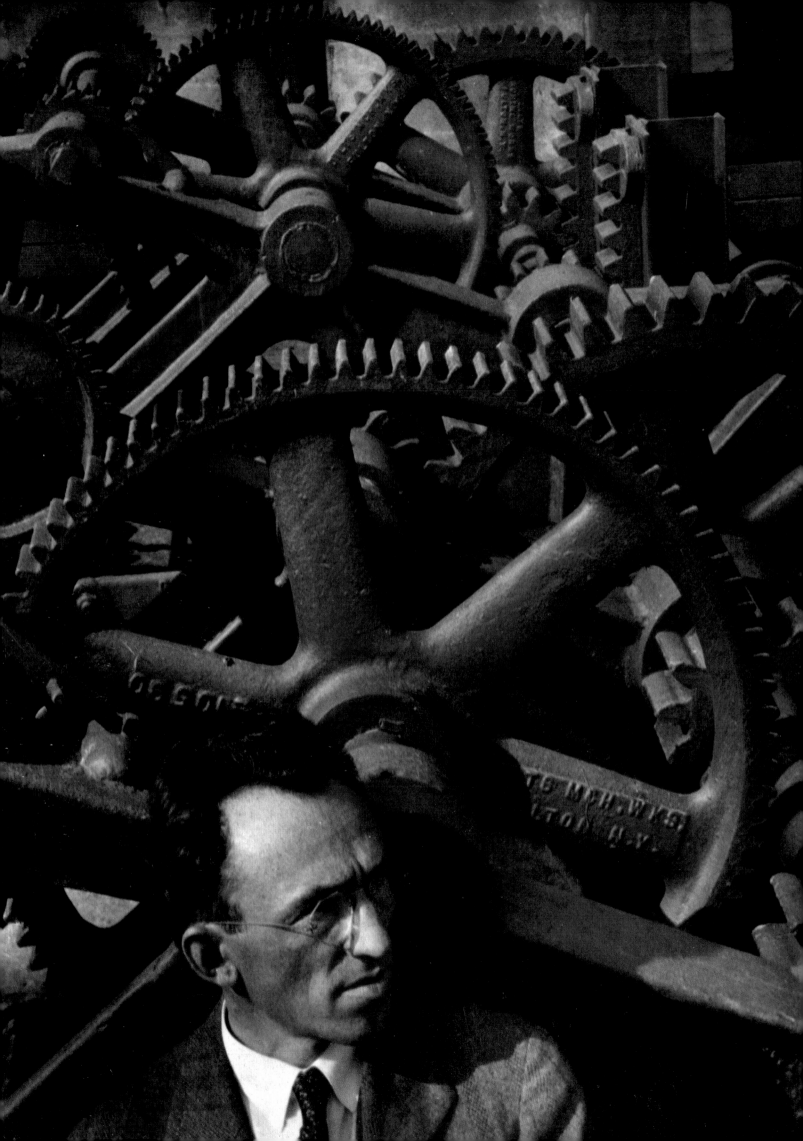

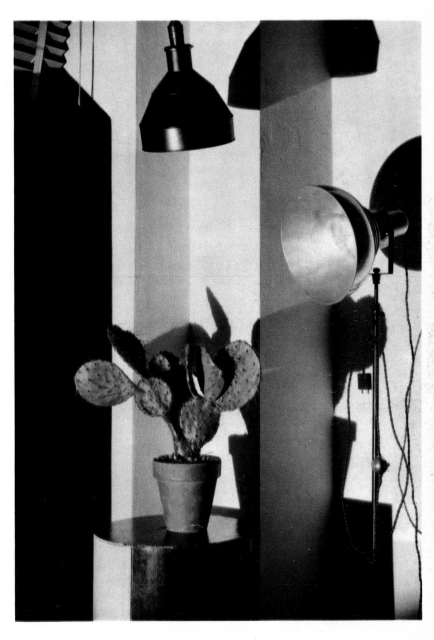

Charles Sheeler 1883–1965
CACTUS AND PHOTOGRAPHER'S LAMP, NEW YORK
*1931. The Museum of Modern Art, New York, gift of Samuel M. Kootz*

**Ralph Steiner** b. 1899
LOUIS LOZOWICK
*1929. Collection of the Photographer*

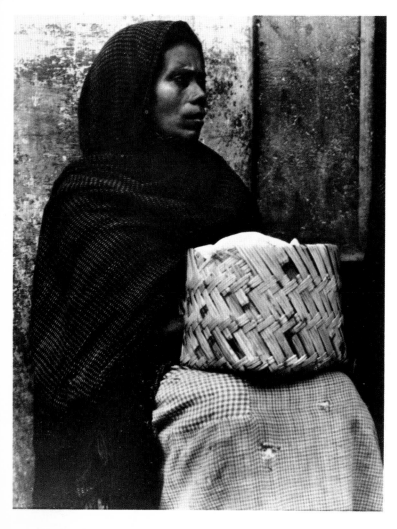

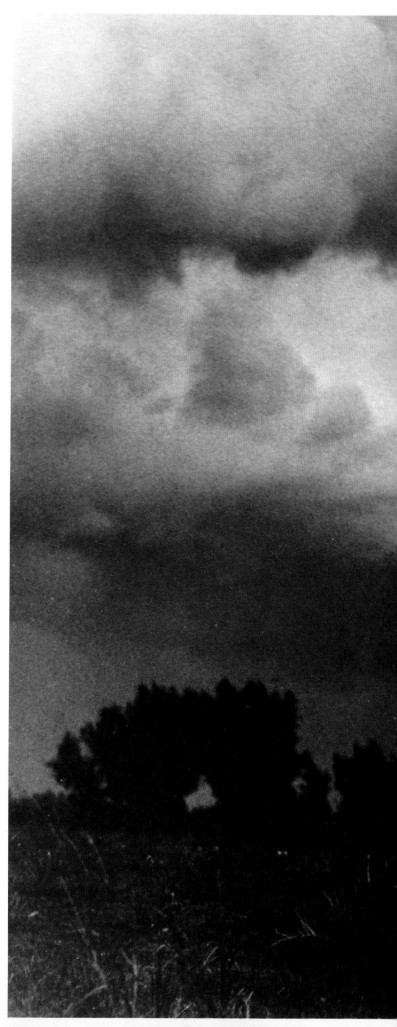

Paul Strand b. 1890
WOMAN–PATZCUARO, MEXICO
*1933. International Museum of Photography at George Eastman House, Rochester, N.Y.*

Paul Strand b. 1890
HORSES AND STORM, NEW MEXICO
*1930. International Museum of Photography at George Eastman House, Rochester, N.Y.*

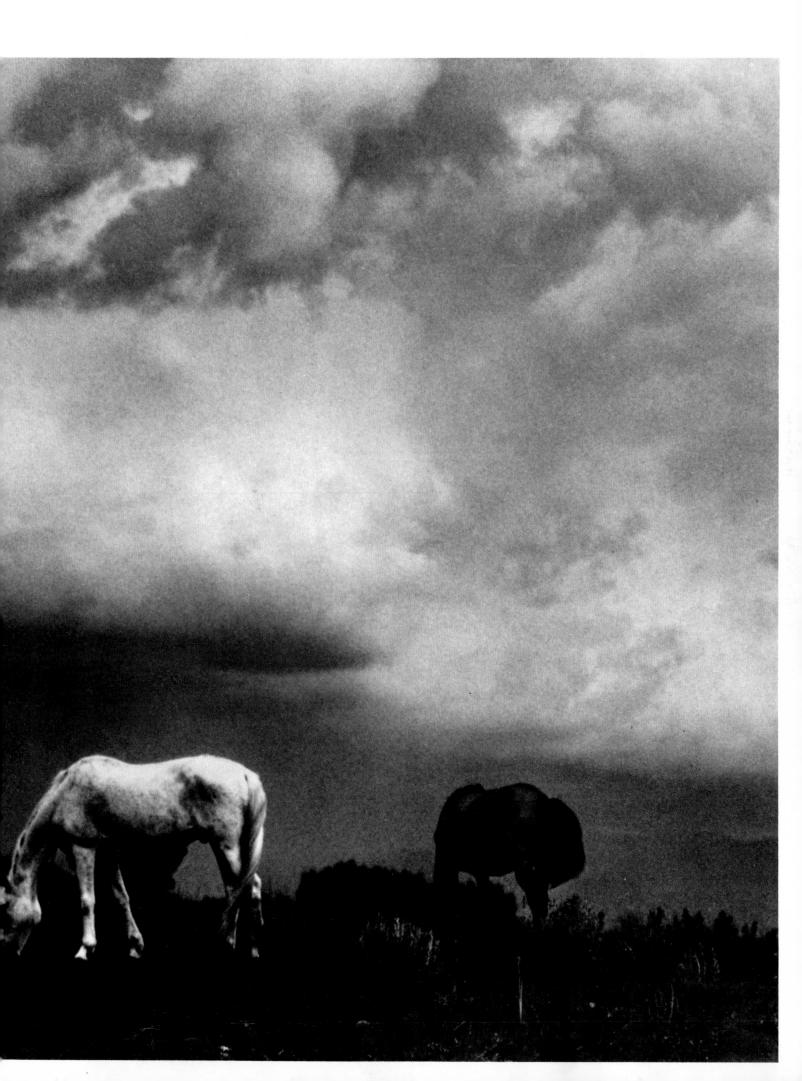

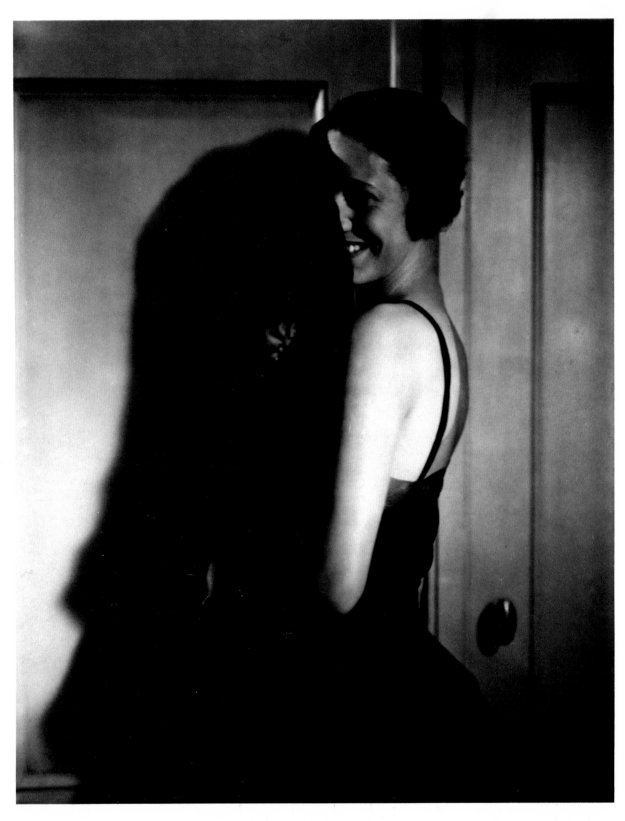

**Edward J. Steichen** 1879–1973
GERTRUDE LAWRENCE
*1928. The Museum of Modern Art, New York, gift of the Photographer*

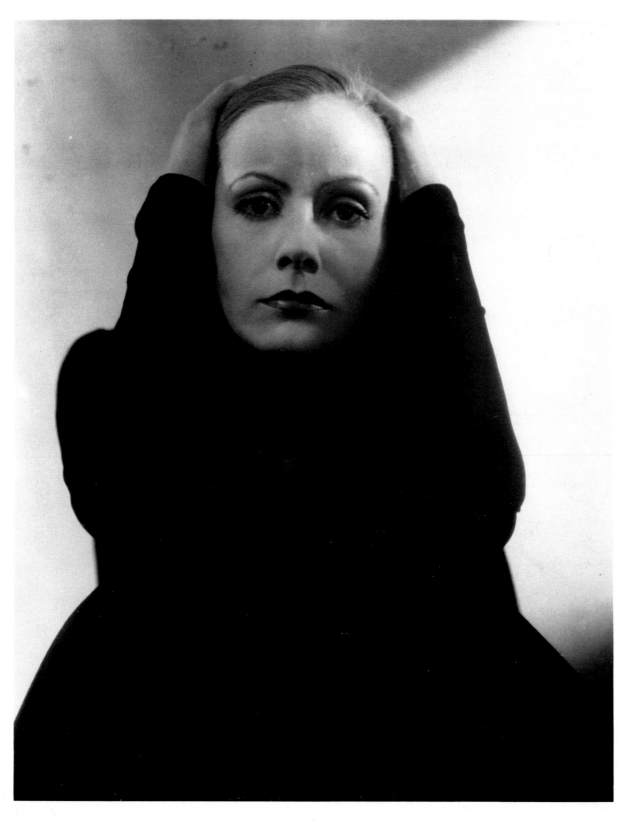

**Edward J. Steichen** 1879–1973
GRETA GARBO
*1928. The Museum of Modern Art, New York, gift of the Photographer*

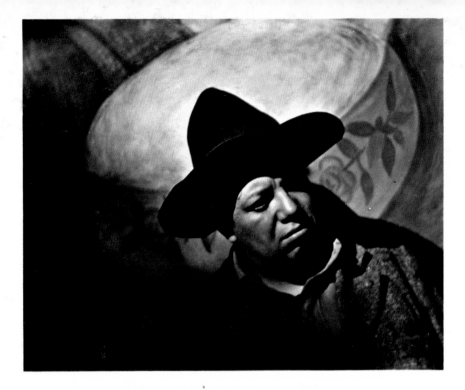

**Edward Weston** 1886–1958
DIEGO RIVERA
*1924. The Art Institute of Chicago*

**Edward Weston** 1886–1958
ONION HALVED
*1930. The Art Institute of Chicago*

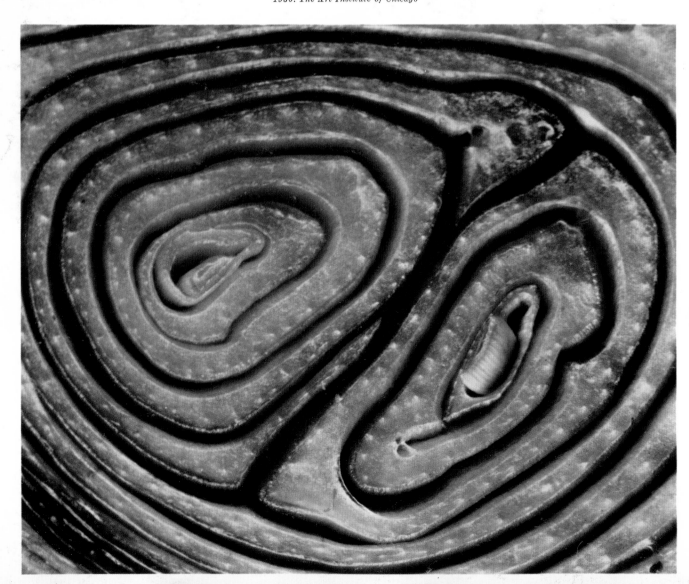

116

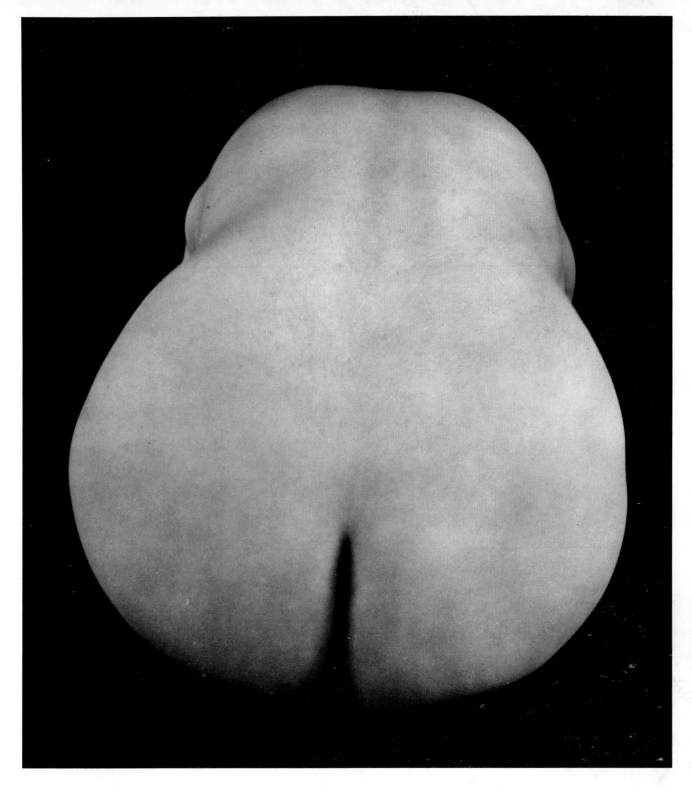

Edward Weston 1886–1958
NUDE
*1925. The Art Institute of Chicago*

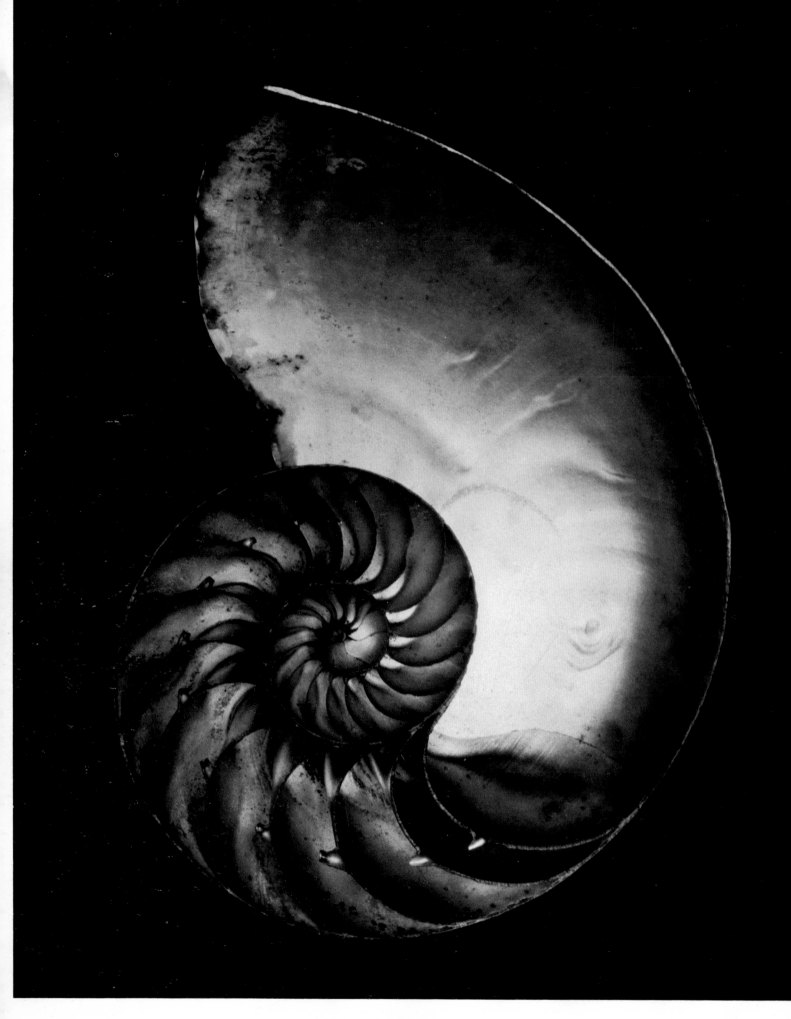

**Edward Weston** 1886–1958
CHAMBERED NAUTILUS
*1927. International Museum of Photography at George Eastman House, Rochester, N.Y.*

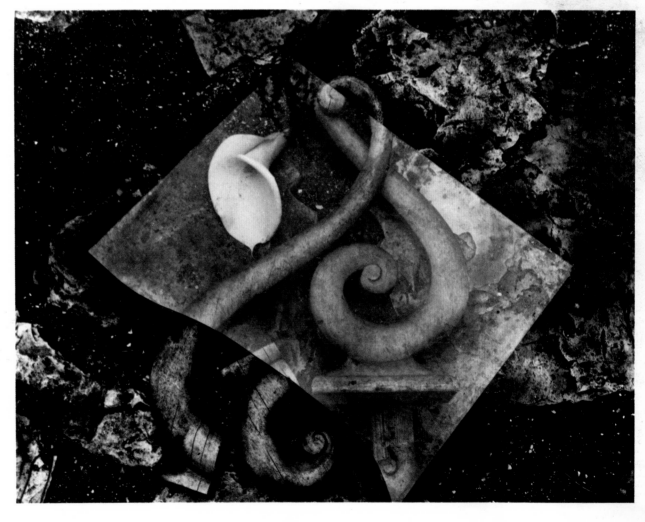

**Edward Weston** 1886–1958

LILY AND RUBBISH

*1939. International Museum of Photography at George Eastman House, Rochester, N.Y.*

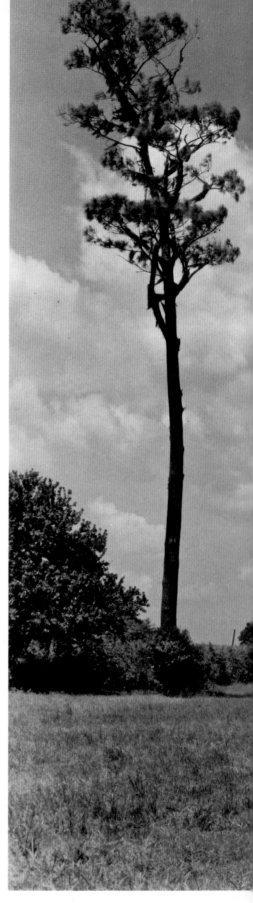

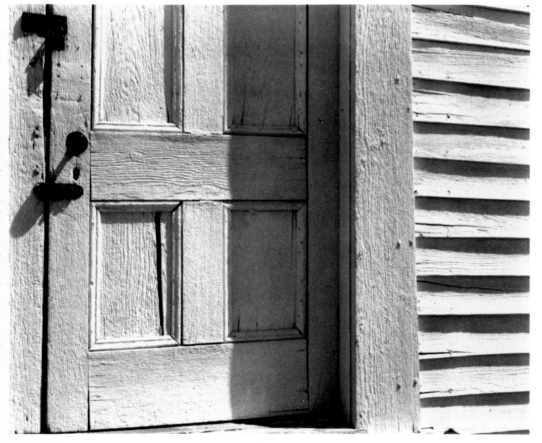

Edward Weston 1886–1958
CHURCH DOOR, HORNITOS
*1940. International Museum of Photography at George Eastman House, Rochester, N.Y.*

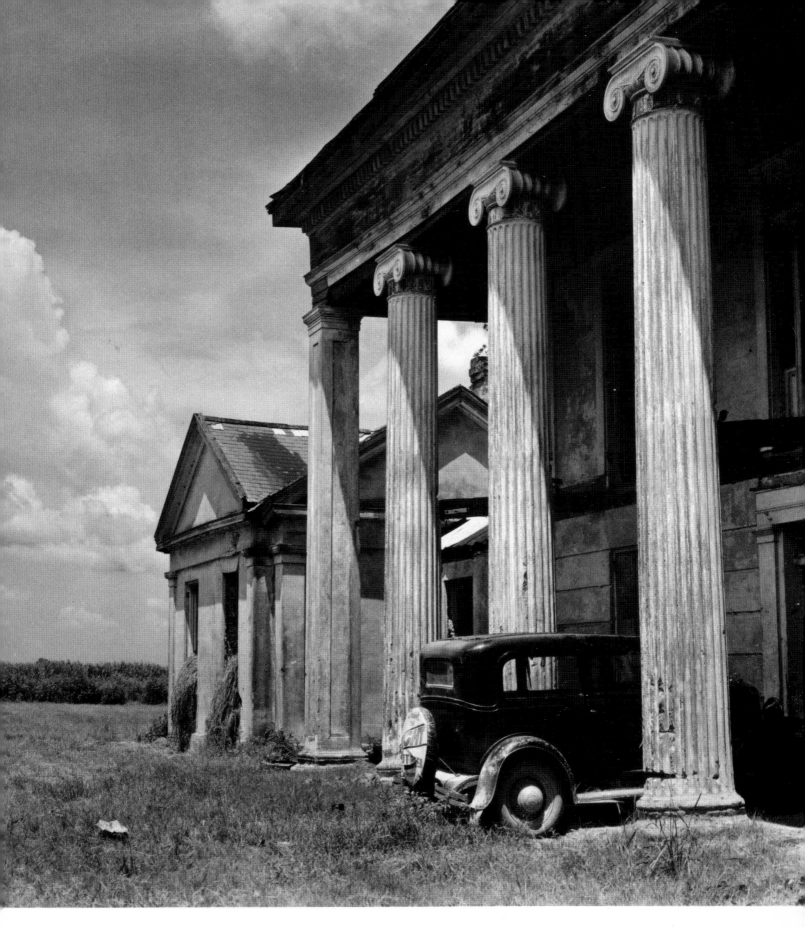

Edward Weston 1886–1958
WOODLAWN, LOUISIANA
*1941. The Art Institute of Chicago*

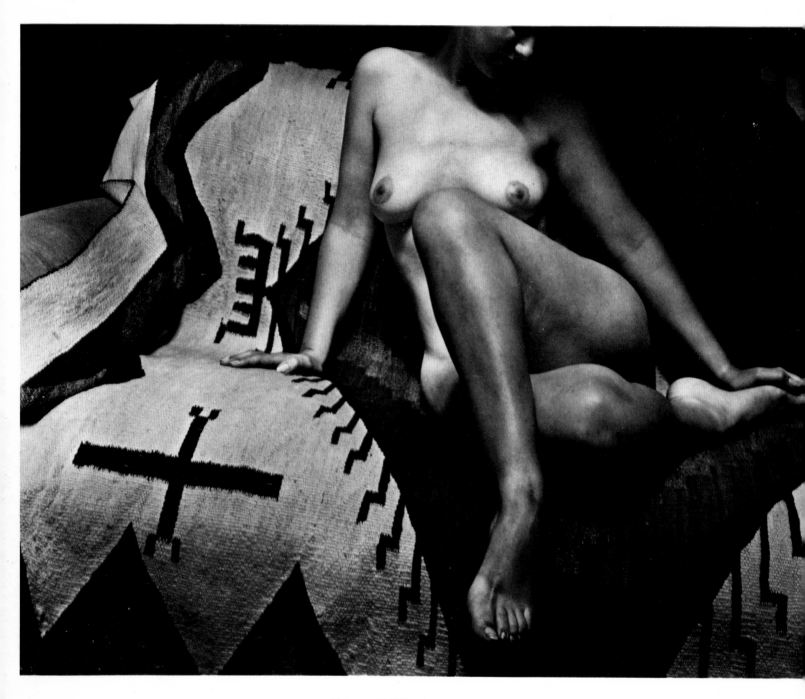

Edward Weston 1886–1958
NUDE
*1945. The Art Institute of Chicago*

122

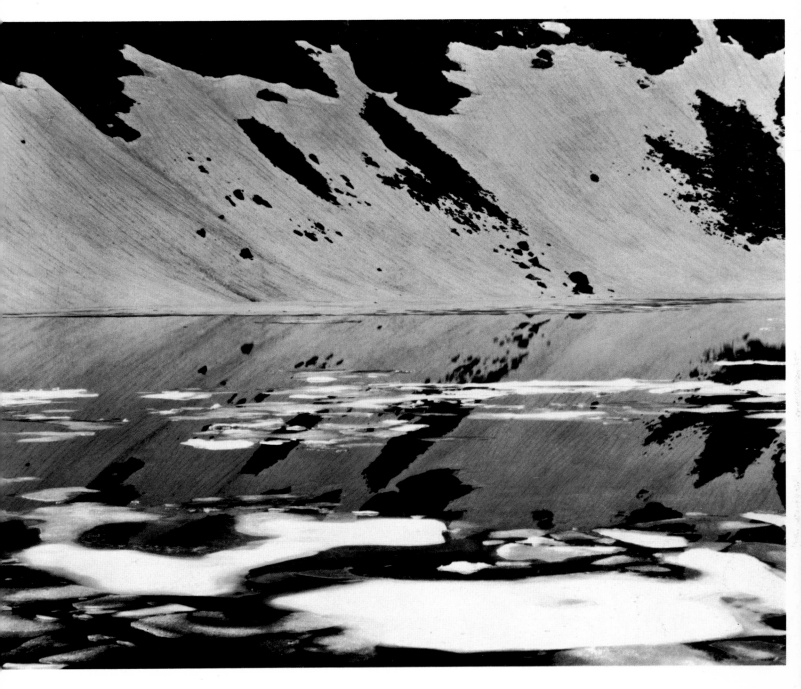

Edward Weston 1886–1958
ICEBERG LAKE
1937. The Art Institute of Chicago

123

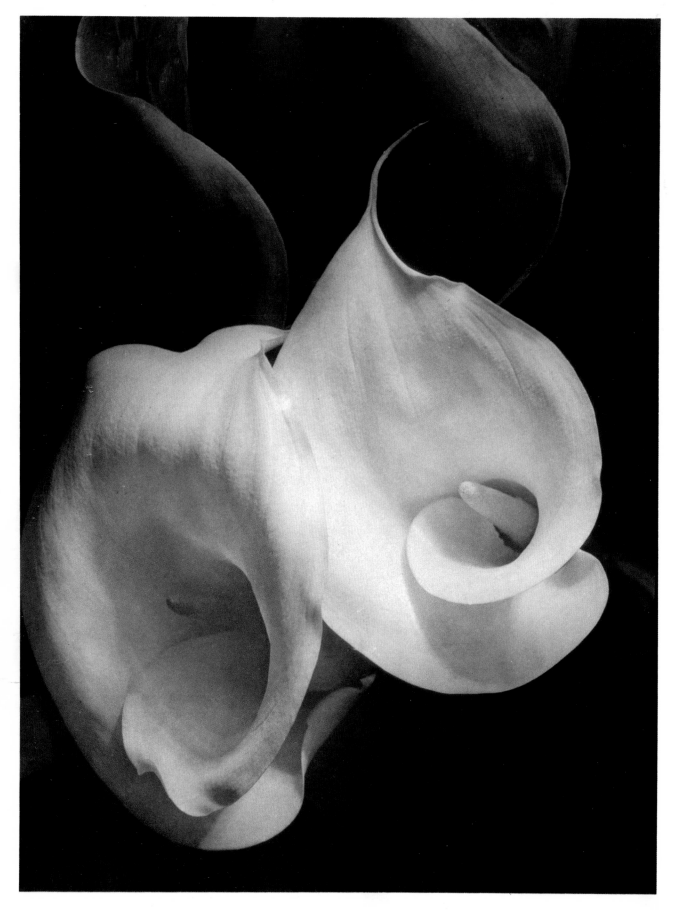

Imogen Cunningham b. 1883

TWO CALLAS

ca. 1929. International Museum of Photography at George Eastman House, Rochester, N.Y.

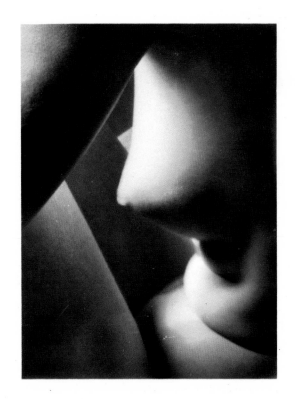

**Imogen Cunningham** b. 1883
TRIANGLES
*1928. Collection of the Photographer*

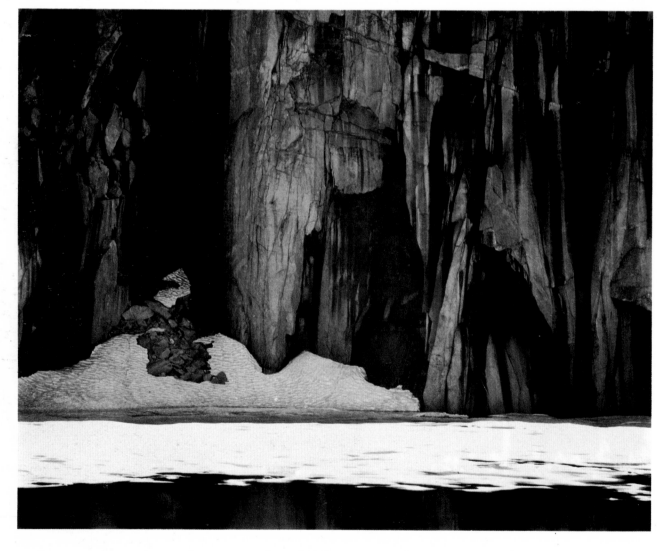

**Ansel Adams** b. 1902
FROZEN LAKE AND CLIFFS, SIERRA NEVADA, CALIFORNIA
*ca. 1934. Collection of the Photographer*

**Ansel Adams** b. 1902
MONOLITH, THE FACE OF HALF DOME, YOSEMITE VALLEY, CALIFORNIA
*ca. 1927. Collection of the Photographer*

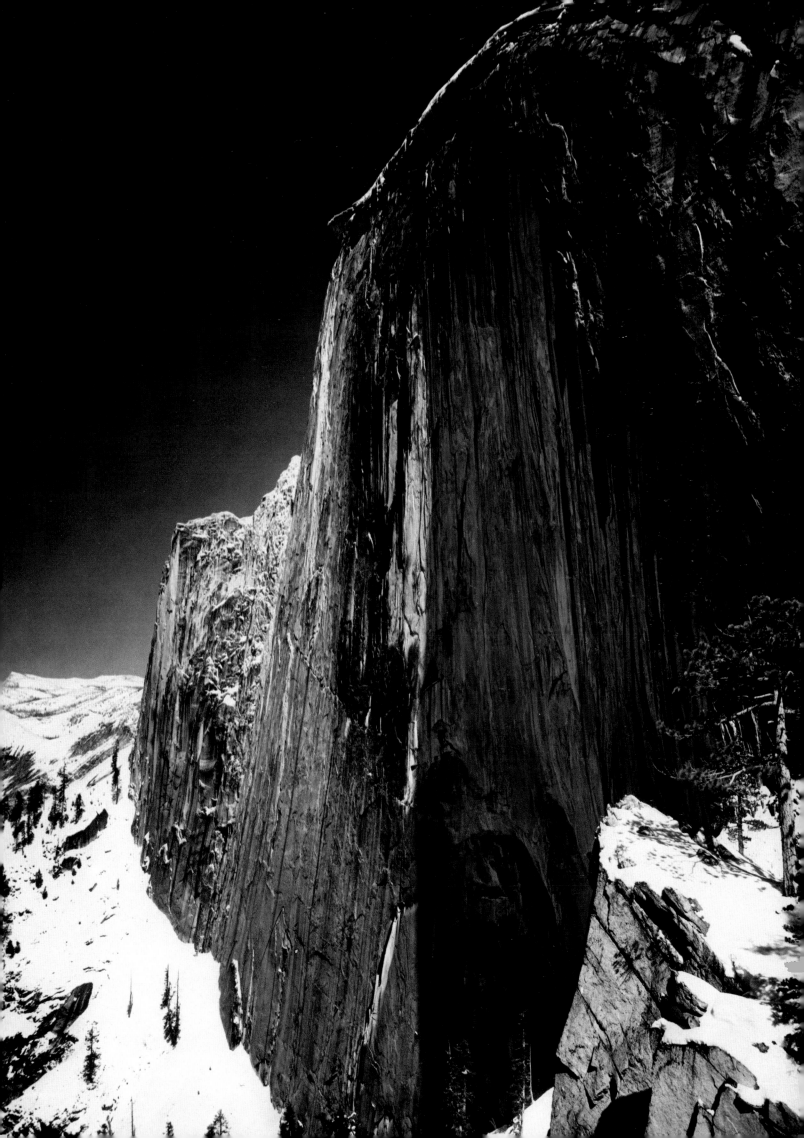

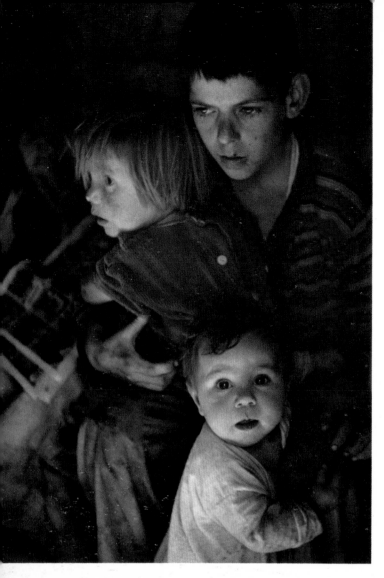

Ansel Adams b. 1902
TRAILER-CAMP CHILDREN, RICHMOND, CALIFORNIA
*ca. 1944. Collection of the Photographer*

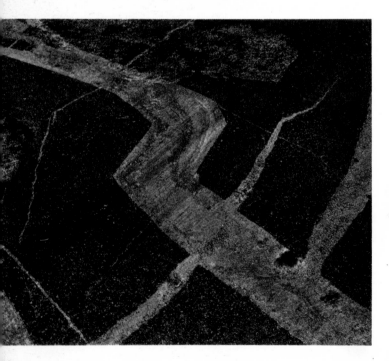

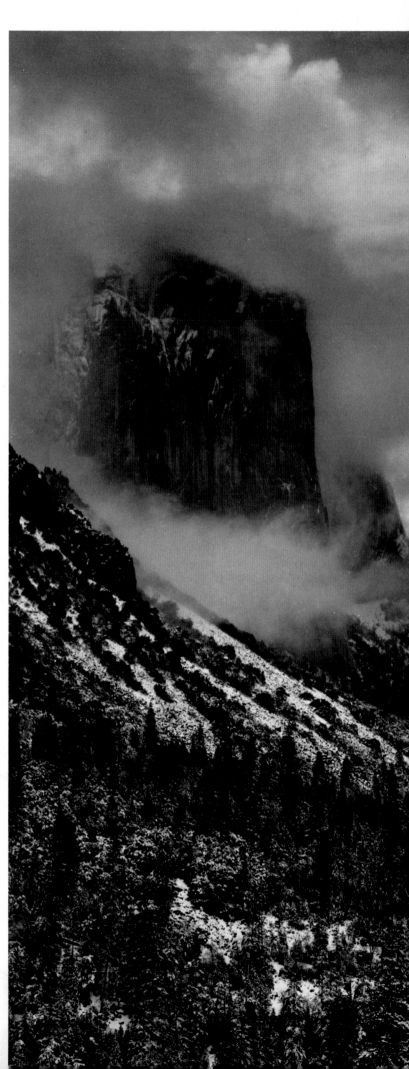

Ansel Adams b. 1902
ROCK VEINS, TENAYA LAKE, YOSEMITE NATIONAL PARK, CALIFORNIA
*ca. 1946. Collection of the Photographer*

# Ansel Adams b. 1902

CLEARING WINTER STORM, YOSEMITE VALLEY, CALIFORNIA

*ca. 1944. Collection of the Photographer*

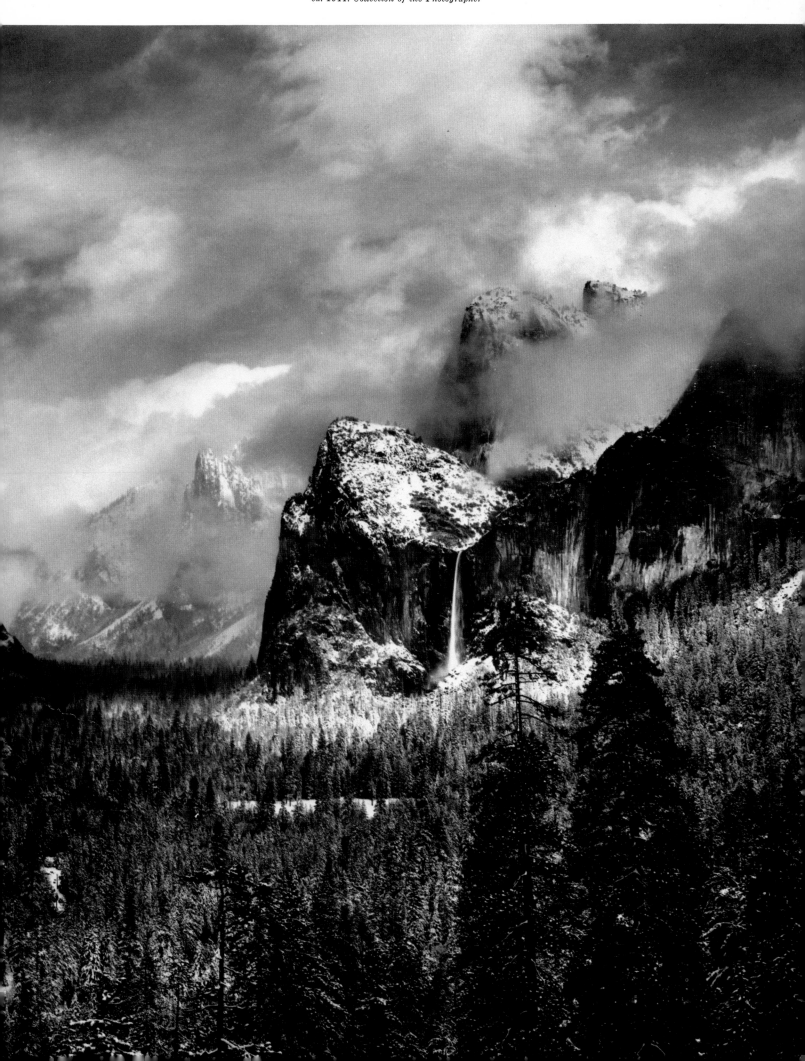

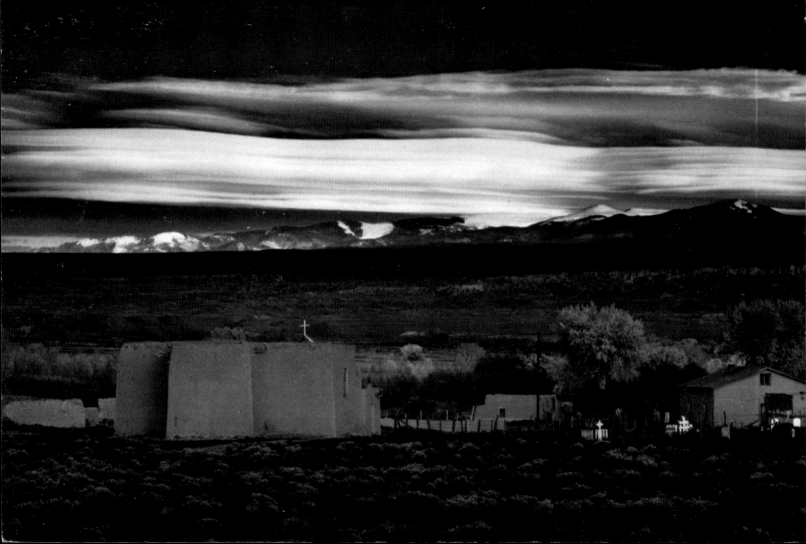

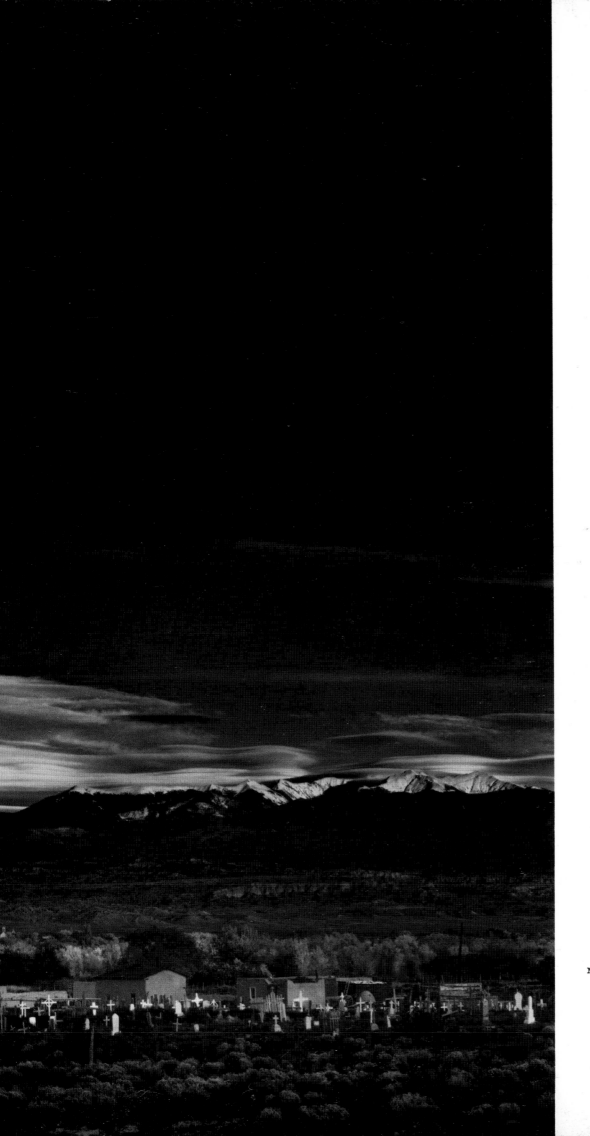

Ansel Adams b. 1902
MOONRISE, HERNANDEZ, NEW MEXICO
*1944. Collection of the Photographer*

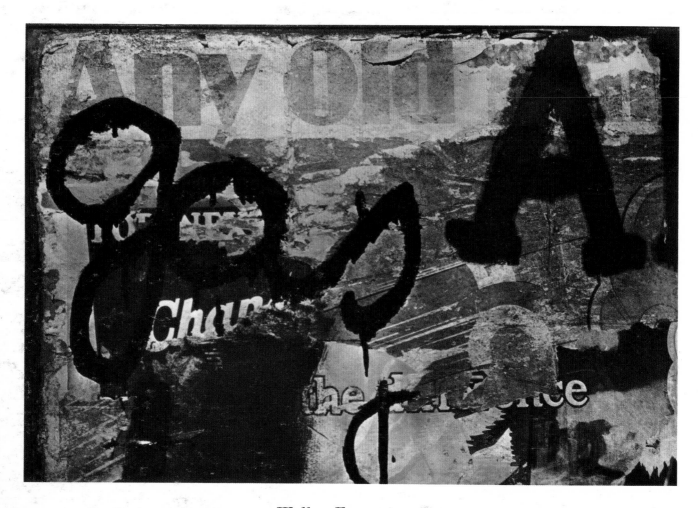

Walker Evans b. 1903
ROADSIDE GAS SIGN
1929. The Art Institute of Chicago, gift of Mrs. James Ward Thorne

Walker Evans b. 1903
TORN MOVIE POSTER, 1930
1930. The Art Institute of Chicago, gift of Mrs. James Ward Thorne

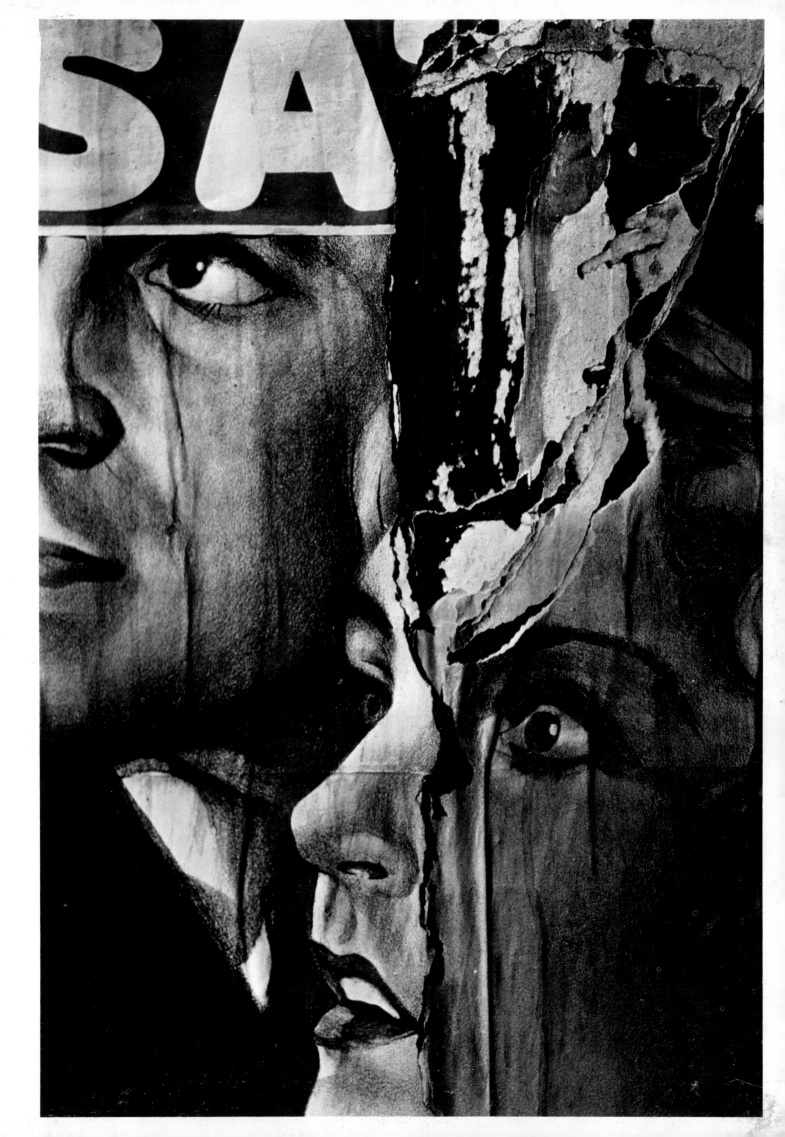

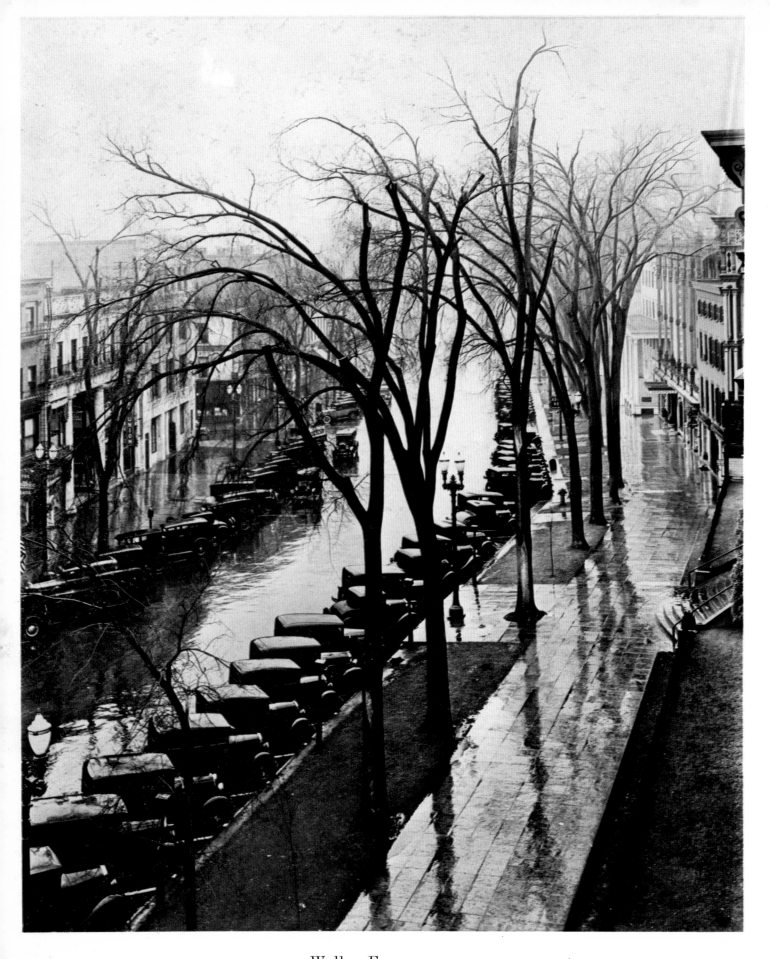

**Walker Evans** b. 1903
MAIN STREET, SARATOGA SPRINGS, NEW YORK
*1931. The Art Institute of Chicago, gift of Mrs. James Ward Thorne*

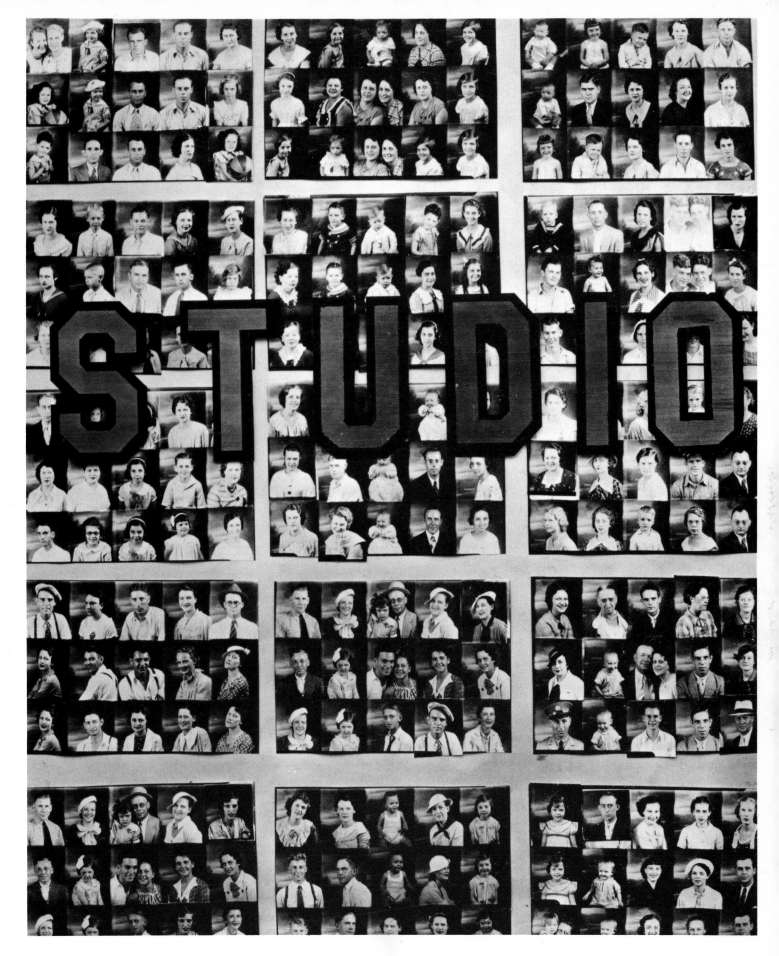

Walker Evans b. 1903
PENNY PICTURE DISPLAY, SAVANNAH
1936. The Art Institute of Chicago, gift of Mrs. James Ward Thorne

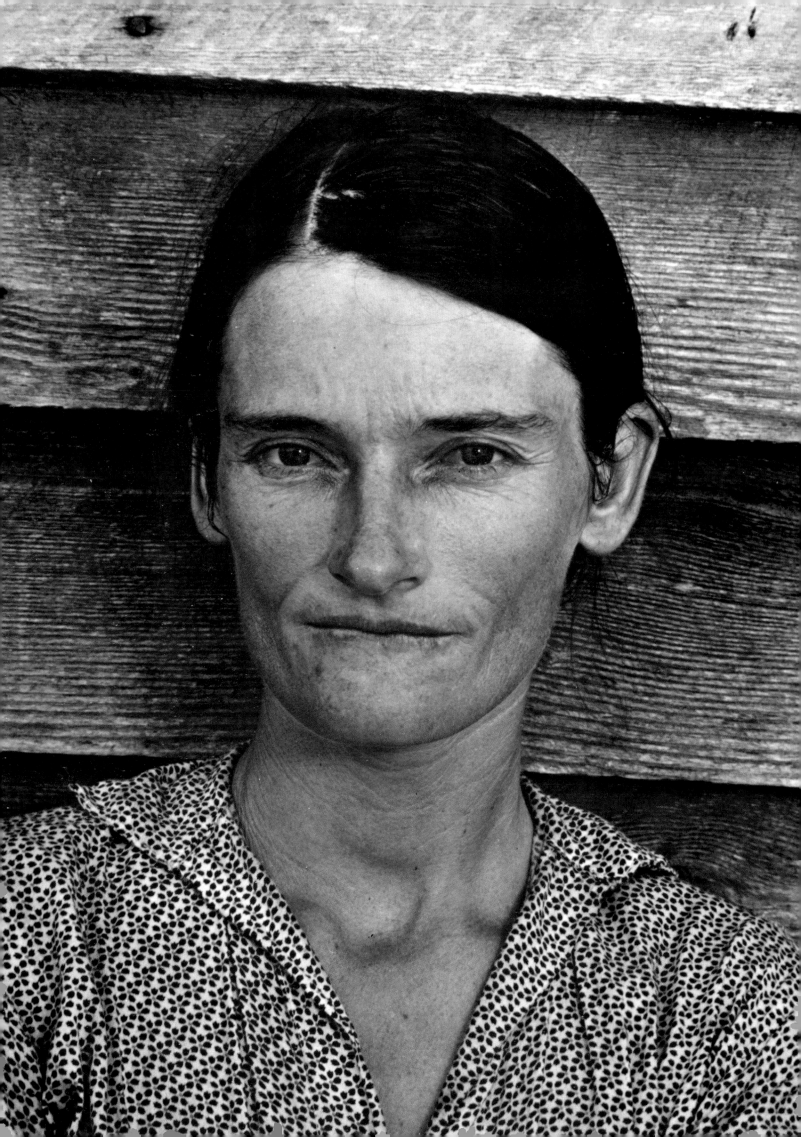

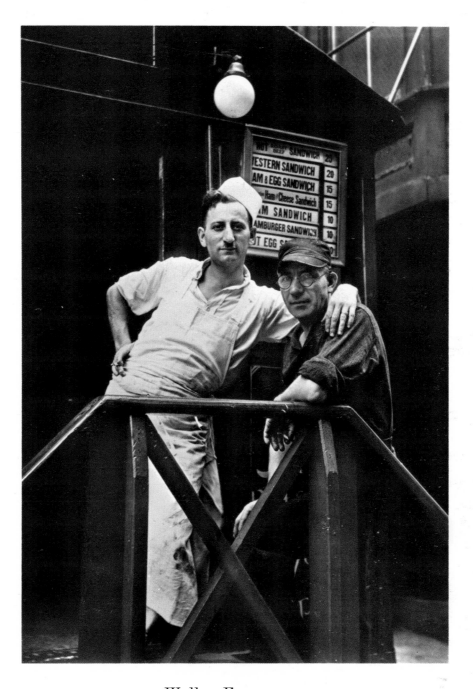

Walker Evans b. 1903
POSED PORTRAITS, NEW YORK
*1931. The Art Institute of Chicago, gift of Mrs. James Ward Thorne*

Walker Evans b. 1903
ALABAMA COTTON TENANT FARMER'S WIFE
*1936. The Art Institute of Chicago, gift of Mrs. James Ward Thorne*

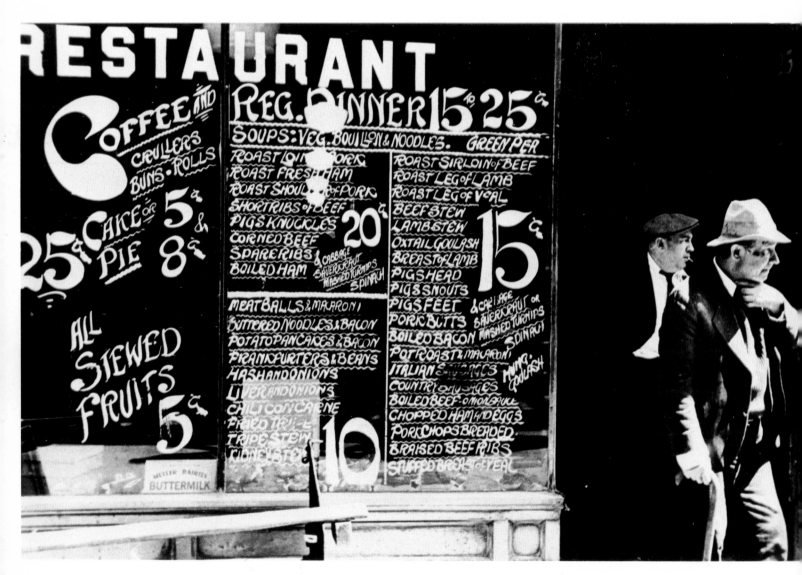

Ben Shahn 1898–1969
UNTITLED
ca. 1935. University of Louisville, Louisville, Ky., Photographic Archives

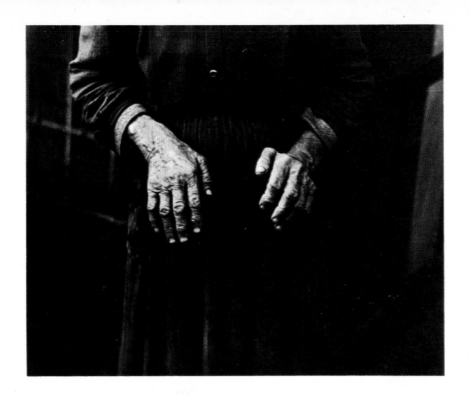

Russell Lee b. 1903
HANDS OF IOWA TENANT FARMER'S WIFE
*1936. The Museum of Modern Art, New York, gift of the Farm Security Administration*

Russell Lee b. 1903
IOWA FARM INTERIOR
*ca. 1937. The Museum of Modern Art, New York, gift of the Farm Security Administration*

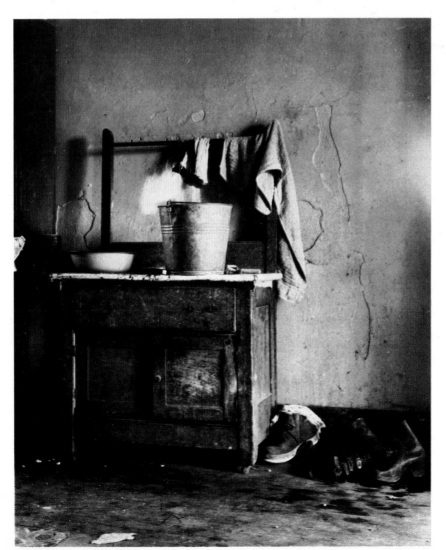

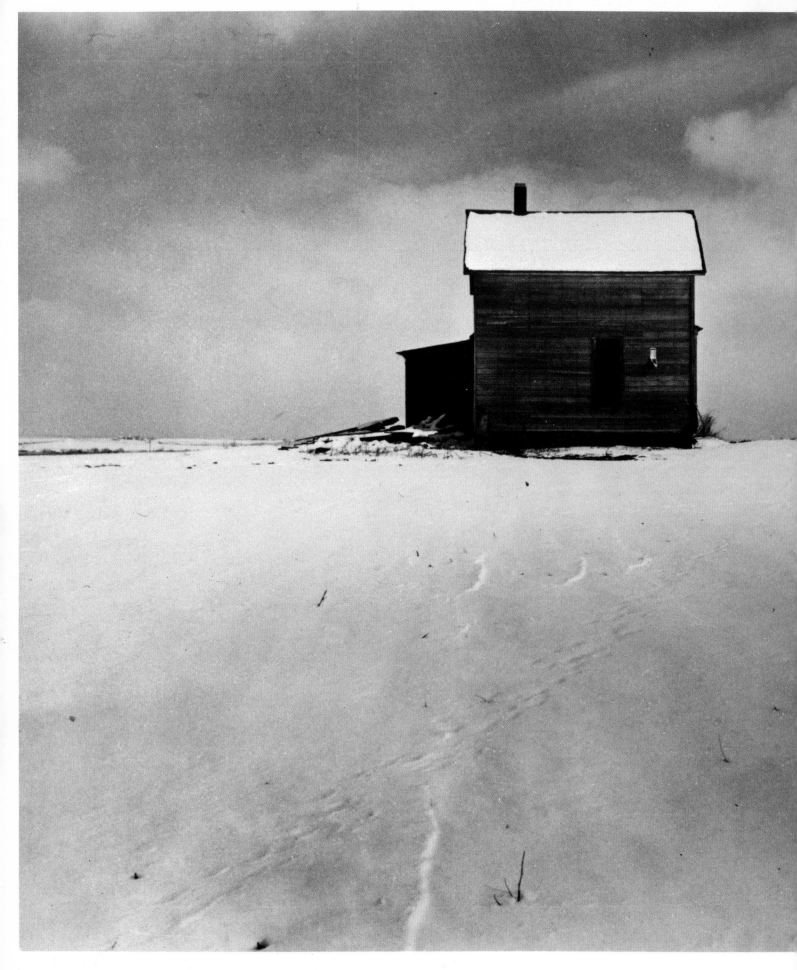

**Wright Morris** b. 1910
WINTER, NEBRASKA
*1941. Collection of the Photographer*

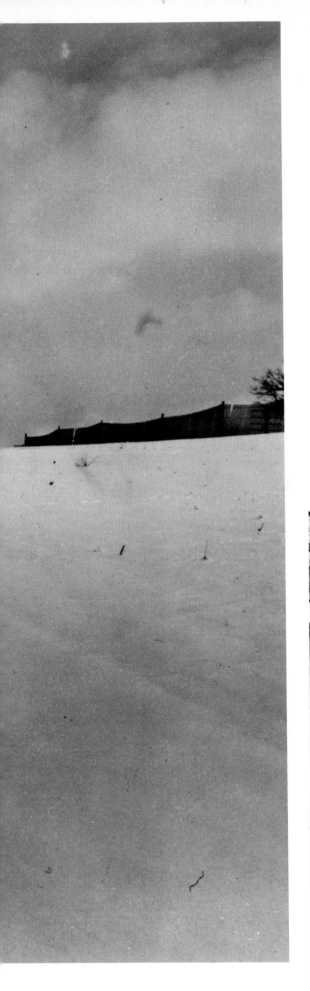

**Wright Morris** b. 1910
MY UNCLE HARRY
*1947. Collection of the Photographer*

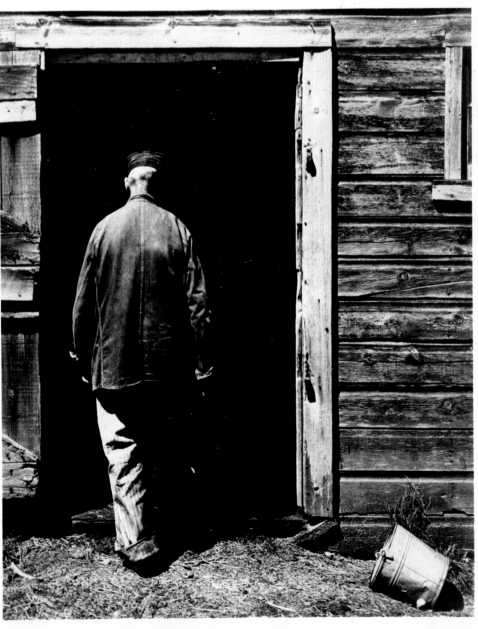

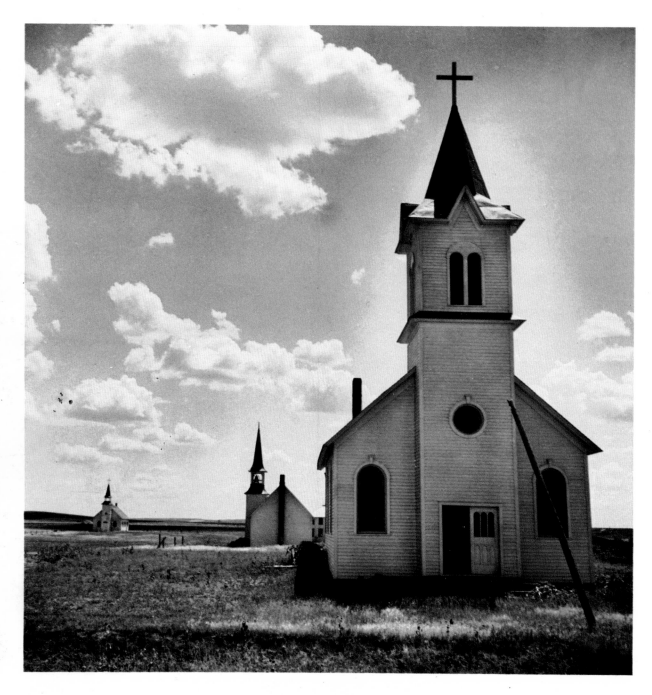

## Dorothea Lange 1895–1965
ON THE GREAT PLAINS, NEAR WINNER, SOUTH DAKOTA
*1938. The Museum of Modern Art, New York, courtesy The Oakland Museum, Dorothea Lange Collection*

## Dorothea Lange 1895–1965
MIGRANT MOTHER, NIPOMO, CALIFORNIA
*1936. The Museum of Modern Art, New York, courtesy The Oakland Museum, Dorothea Lange Collection*

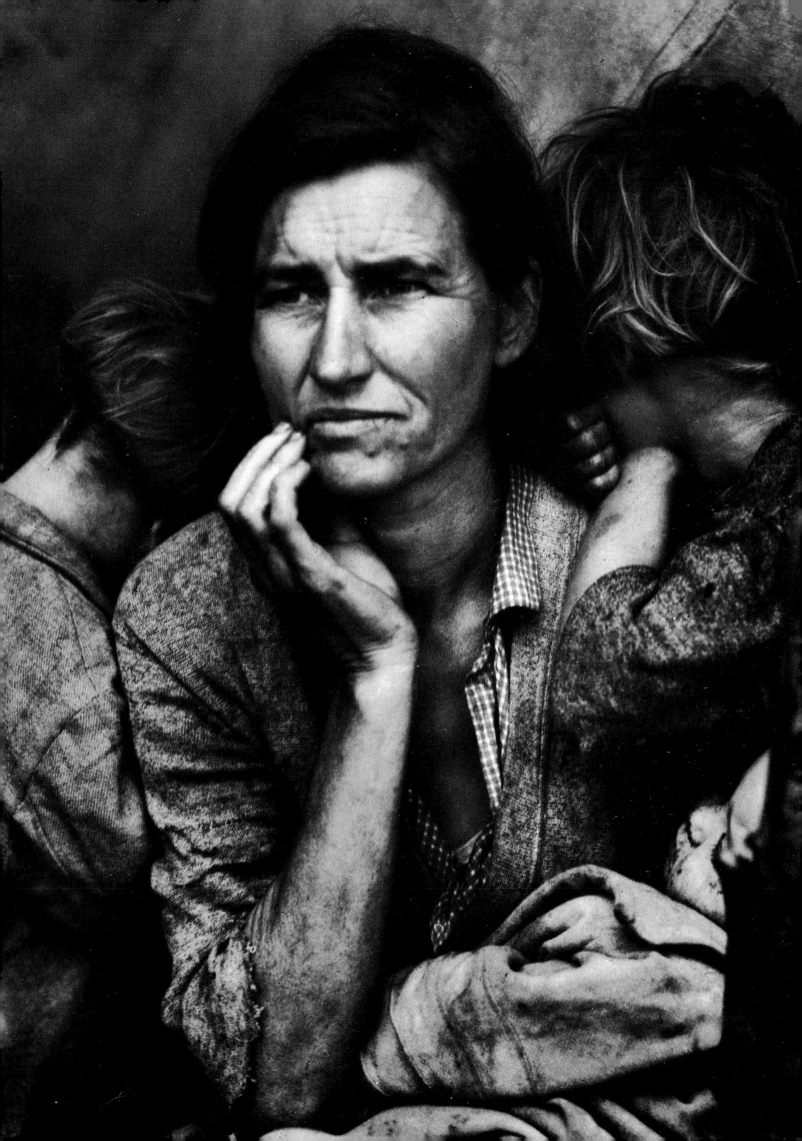

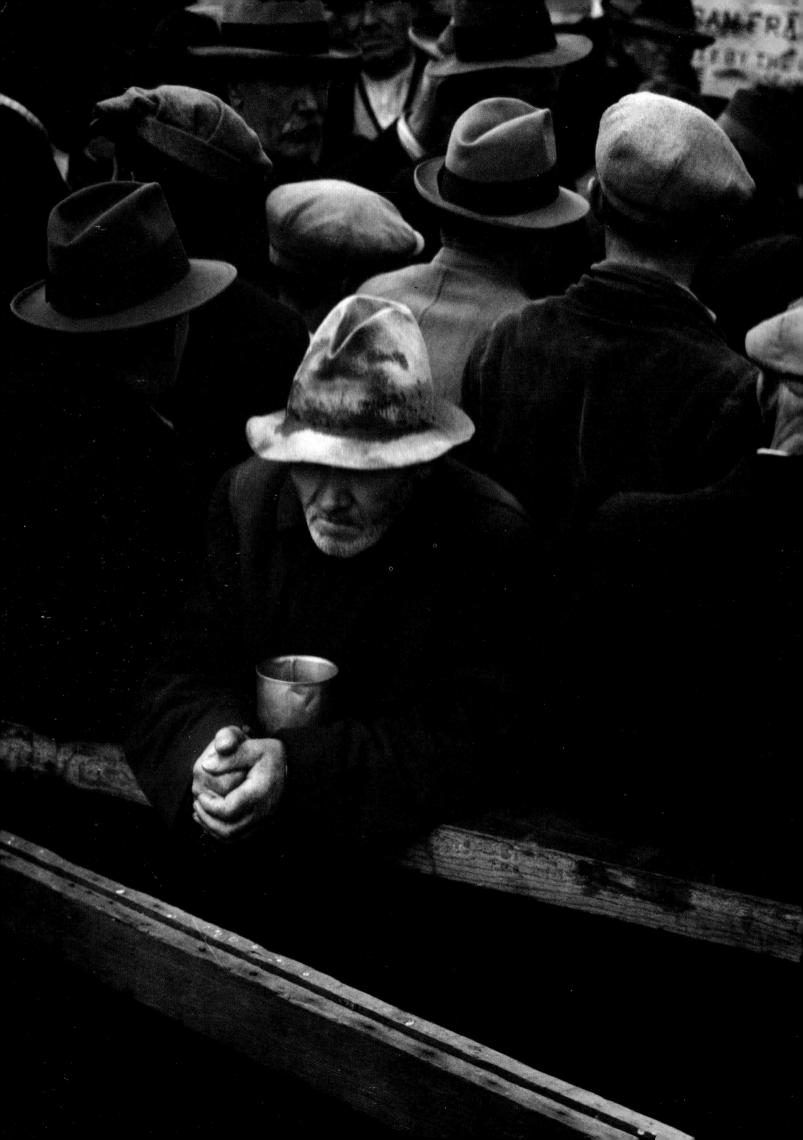

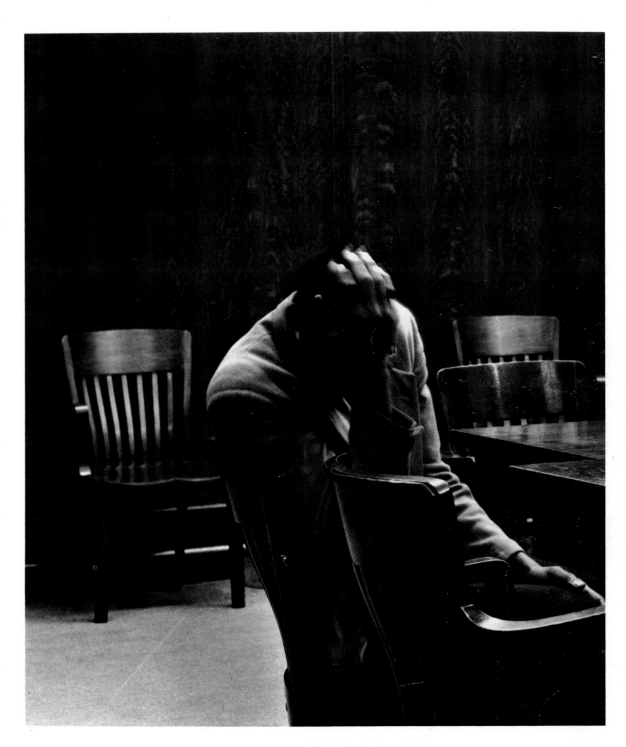

Dorothea Lange 1895–1965
THE DEFENDANT
*1955. The Museum of Modern Art, New York, courtesy The Oakland Museum, Dorothea Lange Collection*

Dorothea Lange 1895–1965
WHITE ANGEL BREADLINE, SAN FRANCISCO
*1933. The Museum of Modern Art, New York, courtesy The Oakland Museum, Dorothea Lange Collection*

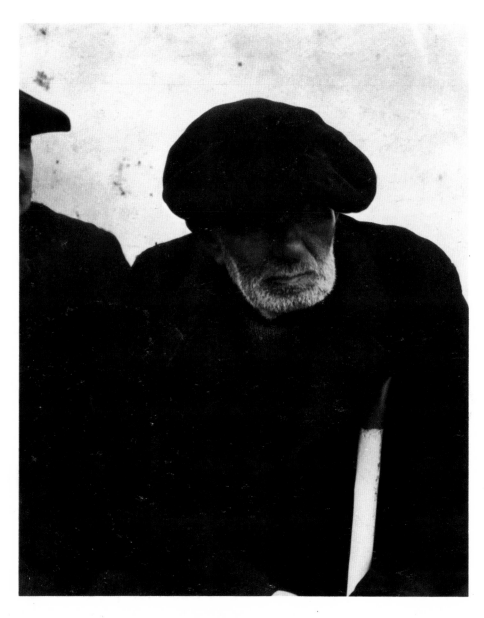

**Paul Strand** b. 1890
OLD SAILOR, PYRENEES, ORIENTALES, FRANCE
*1949. The Museum of Modern Art, New York*

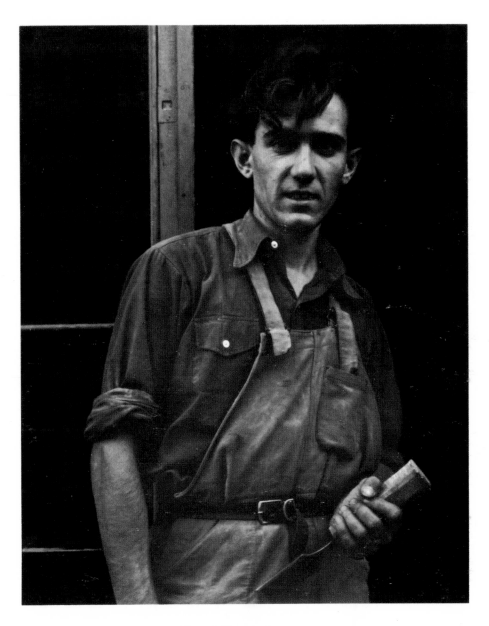

Paul Strand b. 1890
THE YOUNG CARPENTER, JARNAC, FRANCE
*1951. The Museum of Modern Art, New York*

148

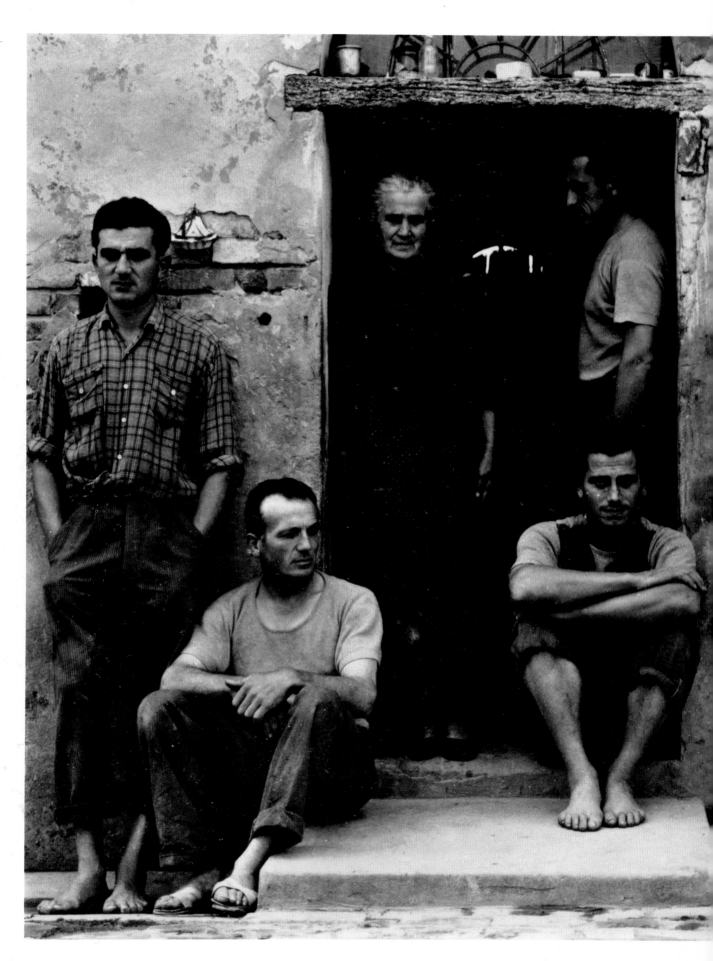

Paul Strand b. 1890
THE FAMILY, LUZZARA, ITALY
1953. The Fogg Art Museum, Harvard University, gift of the Photographer

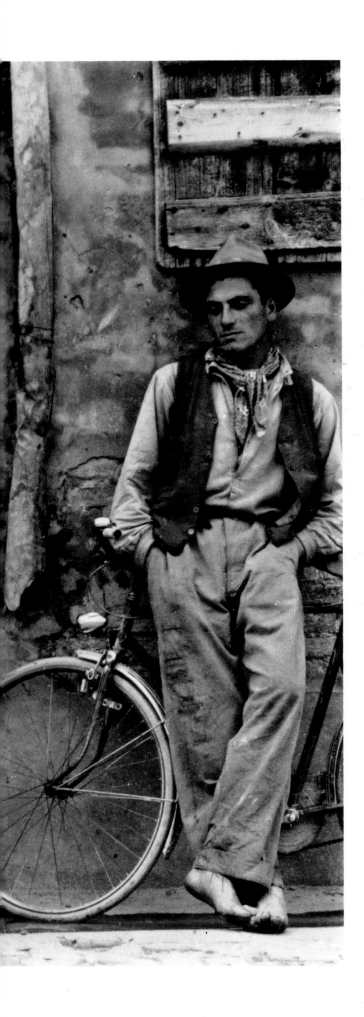

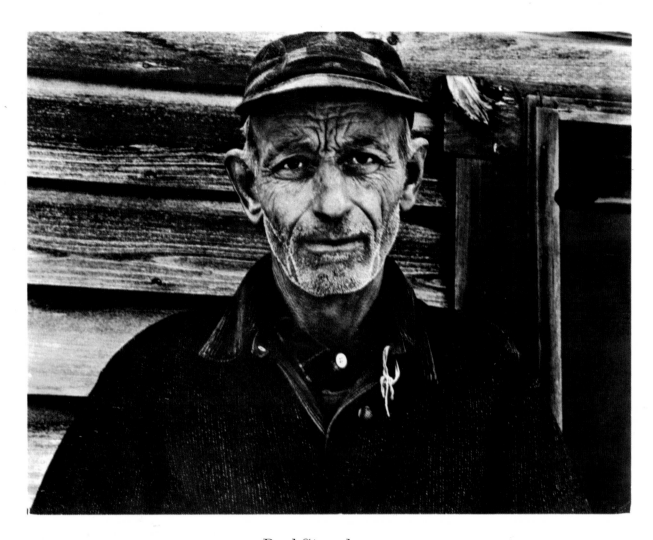

**Paul Strand** b. 1890
MR. BENNETT—WEST RIVER VALLEY, VERMONT
*1944. International Museum of Photography at George Eastman House, Rochester, N.Y.*

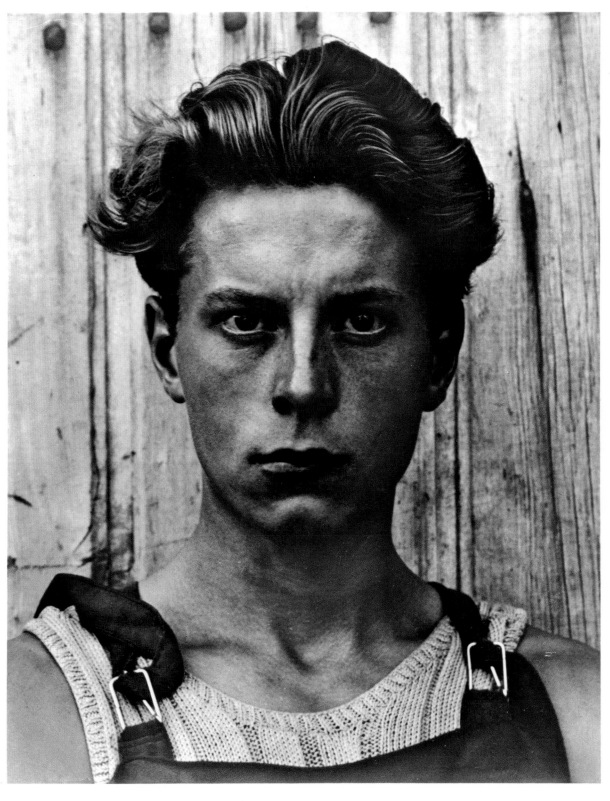

Paul Strand b. 1890
YOUNG BOY, GONDEVILLE, FRANCE
*1951. The Fogg Art Museum, Harvard University, gift of the Photographer*

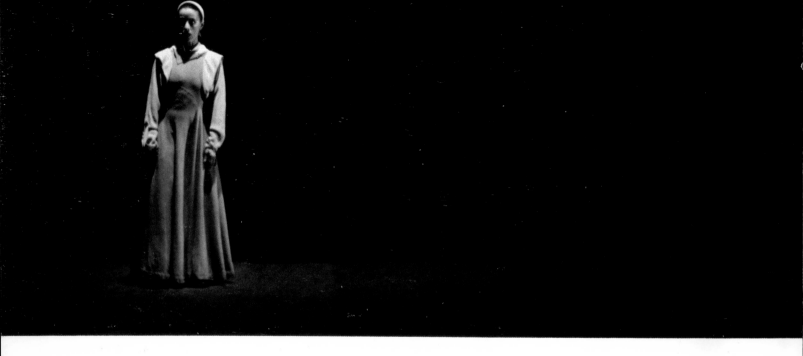

**Barbara Morgan** b. 1900
MARTHA GRAHAM : FRONTIER
*1935. Collection of the Photographer*

152

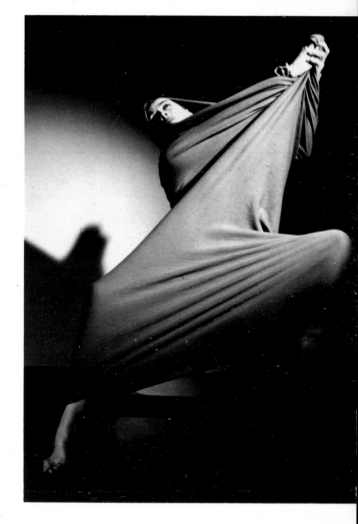

Barbara Morgan b. 1900
MARTHA GRAHAM : LAMENTATION
1935. Collection of the Photographer

153

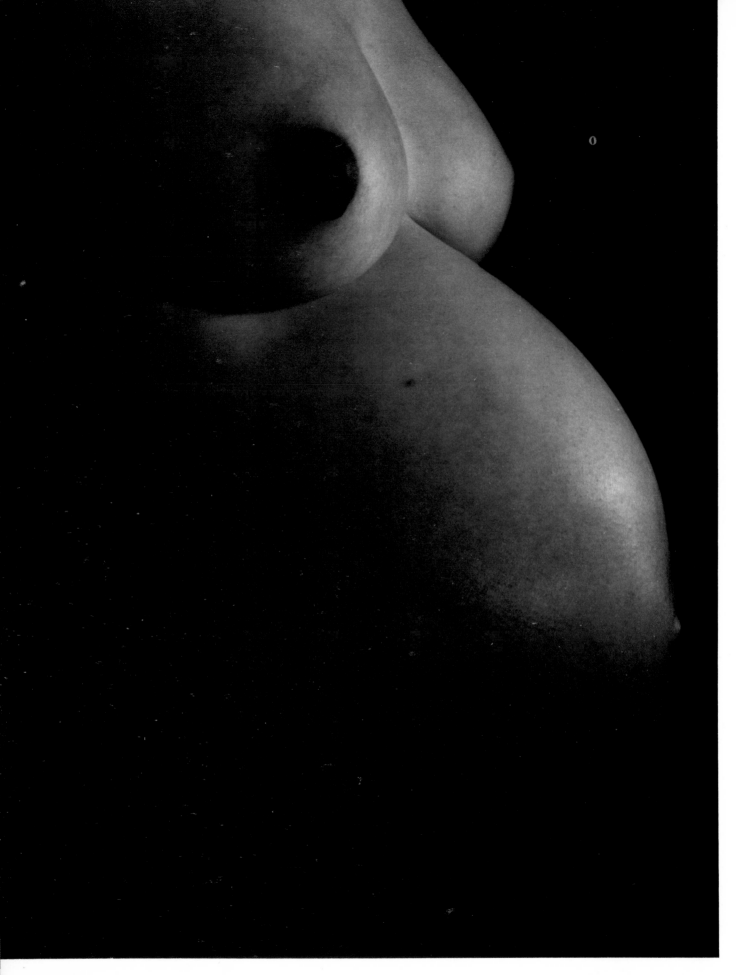

Barbara Morgan b. 1900
PREGNANT
*1940. Collection of the Photographer*

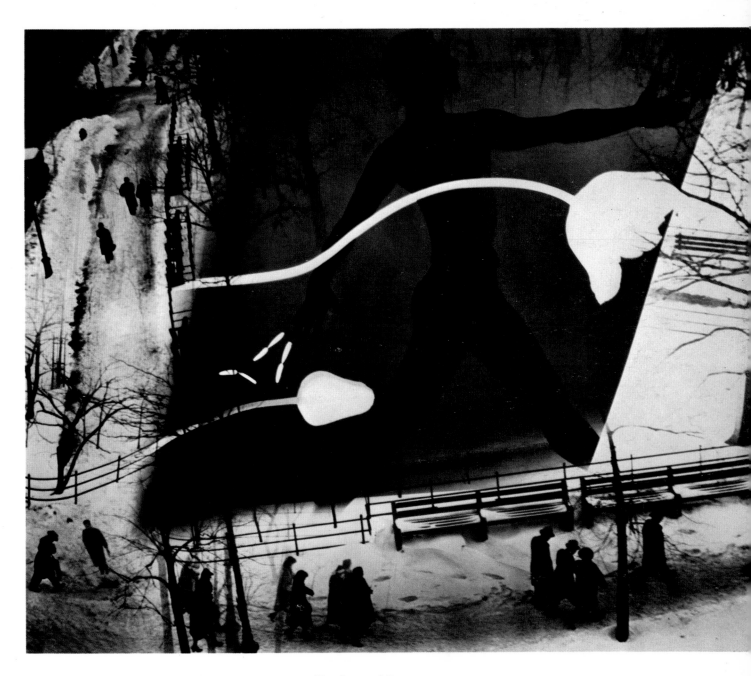

Barbara Morgan b. 1900
SPRING ON MADISON SQUARE
1938. Collection of the Photographer

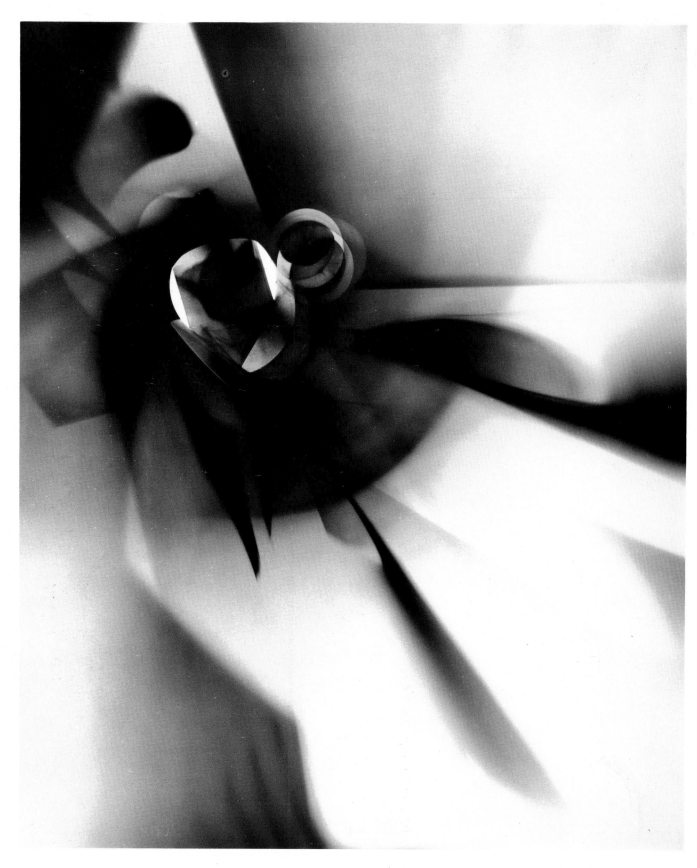

Arthur Siegel b. 1913

PHOTOGRAM #189

*1936. Collection of the Photographer*

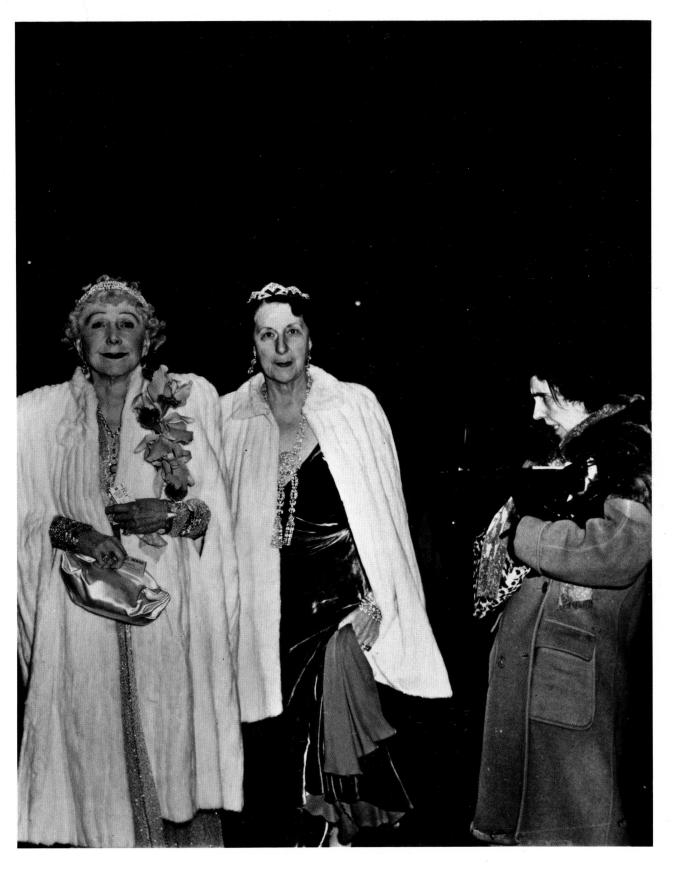

Weegee (Arthur Fellig) 1900–1968
THE CRITIC
*1943. The Art Institute of Chicago*

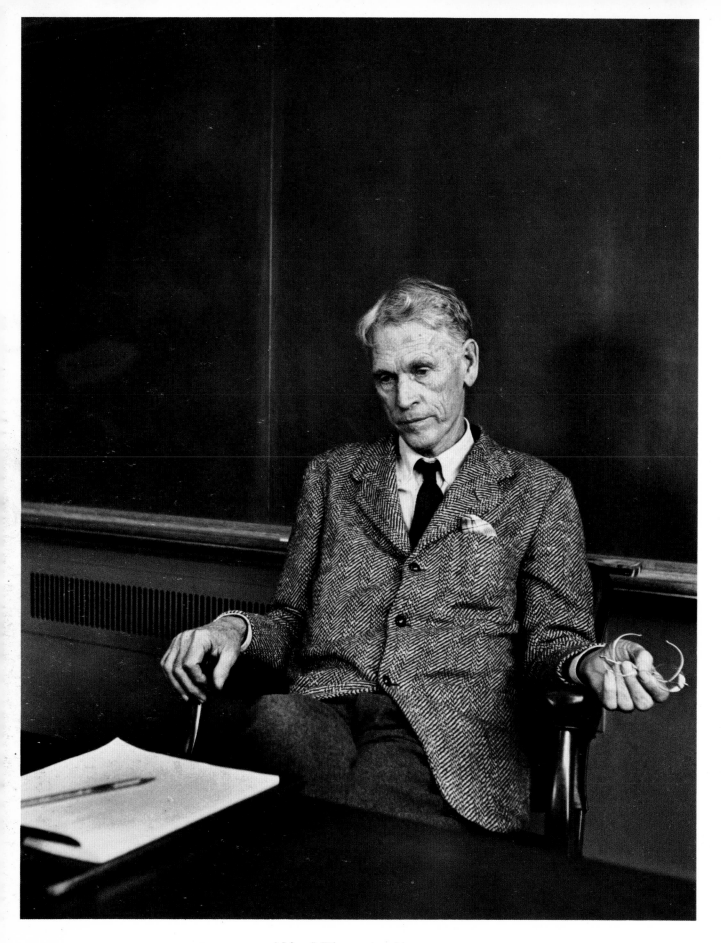

**Alfred Eisenstaedt** b. 1898
PROFESSOR OSWALD VEBLEN, THE INSTITUTE FOR ADVANCED STUDY
*1947. Collection of the Photographer*

W. Eugene Smith b. 1918
UNTITLED
1959. The Art Institute of Chicago

W. Eugene Smith b. 1918
SPANISH VILLAGE SERIES : WEAVING
*1951. The Art Institute of Chicago*

W. Eugene Smith b. 1918
JUANITA
*1953. The Art Institute of Chicago*

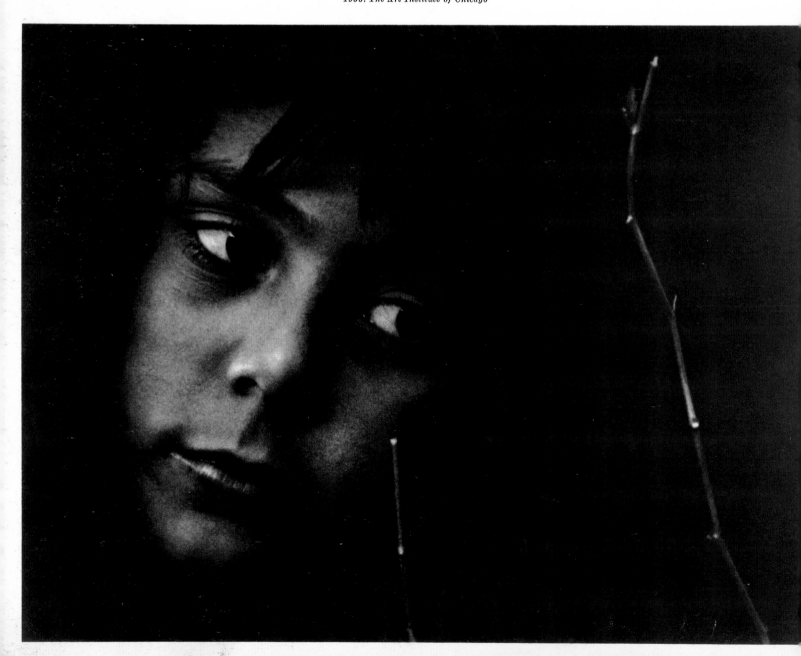

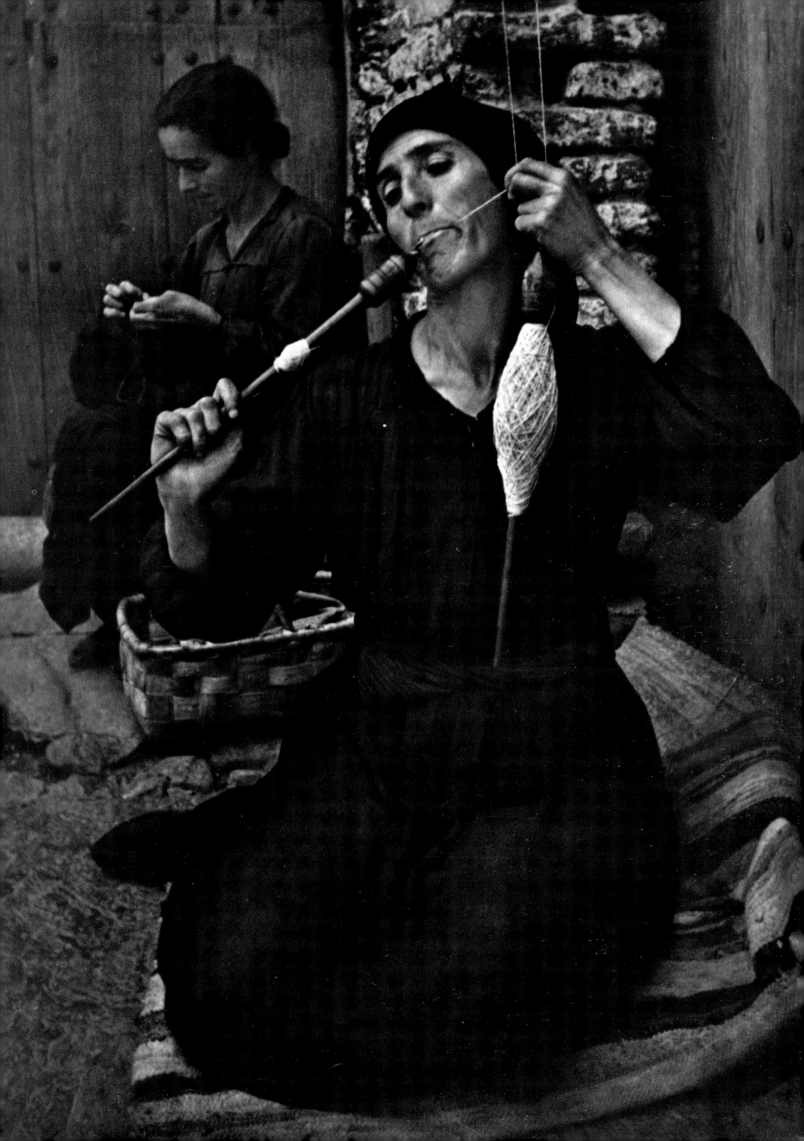

# W. Eugene Smith b. 1918

TOMOKO IN HER BATH, MINAMATA, JAPAN

*1972. The Witkin Gallery, Inc., New York*

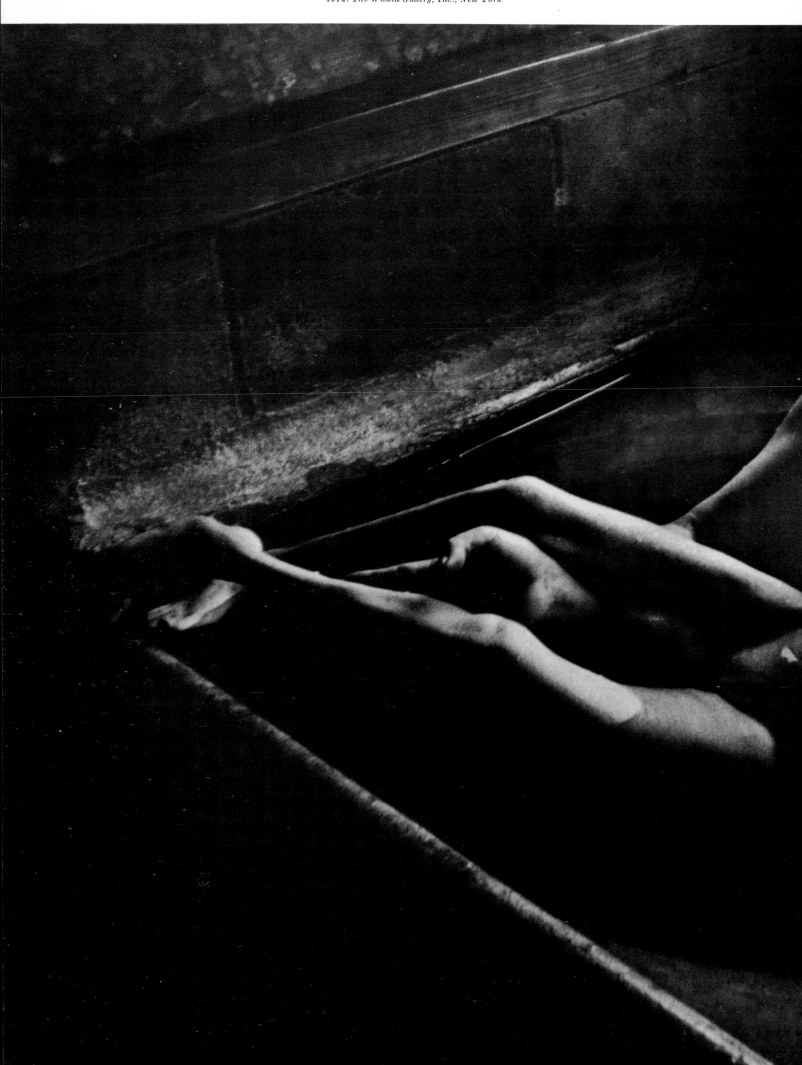

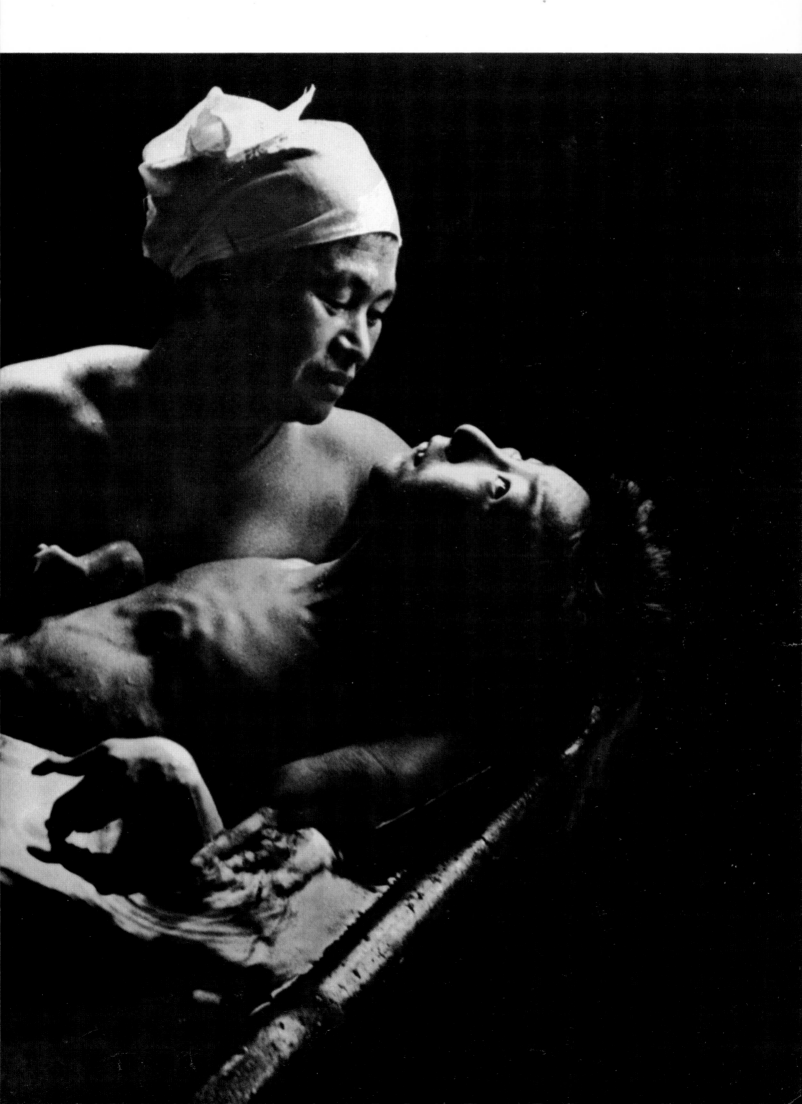

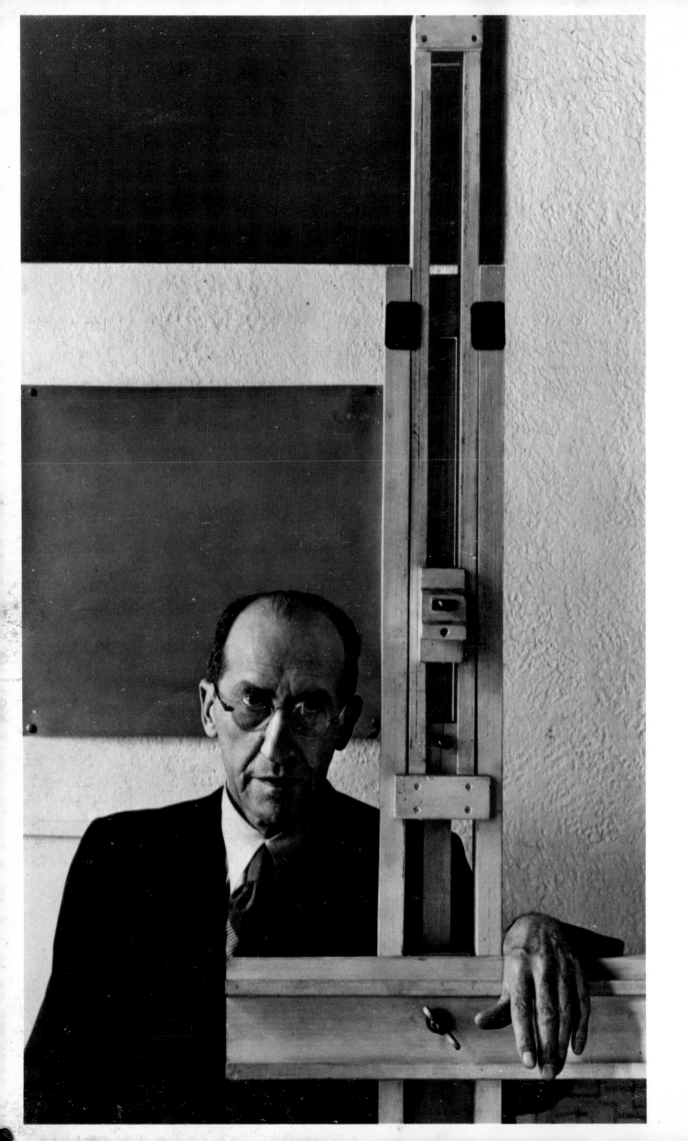

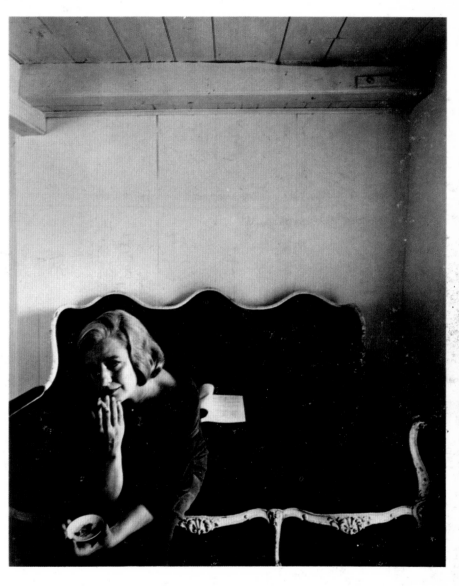

**Arnold Newman** b. 1918
KIM STANLEY
*1963. Light Gallery, New York*

**Arnold Newman** b. 1918
MONDRIAN
*1942. Light Gallery, New York*

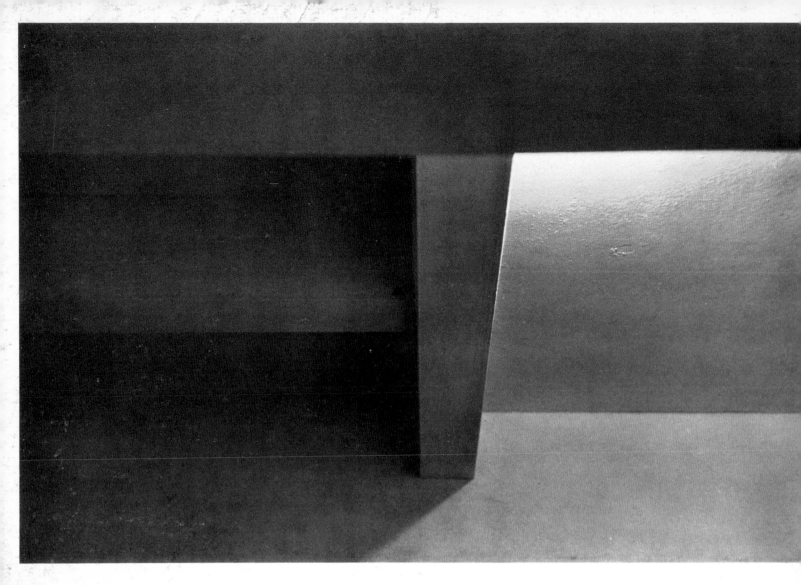

Roy DeCarava b. 1919
UNTITLED
*1969. Collection of the Photographer*

Roy DeCarava b. 1919
UNTITLED
*1952. Collection of the Photographer*

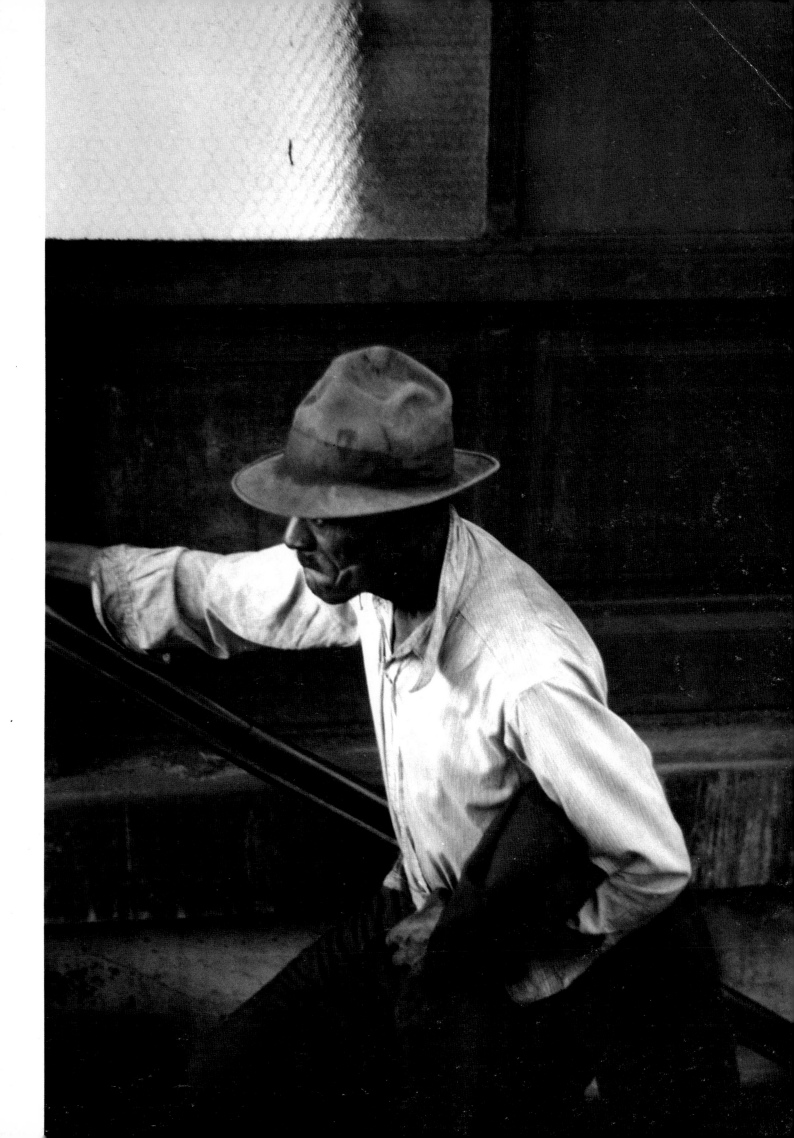

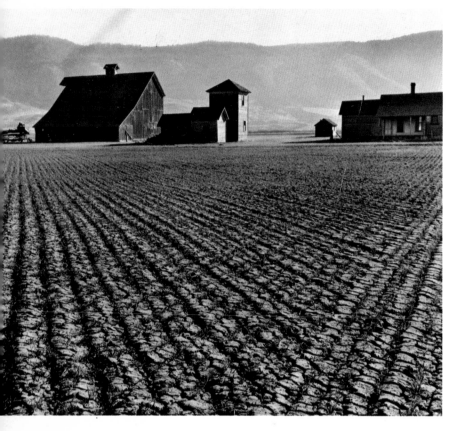

Minor White b. 1908
RANCH, GRANDE RONDE VALLEY
*1941. Collection of the Photographer*

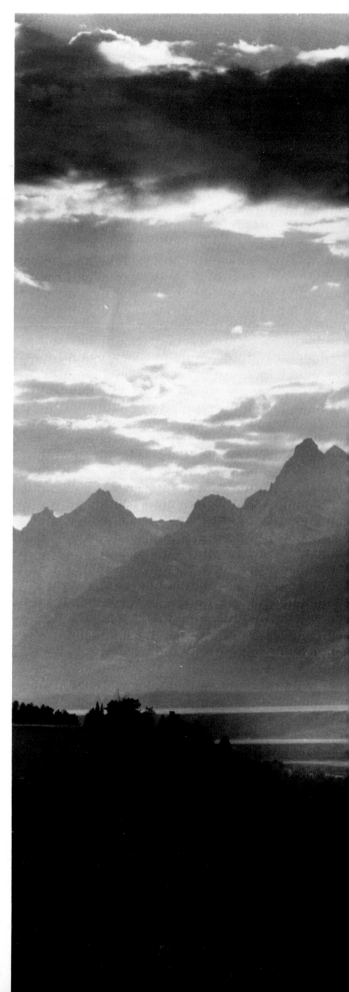

Minor White b. 1908
GRAND TETONS, WYOMING
*1959. Collection of the Photographer*

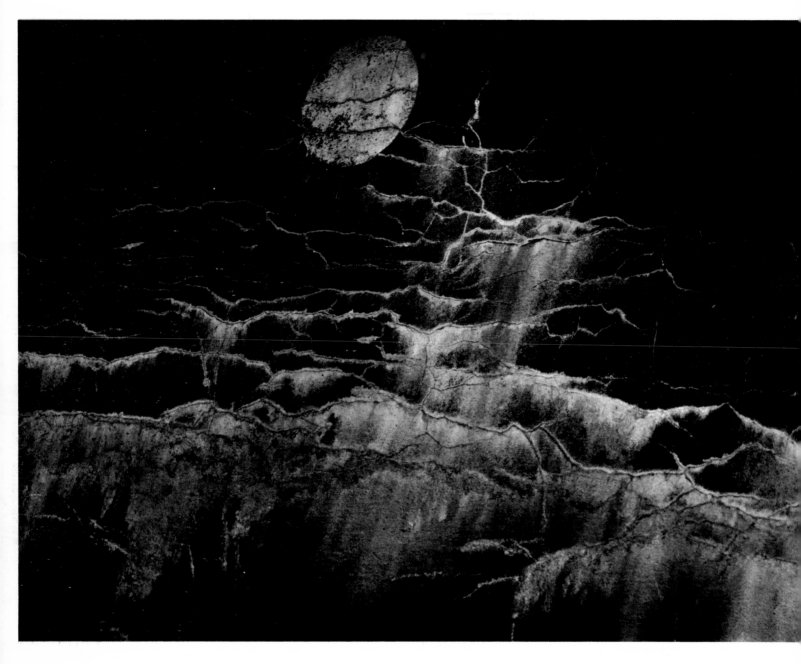

**Minor White** b. 1908
MOON AND WALL ENCRUSTATIONS
*1964. Collection of the Photographer*

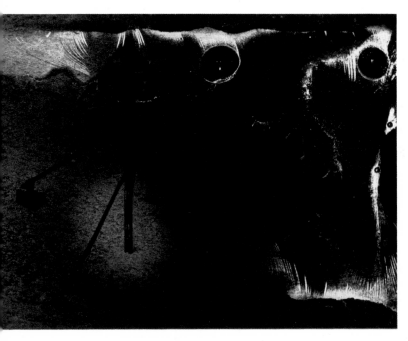

**Minor White** b. 1908
NAVIGATION MARKER, NOVA SCOTIA
*1970. Collection of the Photographer*

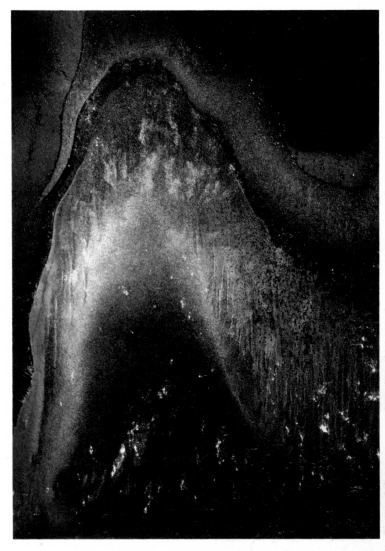

**Minor White** b. 1908
FROST WAVE, ROCHESTER, NEW YORK
*1959. Collection of the Photographer*

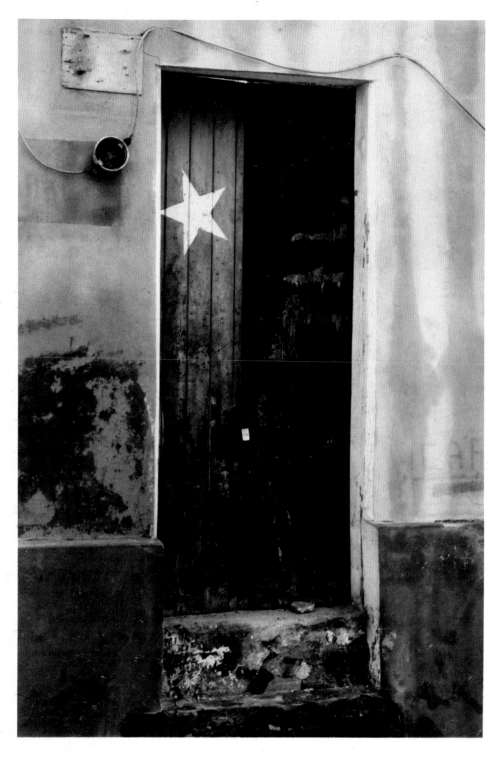

**Minor White** b. 1908
DOOR AND STAR, SAN JUAN, PUERTO RICO
*1973. Collection of the Photographer*

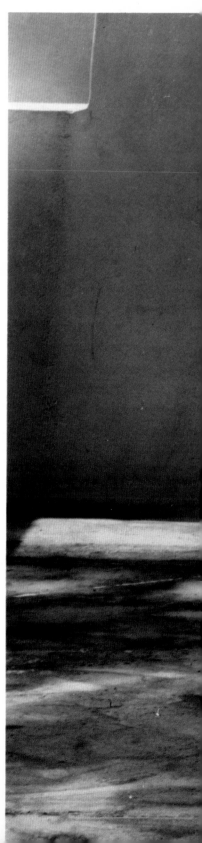

Minor White b. 1908
CEMETERY, PONCE, PUERTO RICO
*1973. Collection of the Photographer*

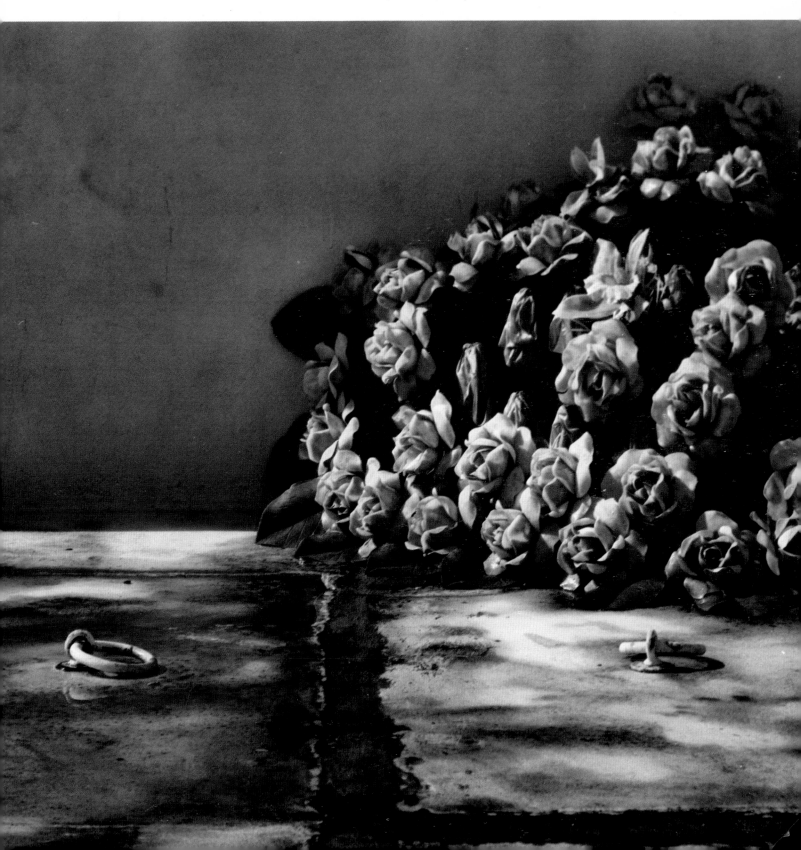

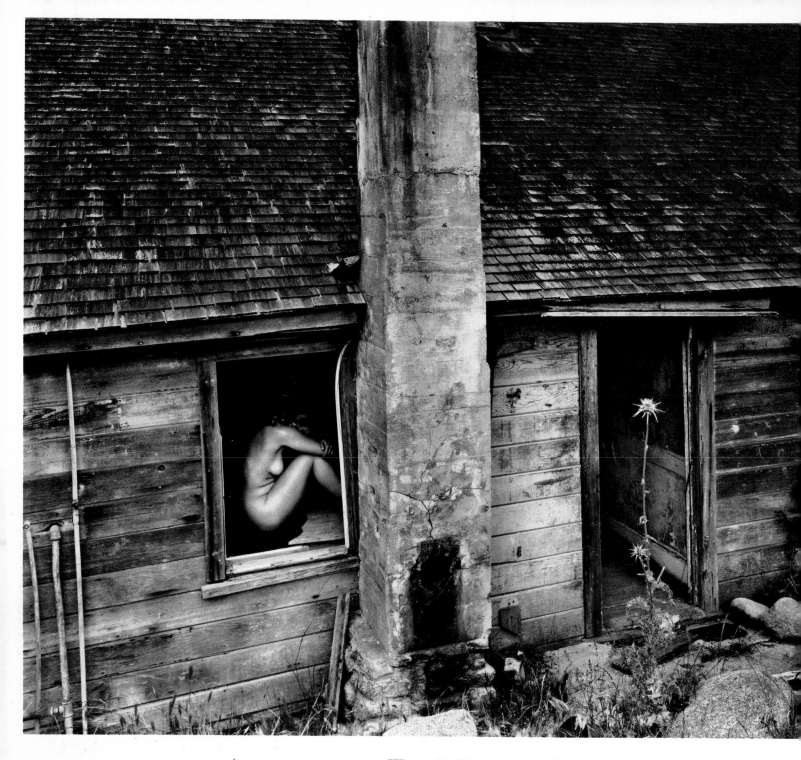

Wynn Bullock b. 1902
WOMAN AND THISTLE
1953. Collection of the Photographer

174

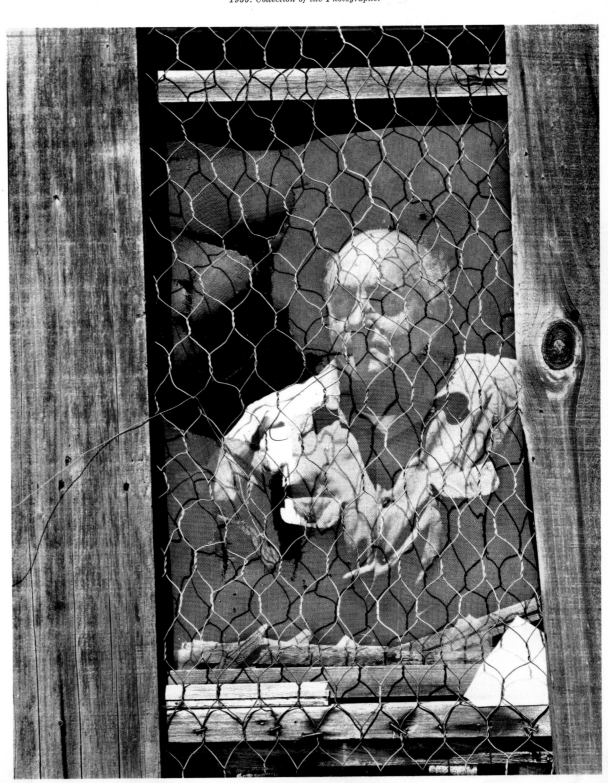

**Wynn Bullock** b. 1902
SAWED-OFF TREE TRUNK
*1972. Collection of the Photographer*

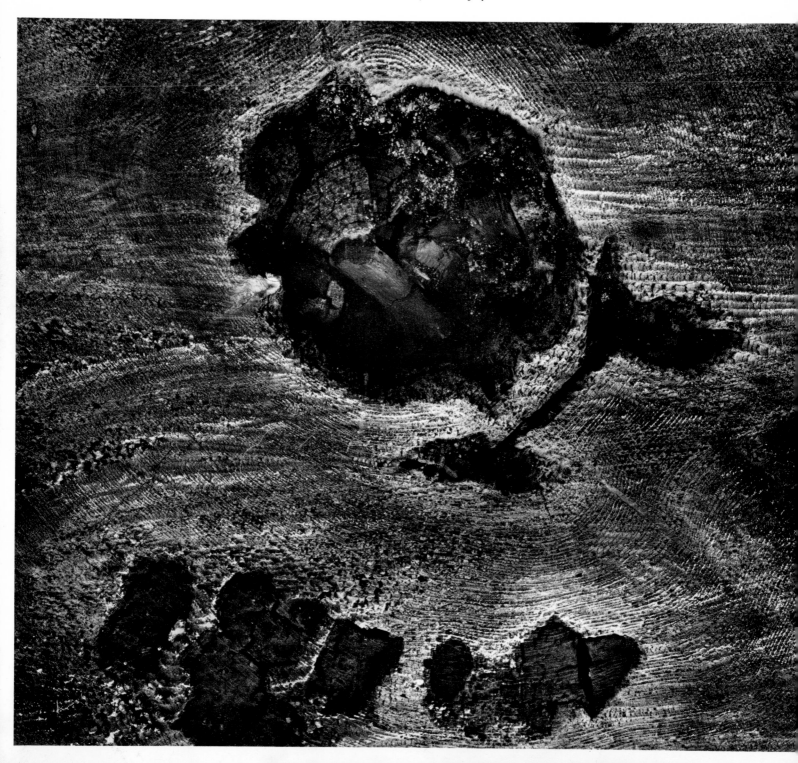

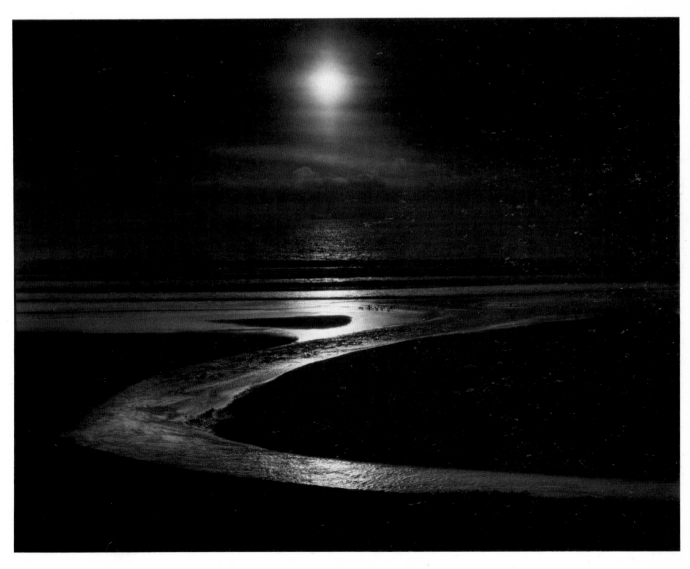

**Wynn Bullock** b. 1902
LET THERE BE LIGHT
*1954. Collection of the Photographer*

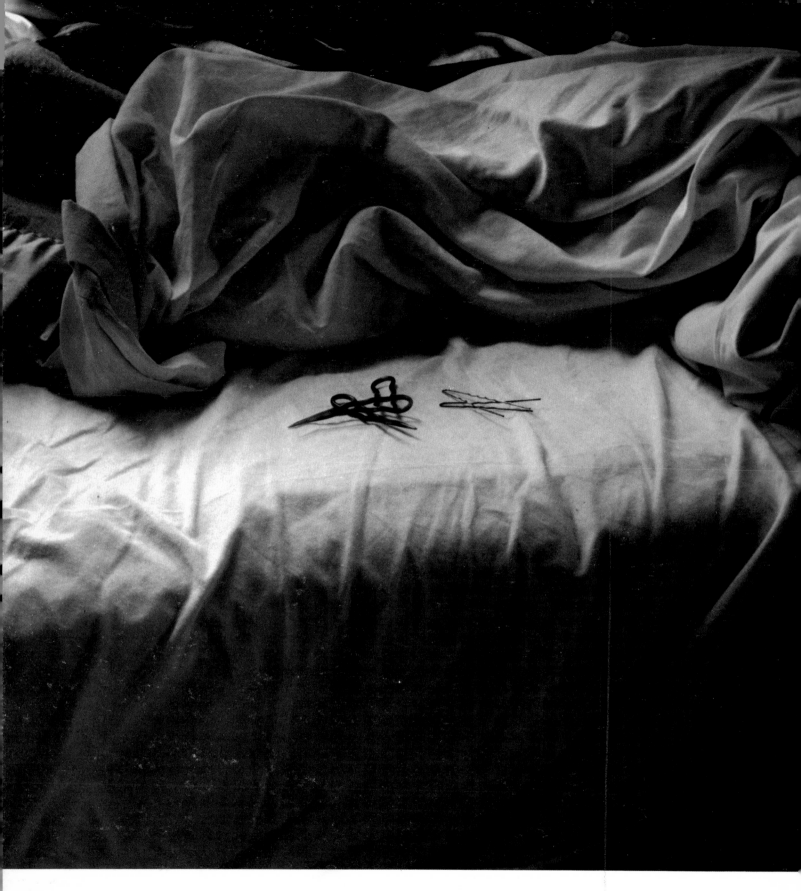

Imogen Cunningham b. 1883
THE UNMADE BED
*1957. Collection of the Photographer*

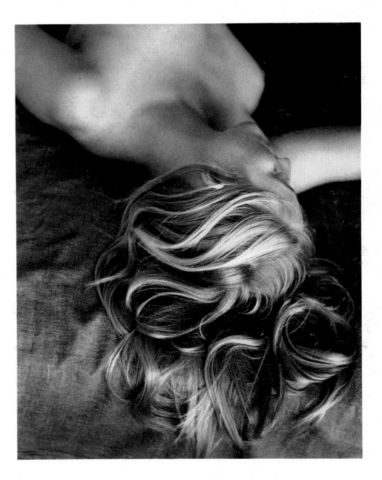

Imogen Cunningham b. 1883
PHOENIX RECUMBENT
*1968. Collection of the Photographer*

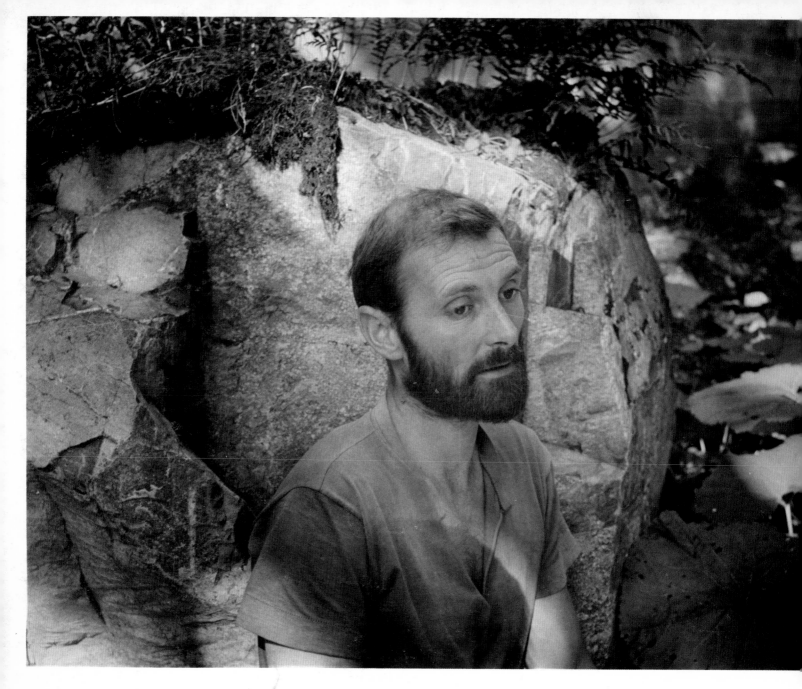

Imogen Cunningham b. 1883
MORRIS GRAVES, PAINTER
*1950. Collection of the Photographer*

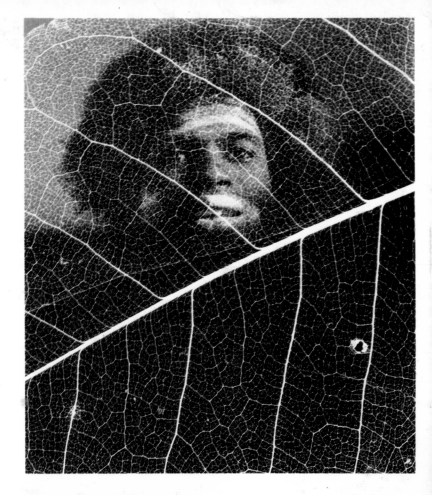

**Imogen Cunningham** b. 1883
CHRIS
*1973. Collection of the Photographer*

**Imogen Cunningham** b. 1883
DREAM WALKING
*1968. Collection of the Photographer*

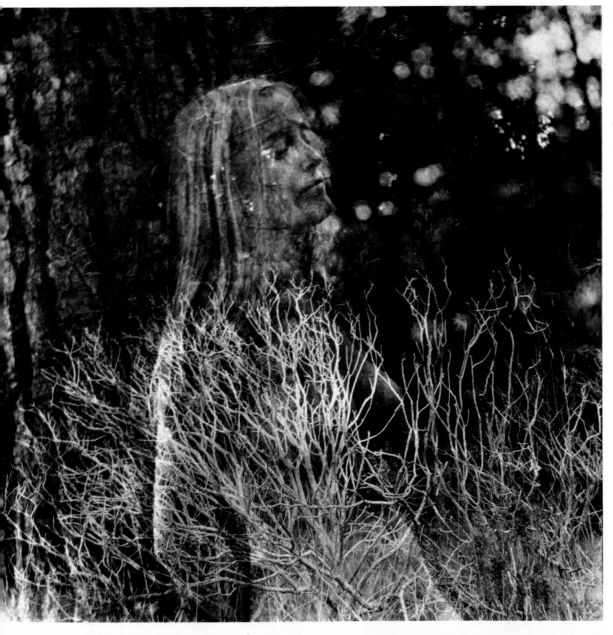

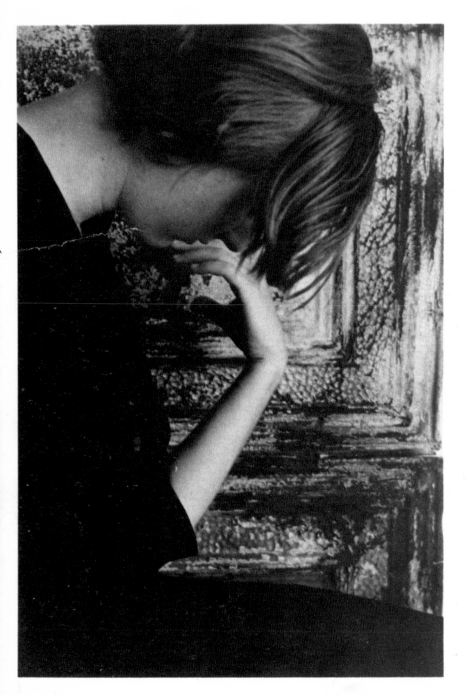

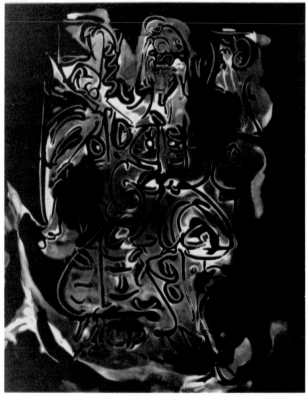

**Frederick Sommer** b. 1905
LEE NEVIN
*1960. Light Gallery, New York*

**Frederick Sommer** b. 1905
SMOKE ON GLASS
*1964. Light Gallery, New York*

182

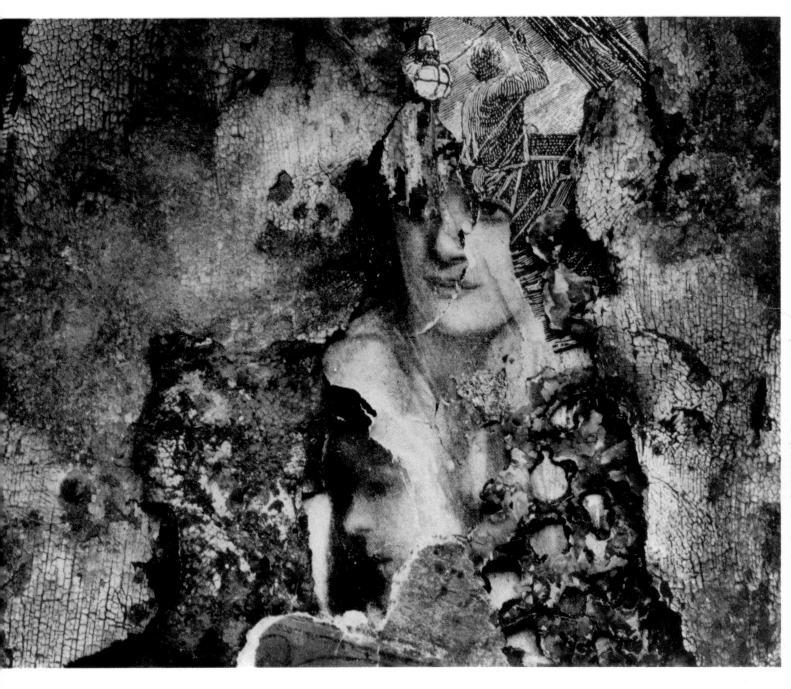

Frederick Sommer b. 1905
CIRCUMNAVIGATION OF THE BLOOD
*1950. Light Gallery, New York*

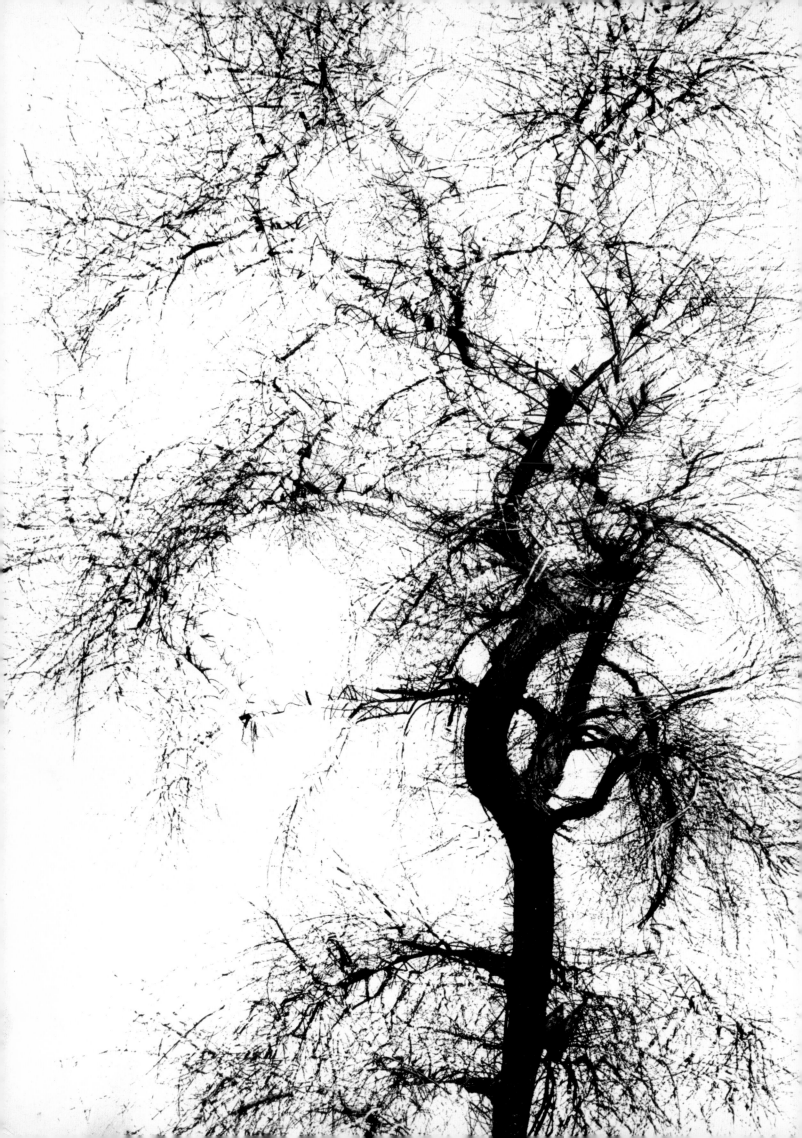

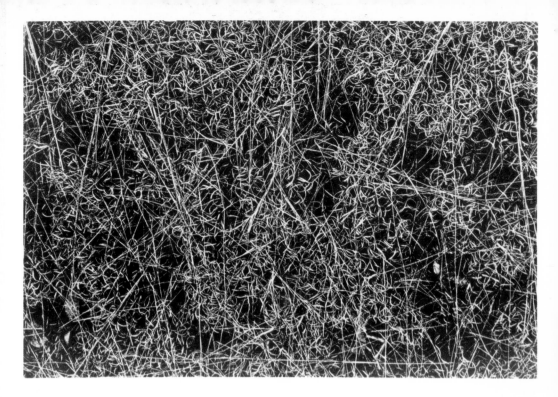

**Harry Callahan** b. 1912
RHODE ISLAND
*1964. Light Gallery, New York*

**Harry Callahan** b. 1912
MULTIPLE EXPOSURE TREE, CHICAGO
*1956. Light Gallery, New York*

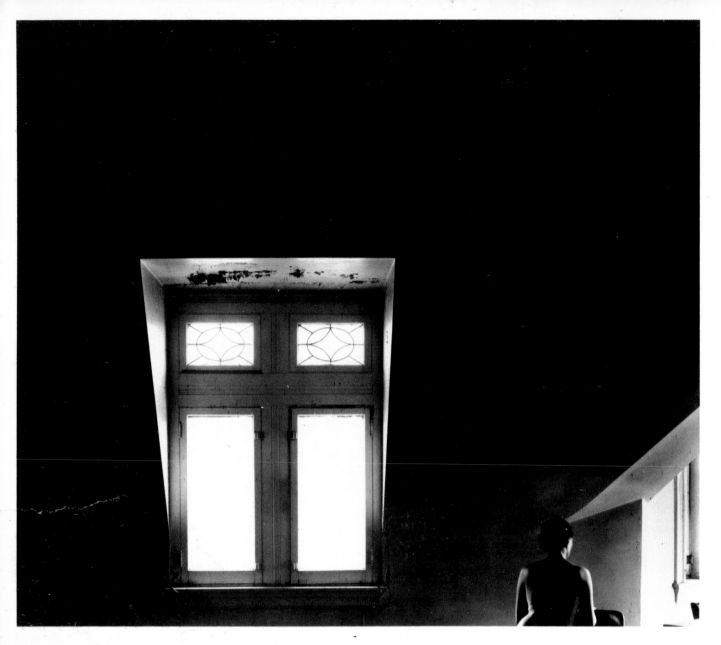

Harry Callahan b. 1912
ELEANOR
*1948. Light Gallery, New York*

Harry Callahan b. 1912
UNTITLED
*1972. Light Gallery, New York*

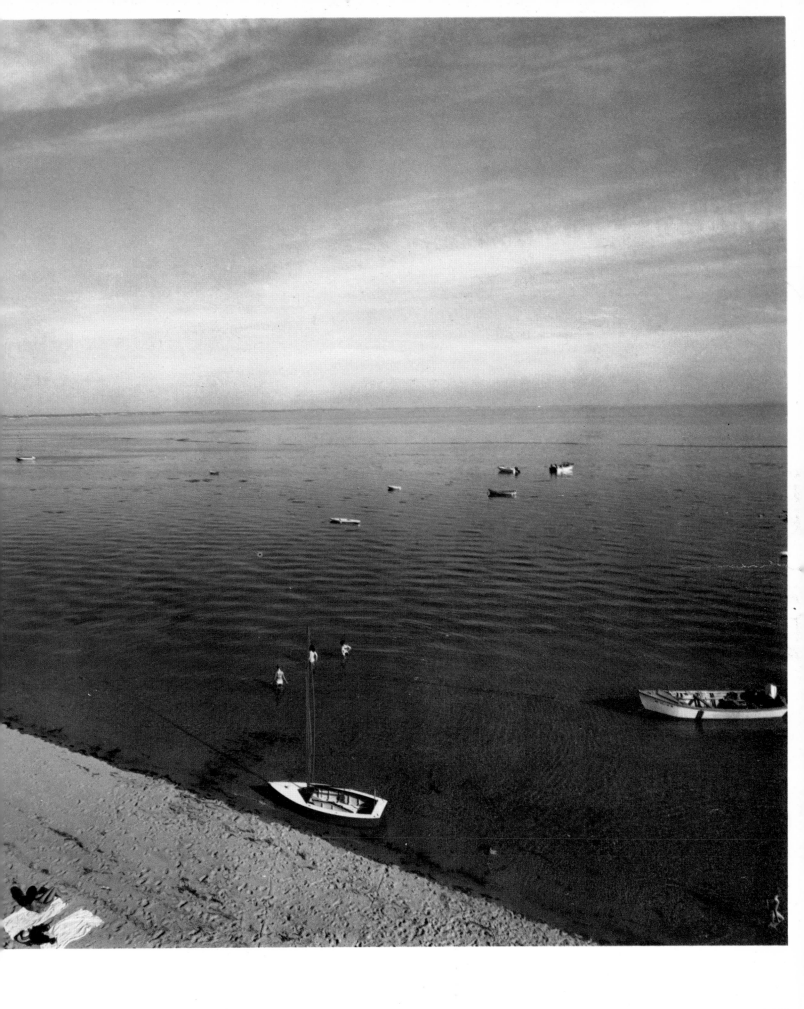

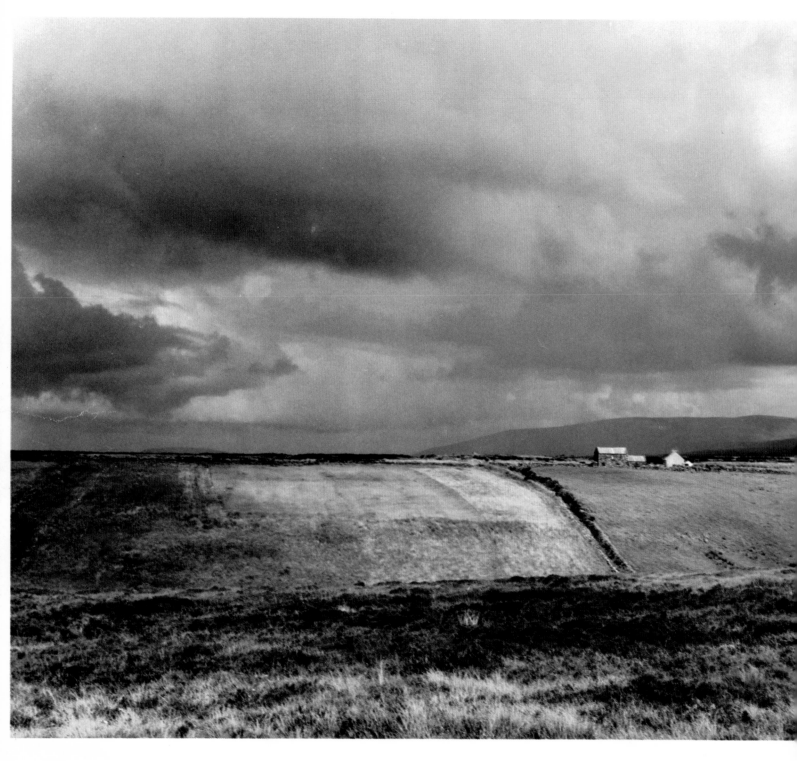

**Paul Caponigro** b. 1932
IRELAND, COUNTY SLIGO
*1967. Collection of the Photographer*

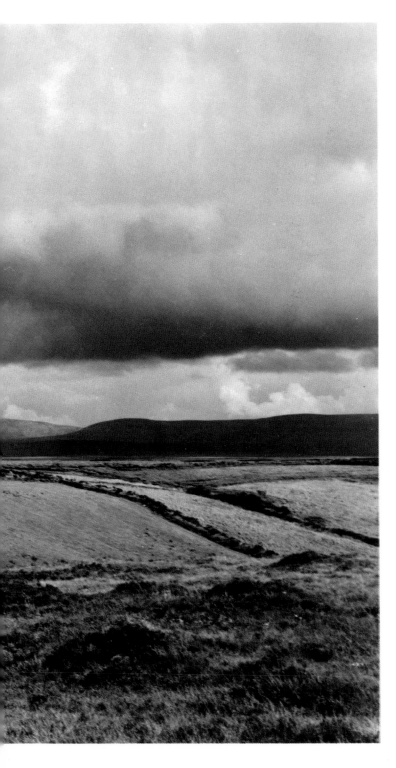

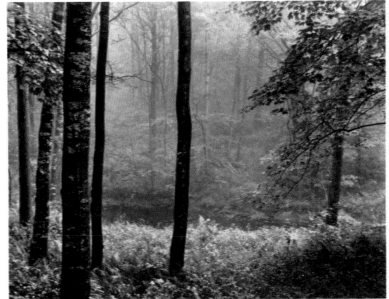

Paul Caponigro b. 1932
REDDING WOODS
*1969. Collection of the Photographer*

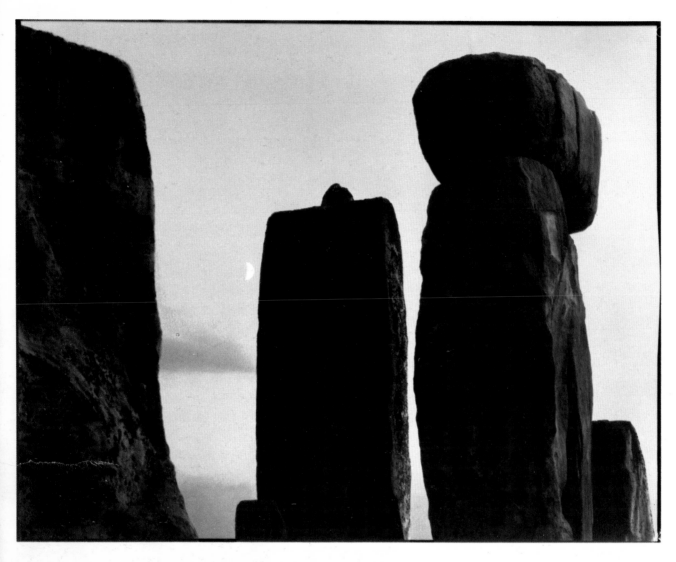

Paul Caponigro b. 1932
STONEHENGE
*1972. Collection of the Photographer*

Paul Caponigro b. 1932
ROCK WALL NUMBER 2, WEST HARTFORD, CONNECTICUT
*1959. Collection of the Photographer*

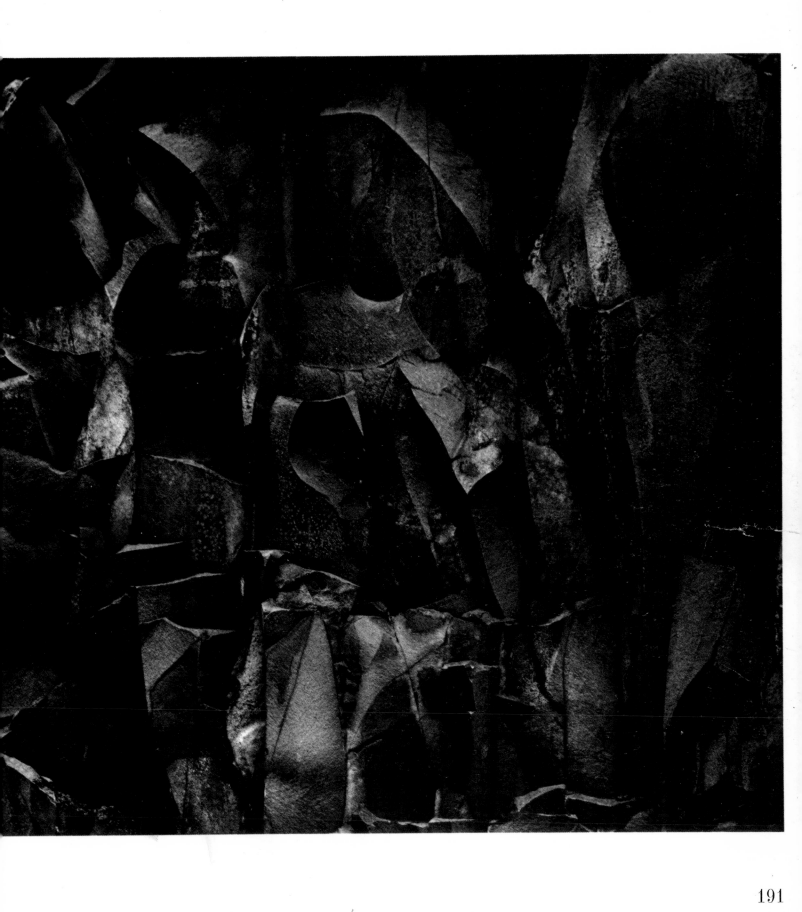

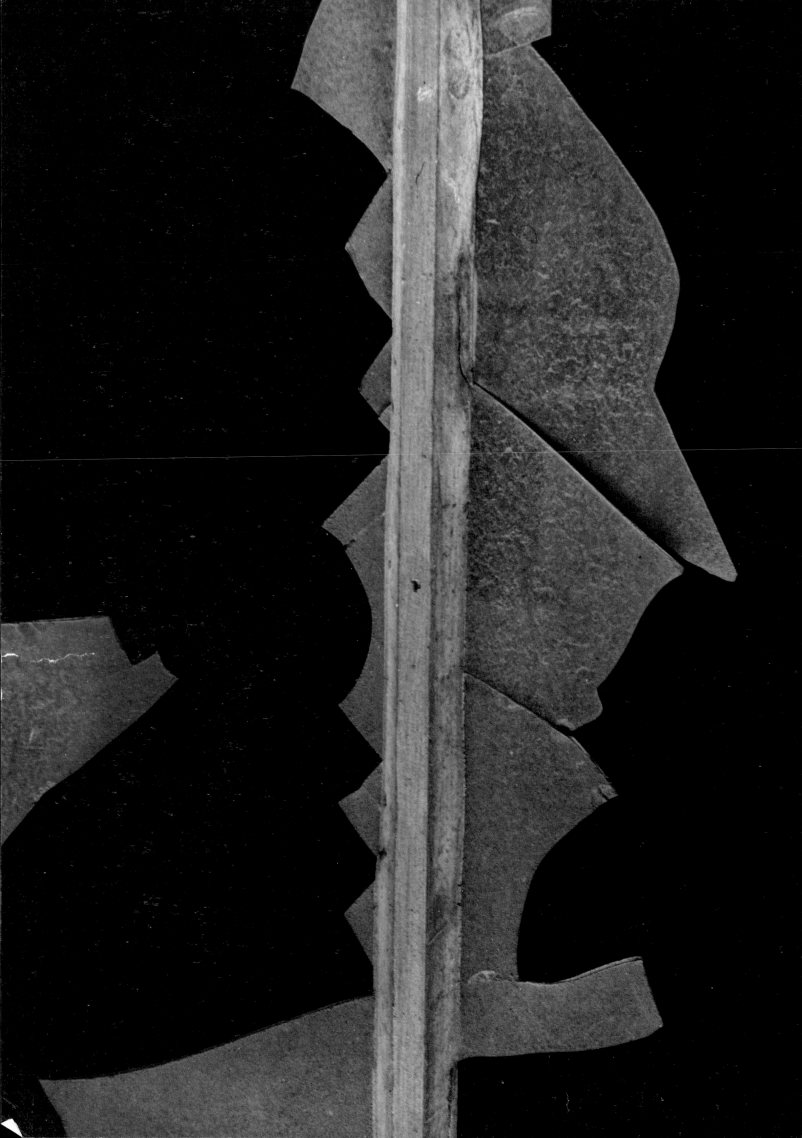

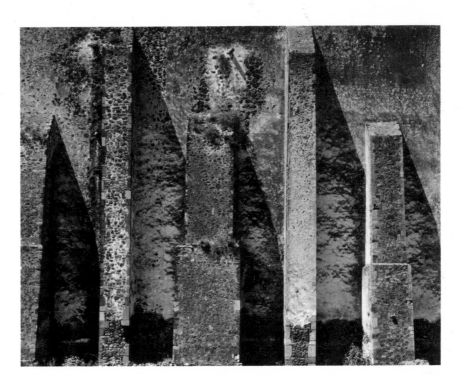

Aaron Siskind b. 1903
CHICAGO 25
1960. Light Gallery, New York

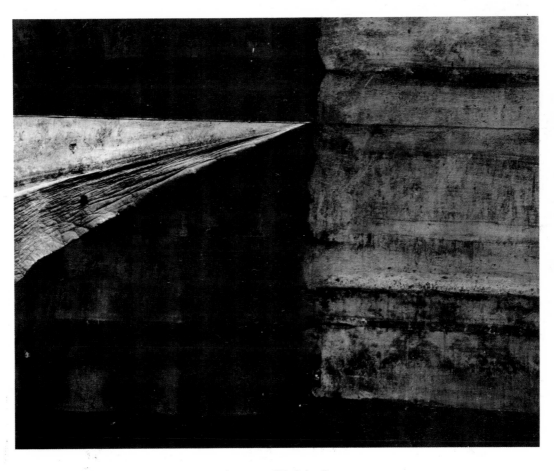

Aaron Siskind b. 1903
NEW YORK
1948. Light Gallery, New York

Aaron Siskind b. 1903
ACOLMAN, MEXICO 2
1955. Light Gallery, New York

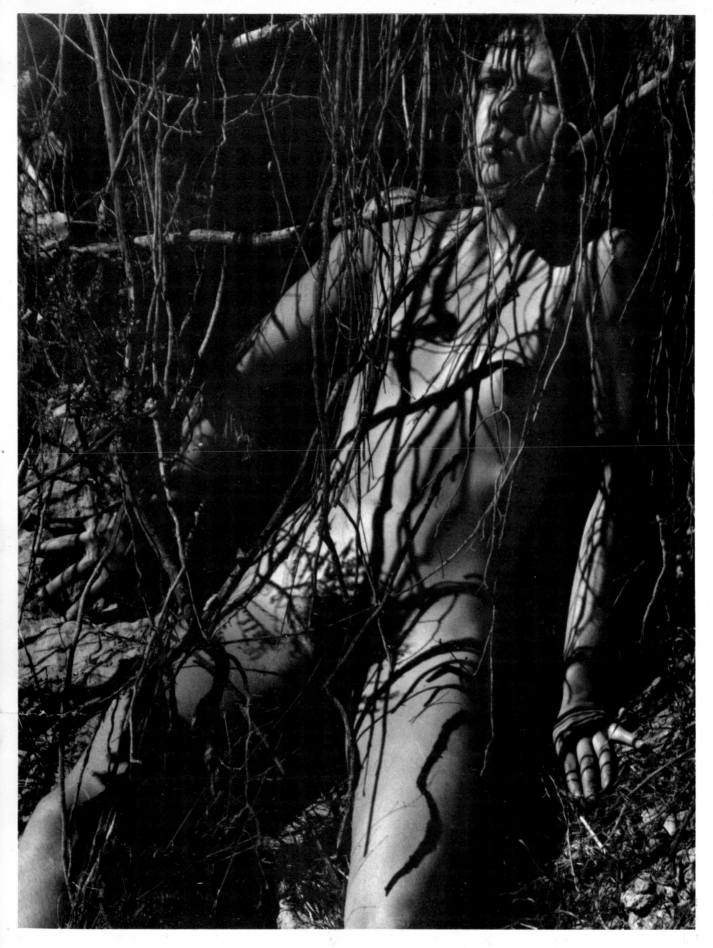

Walter Chappell b. 1925
NUDE WITH ROOT PATTERN, SANTA CRUZ
*1972. Collection of the Photographer*

**Walter Chappell** b. 1925
NUDE
*1973. Collection of the Photographer*

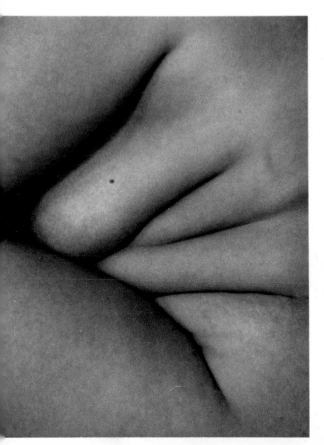

**Walter Chappell** b. 1925
MALE TORSO WITH SHADOWS
*1973. Collection of the Photographer*

195

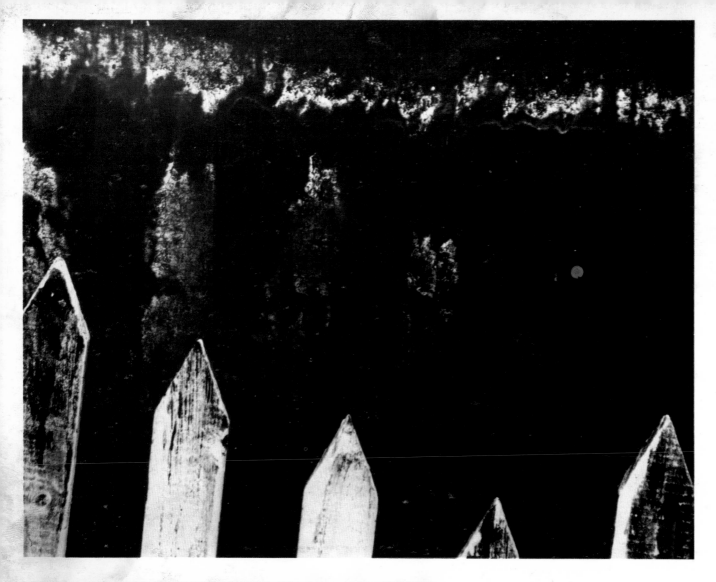

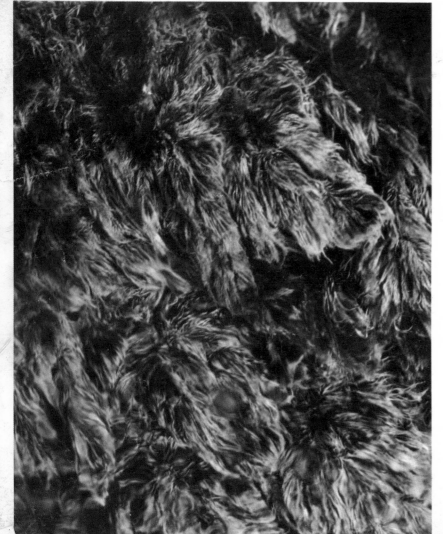

Walter Chappell b. 1925
PICKET FENCE
*1958. Collection of the Photographer*

Walter Chappell b. 1925
MINERAL GRASS
*1963. Collection of the Photographer*

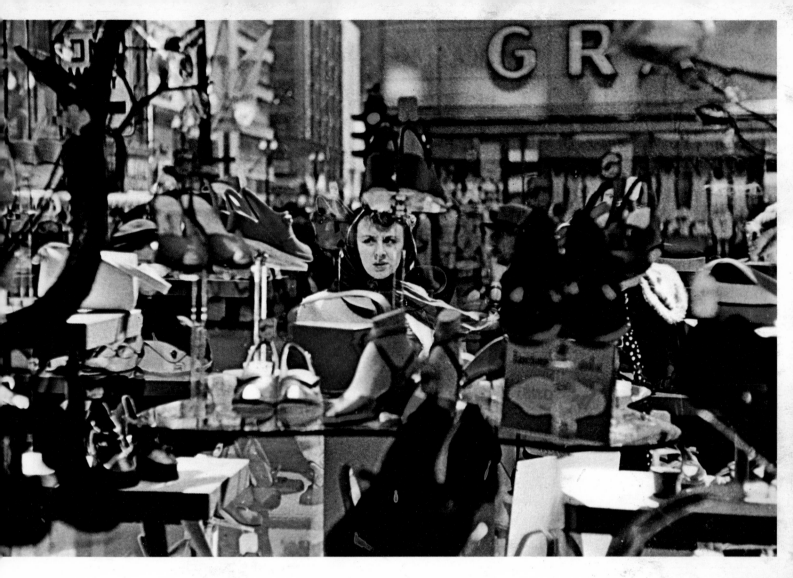

**Arthur Siegel** b. 1913
FROM THE SERIES: "IN SEARCH OF MYSELF"
*1951. Collection of the Photographer*

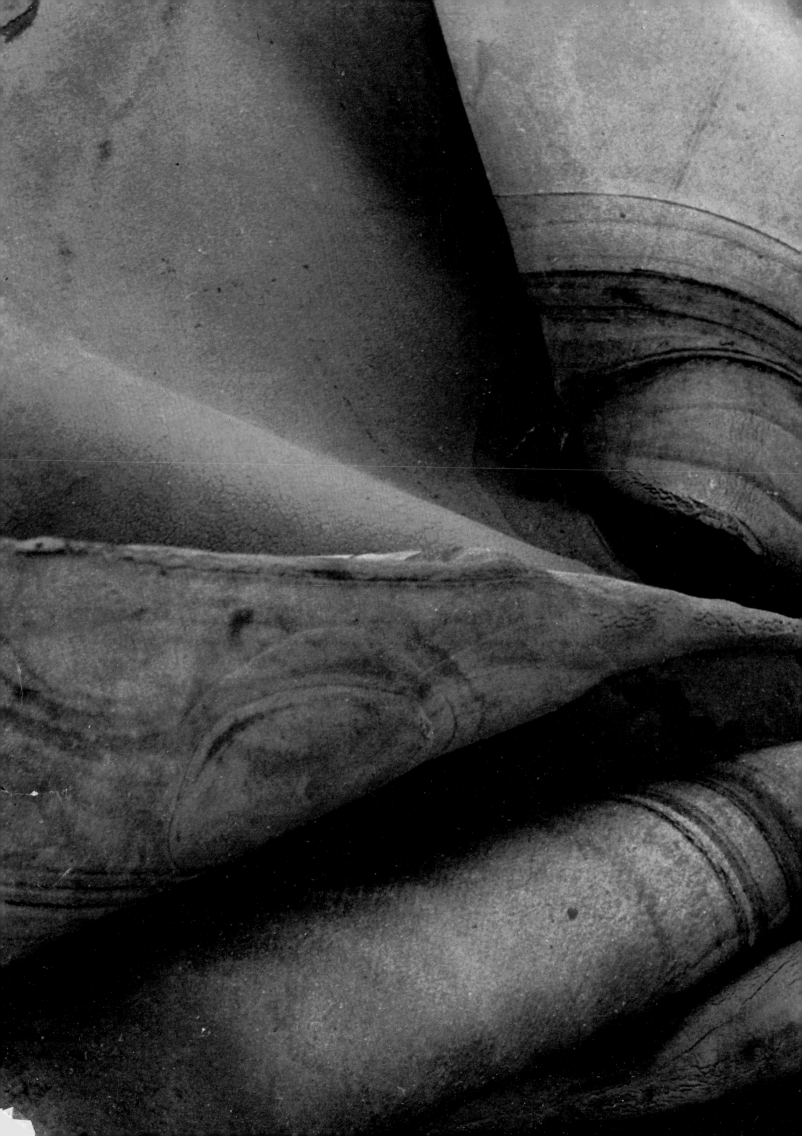

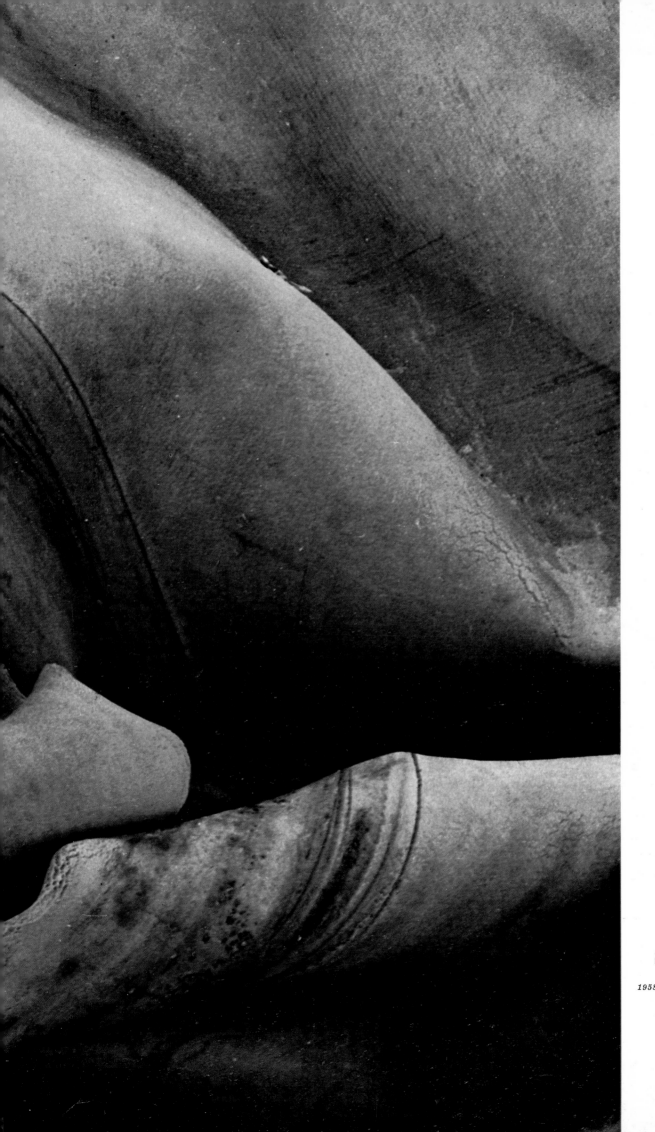

Syl Labrot b. 1929
INNER TUBES
1958. Collection of the Photographer

199

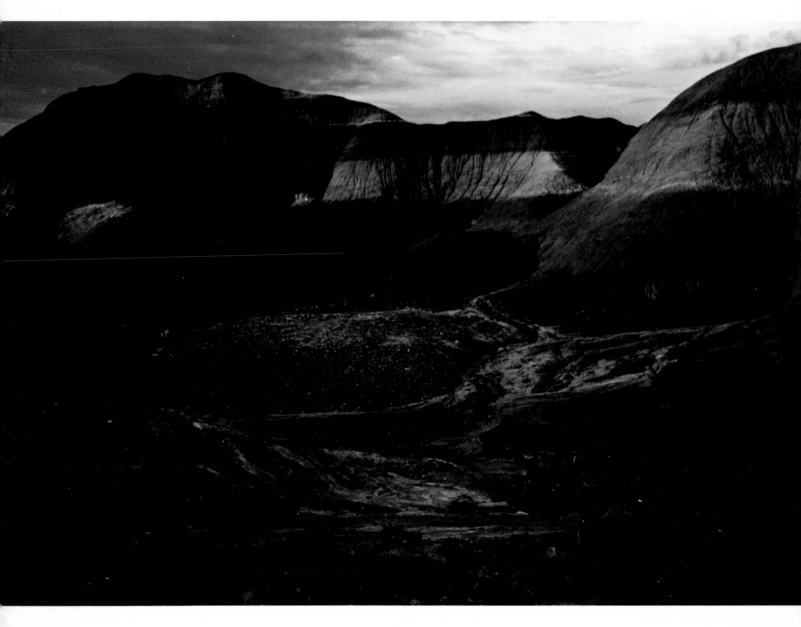

Dean Brown 1936–1973
RED STRIPED HILLS
*1969. Collection of Carol Brown, New York*

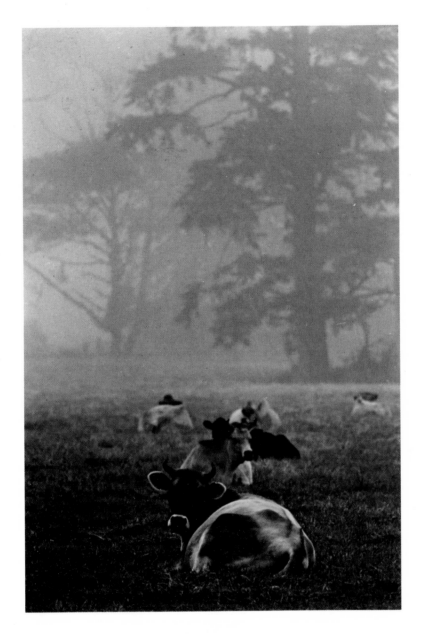

Dean Brown 1936–1973
CALIFORNIA COWS
*1969. Collection of Carol Brown, New York*

**Eliot Porter** b. 1901
LICHENS ON ROUND STONES, SOUTH COAST, ICELAND
*1972. Collection of the Photographer*

**Eliot Porter** b. 1901
TENT CATERPILLARS, TAMWORTH, NEW HAMPSHIRE
*1953. Collection of the Photographer*

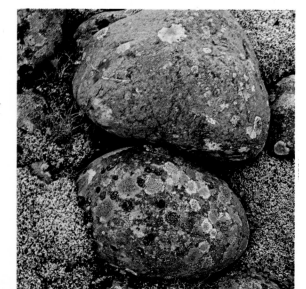

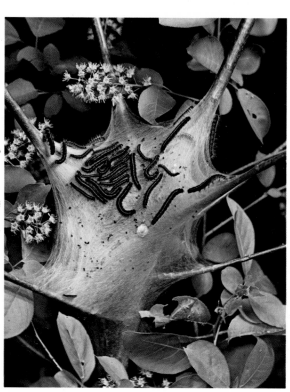

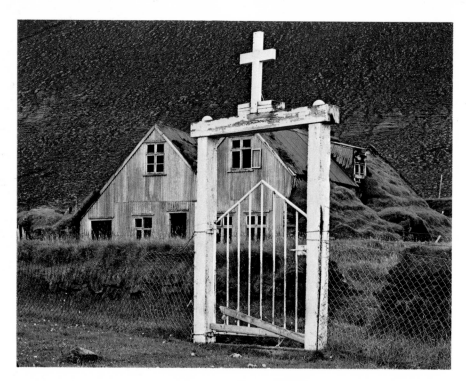

**Eliot Porter** b. 1901
ABANDONED FARM, ICELAND
*1972. Collection of the Photographer*

**Eliot Porter** b. 1901
HIGHEST WATERFALL, DAVIS GULCH, ESCALANTE RIVER, LAKE POWELL, UTAH
*1965. Collection of the Photographer*

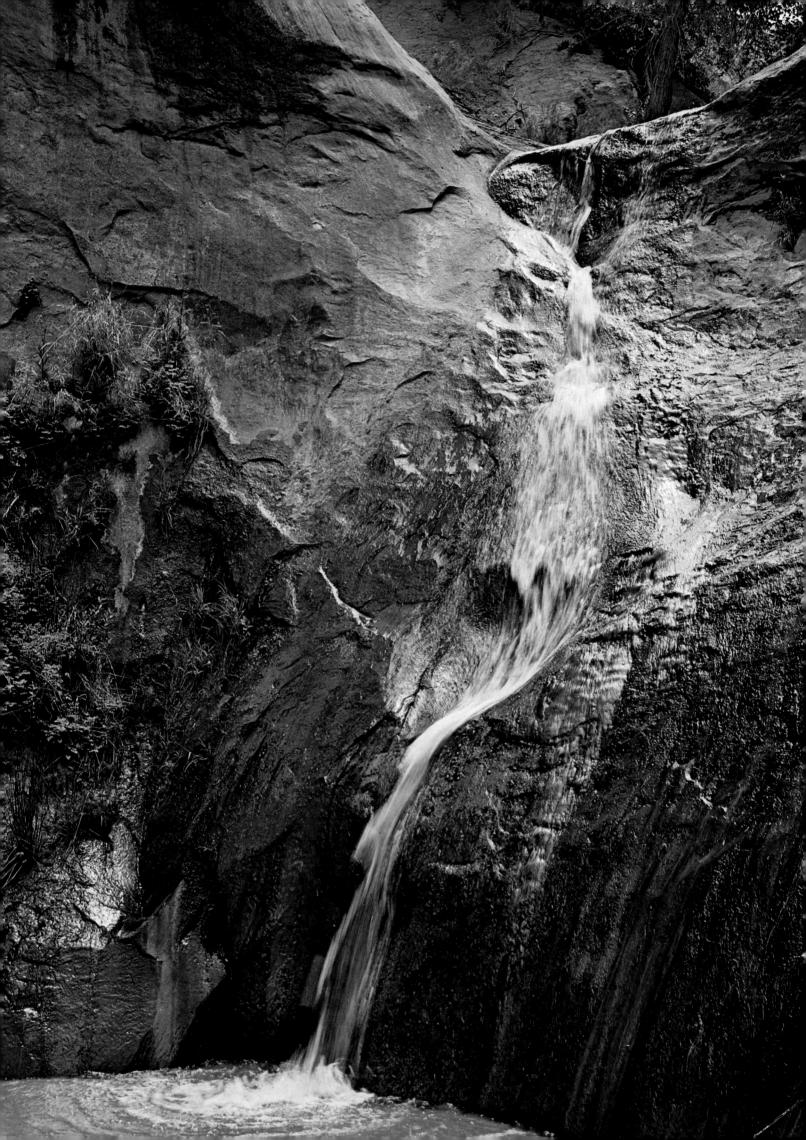

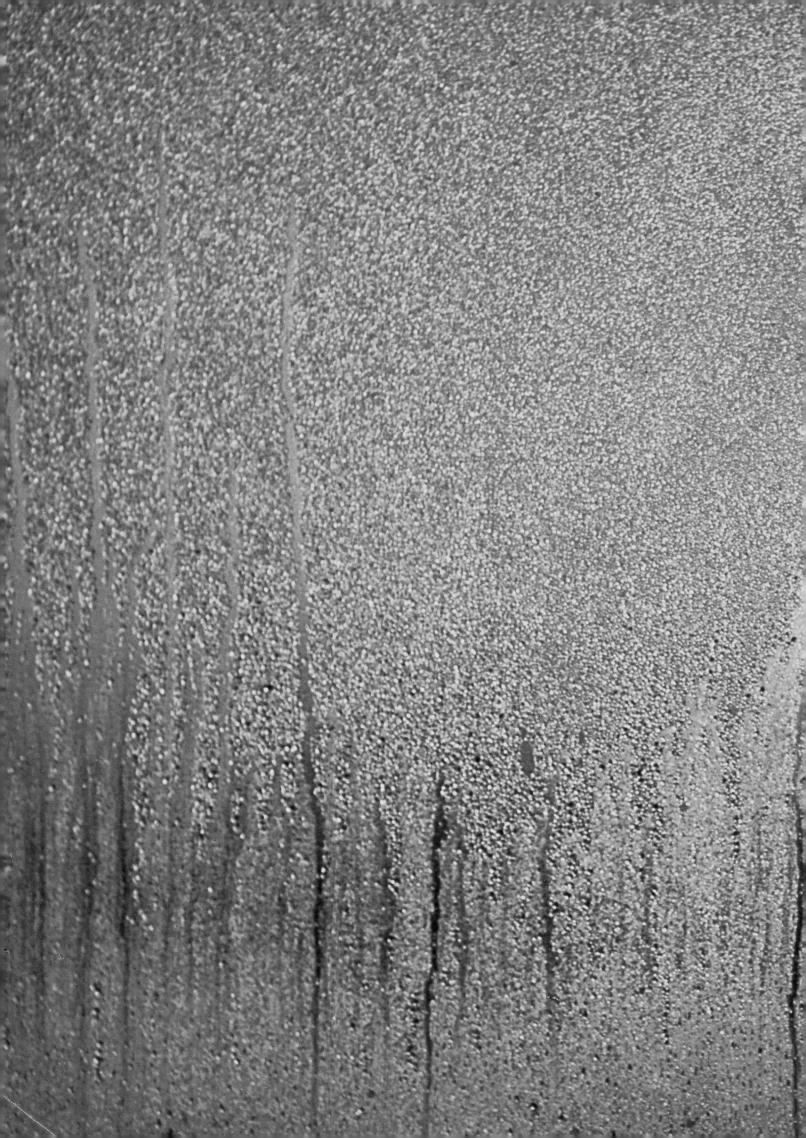

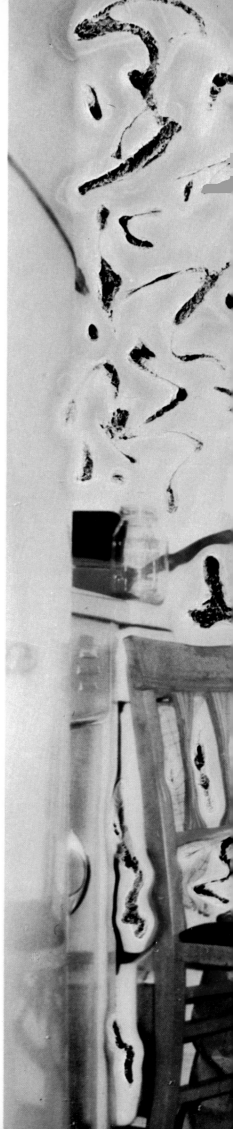

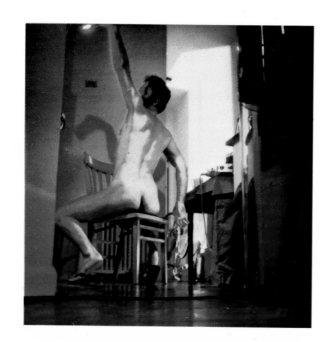

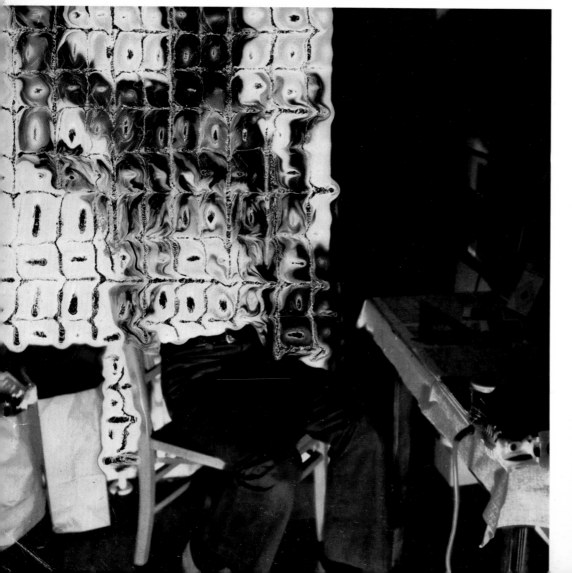

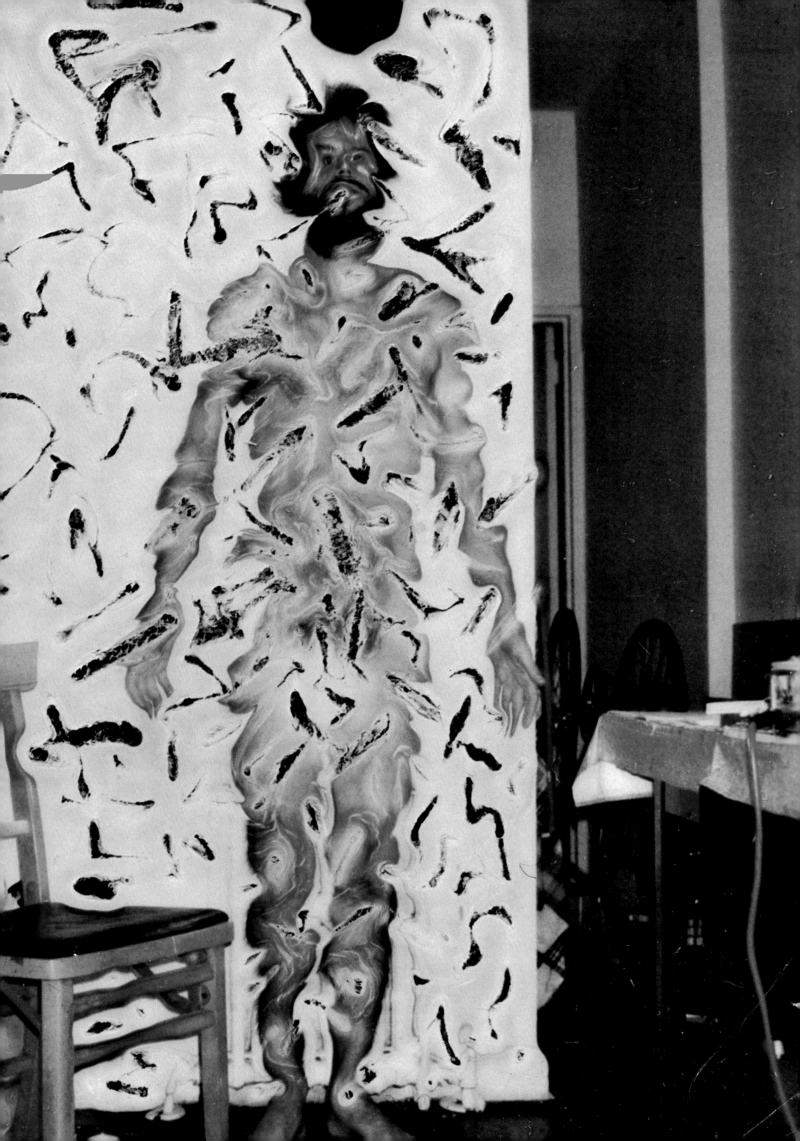

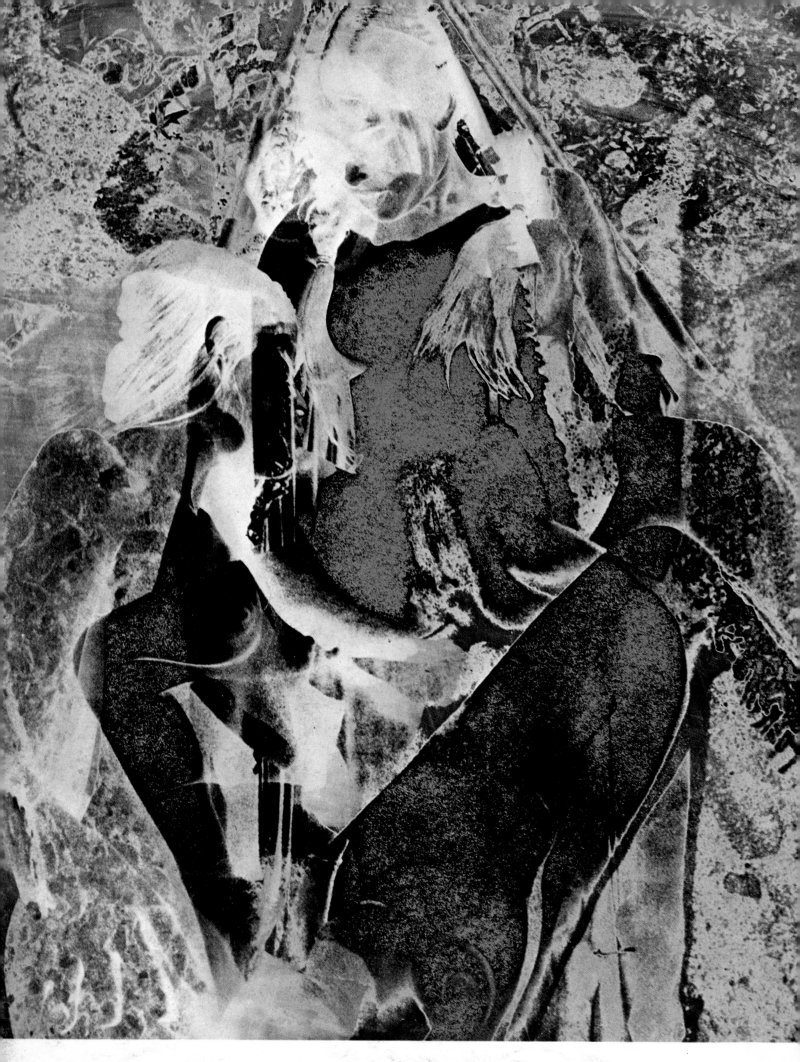

Robert Heinecken b. 1931
FOUR FIGURES #3
1970. Light Gallery, New York

Syl Labrot b. 1929

HEADLIGHT

*1960. Collection of the Photographer*

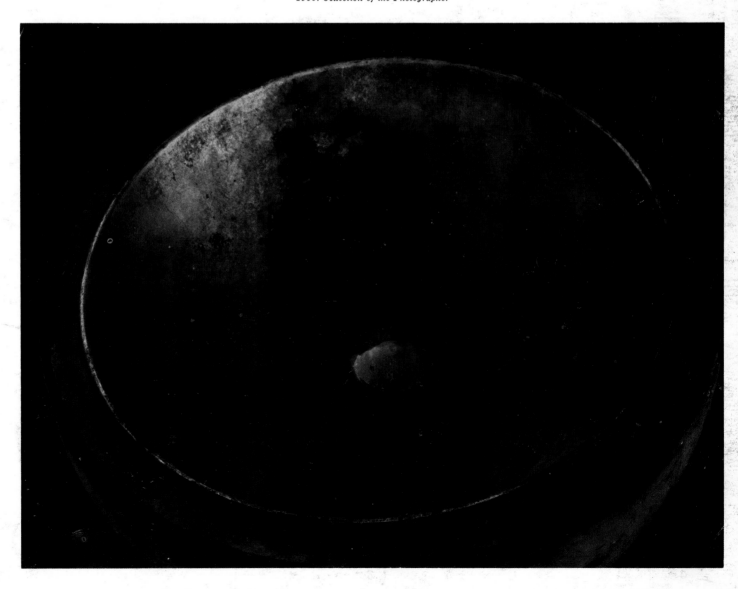

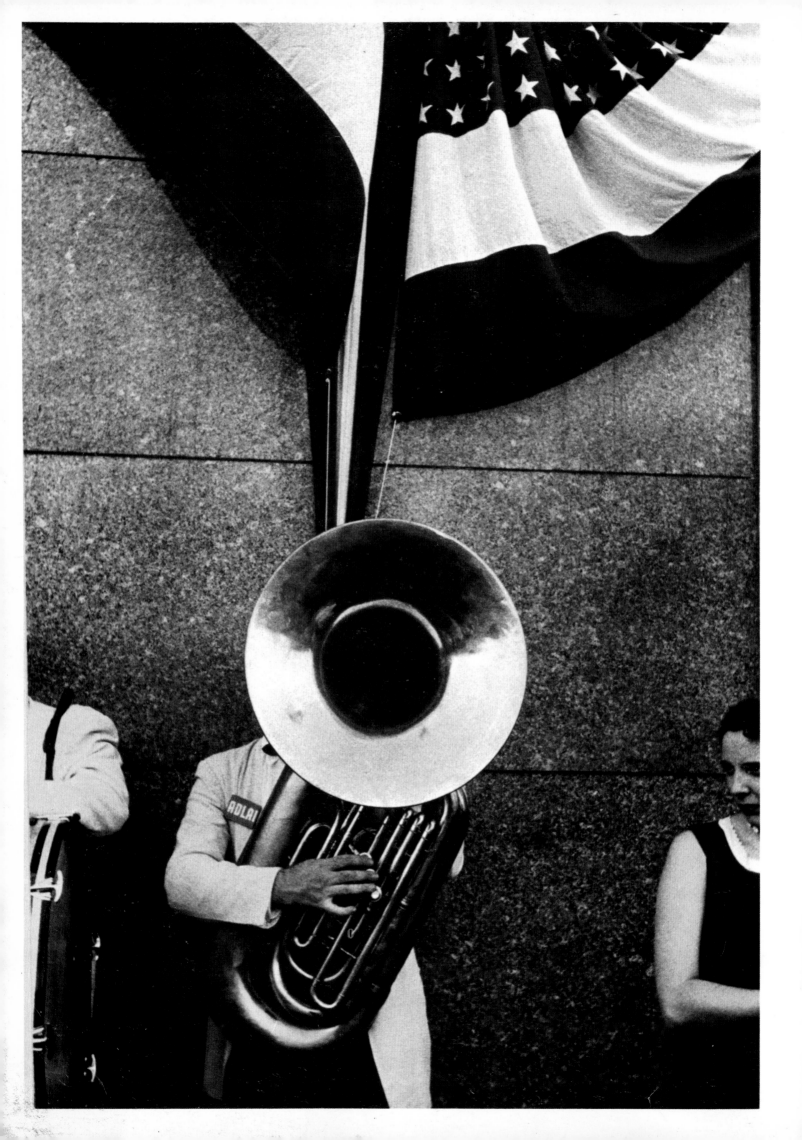

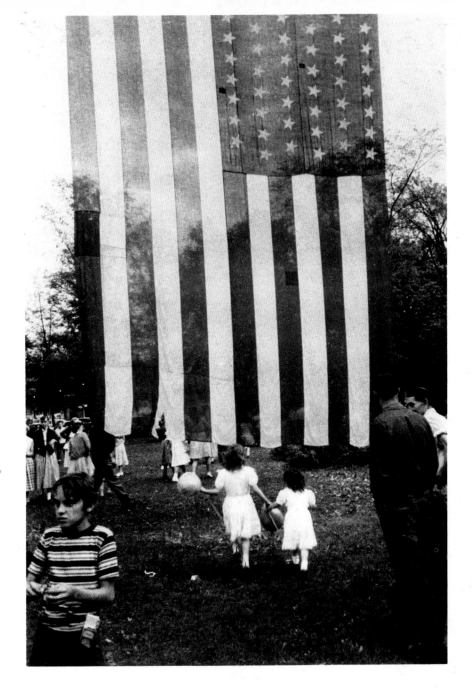

Robert Frank b. 1924
FOURTH OF JULY, JAY, NEW YORK
*1958. The Art Institute of Chicago*

Robert Frank b. 1924
POLITICAL RALLY, CHICAGO
*1958. The Art Institute of Chicago*

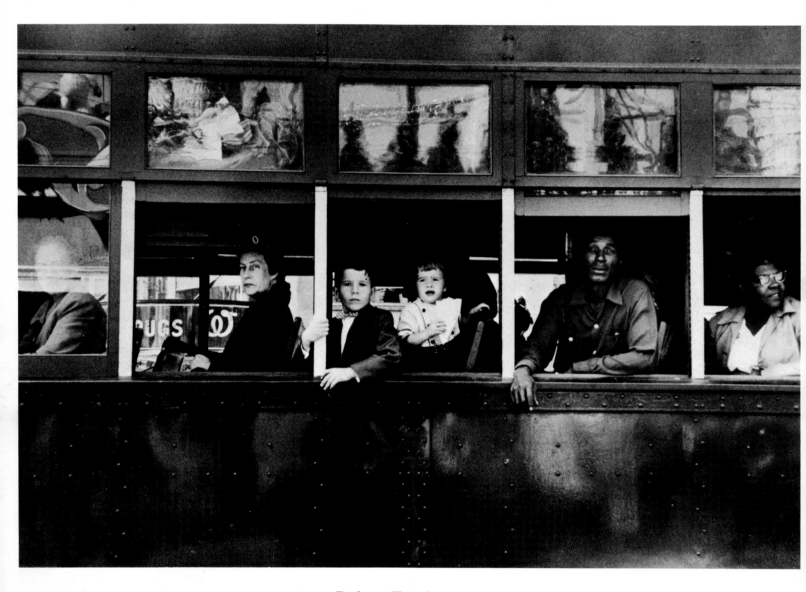

Robert Frank b. 1924
TROLLEY, NEW ORLEANS
1958. *The Art Institute of Chicago*

Robert Frank b. 1924
NEWBURGH, NEW YORK
1955. *The Art Institute of Chicago*

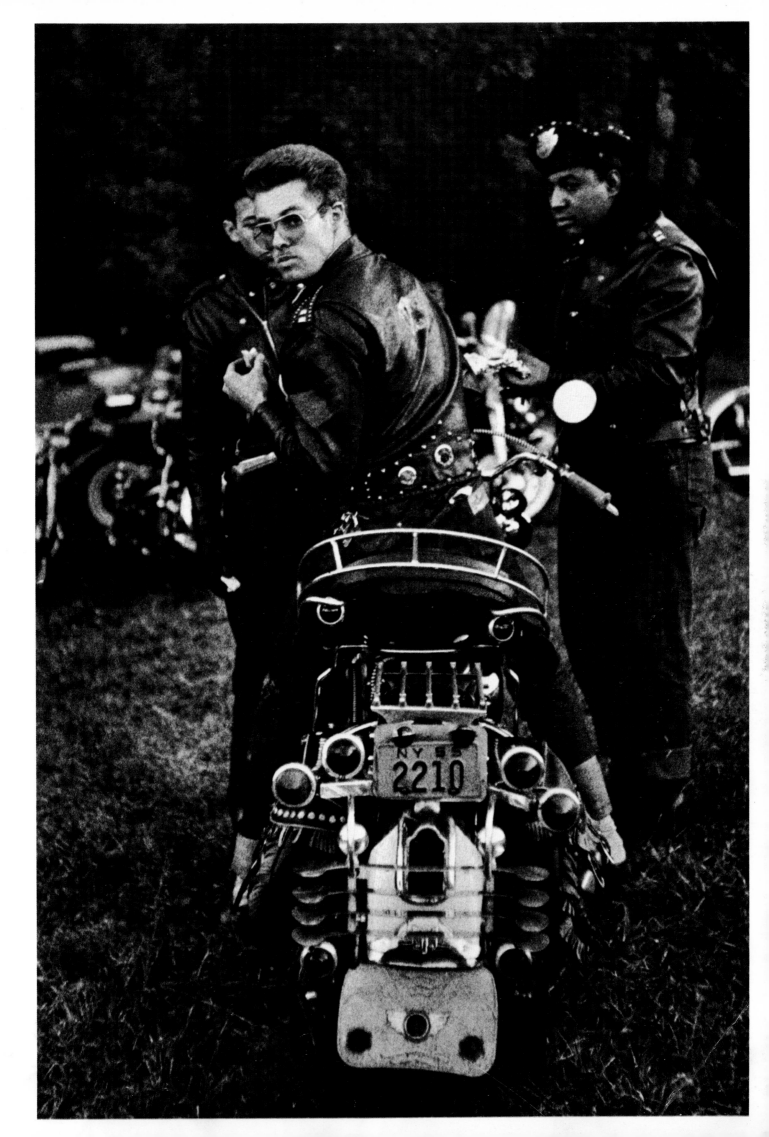

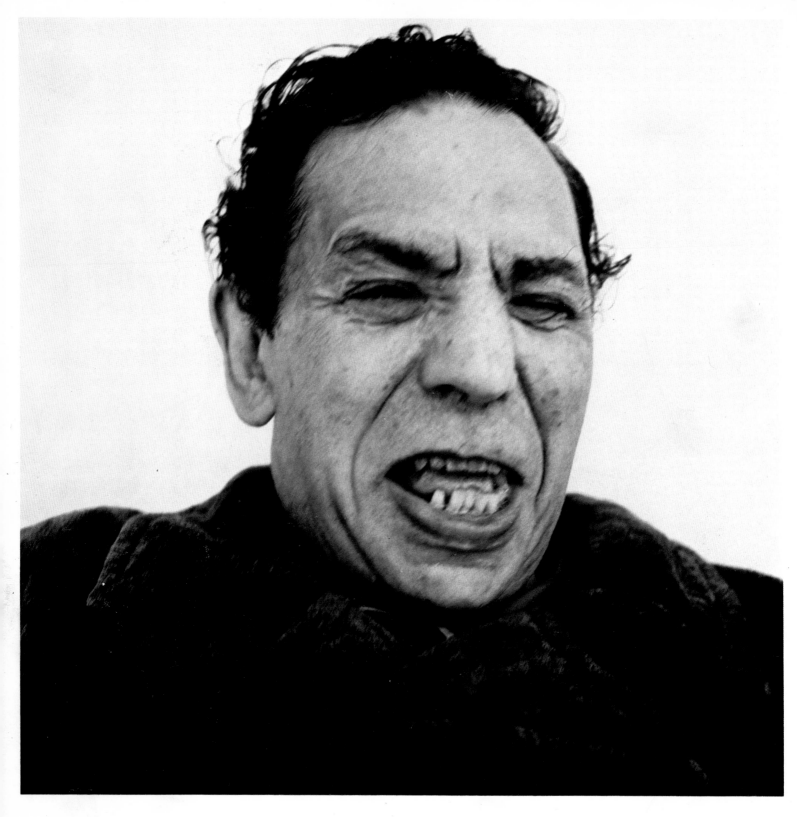

Richard Avedon b. 1923
OSCAR LEVANT
*1972. Collection of the Photographer*

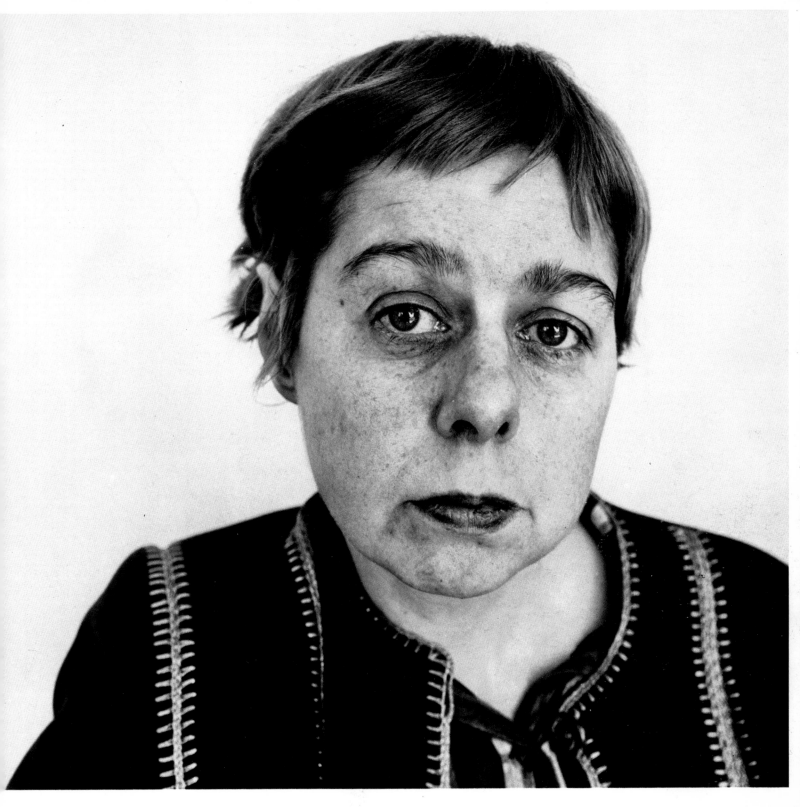

Richard Avedon b. 1923
CARSON MC CULLERS
1950. Collection of the Photographer

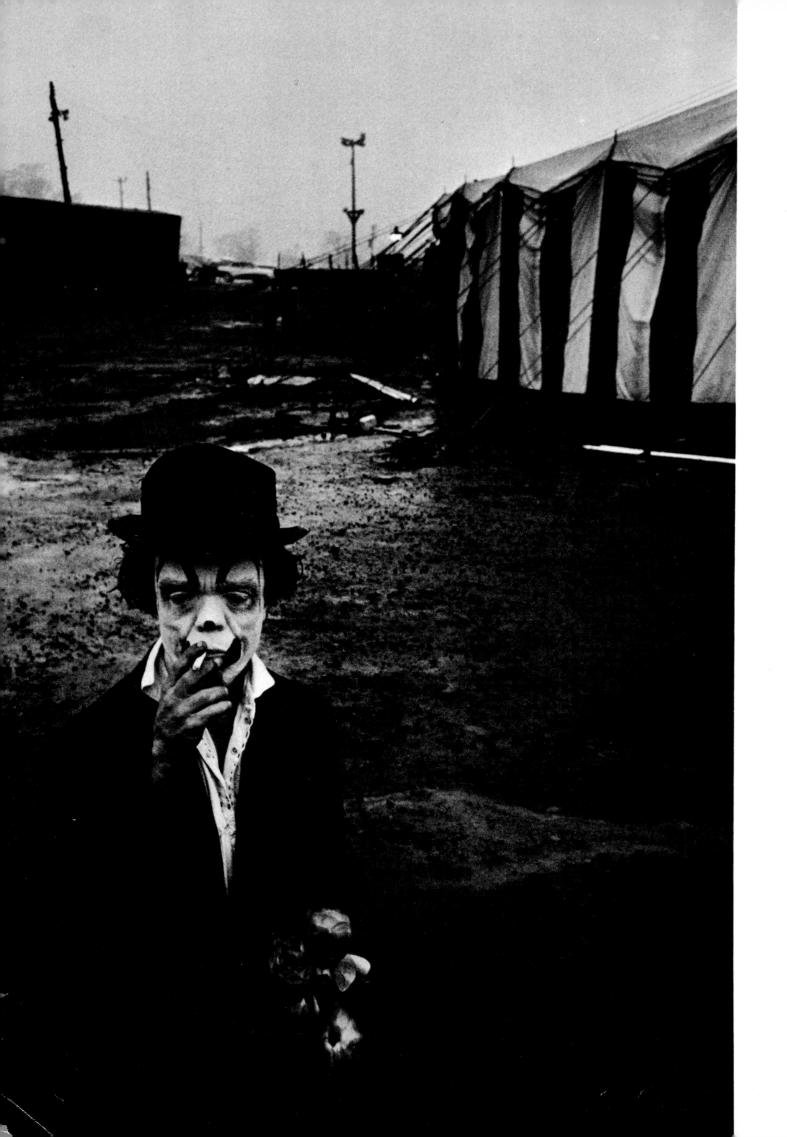

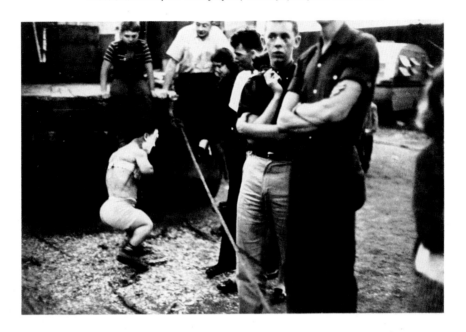

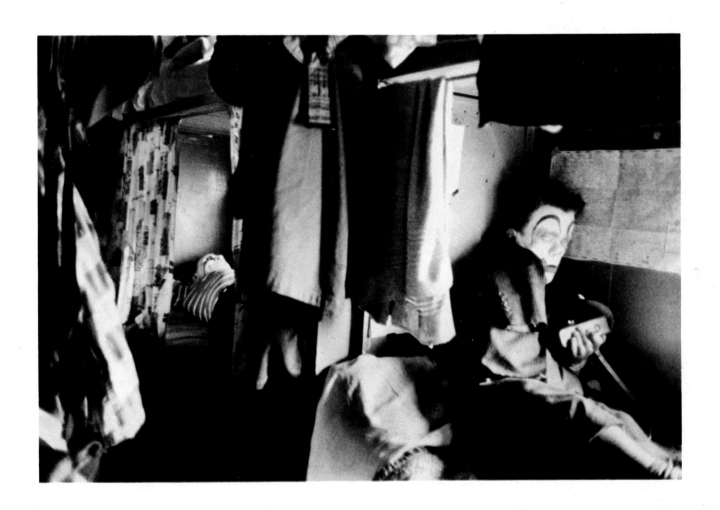

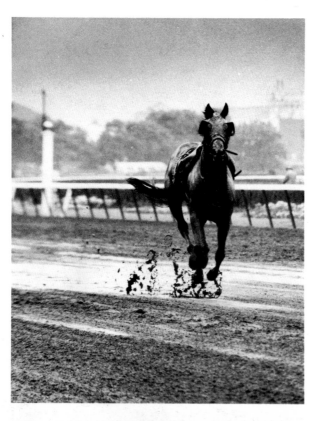

Robert Riger b. 1924
ARCARO IS DOWN, BELMONT STAKES
*1959. Collection of the Photographer*

Robert Riger b. 1924
OVER THE TOP FOR SIX, WASHINGTON AT NEW YORK 1960
*Collection of the Photographer*

Robert Riger b. 1924
WILLIE MAYS STEALS THIRD, NEW YORK AT BROOKLYN
*1955. Collection of the Photographer*

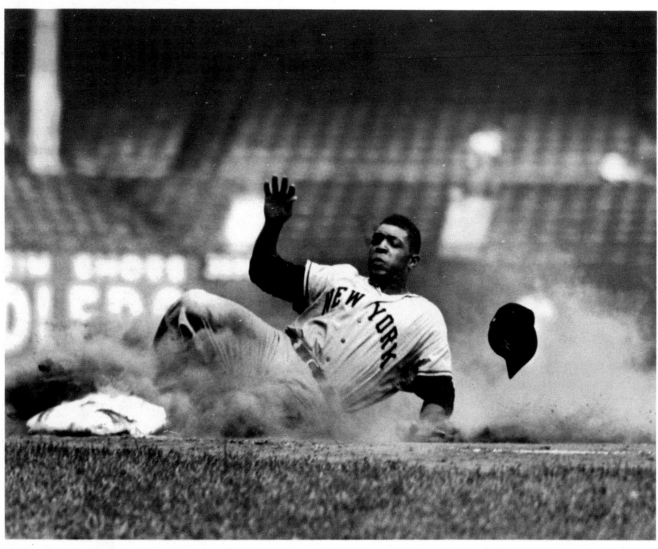

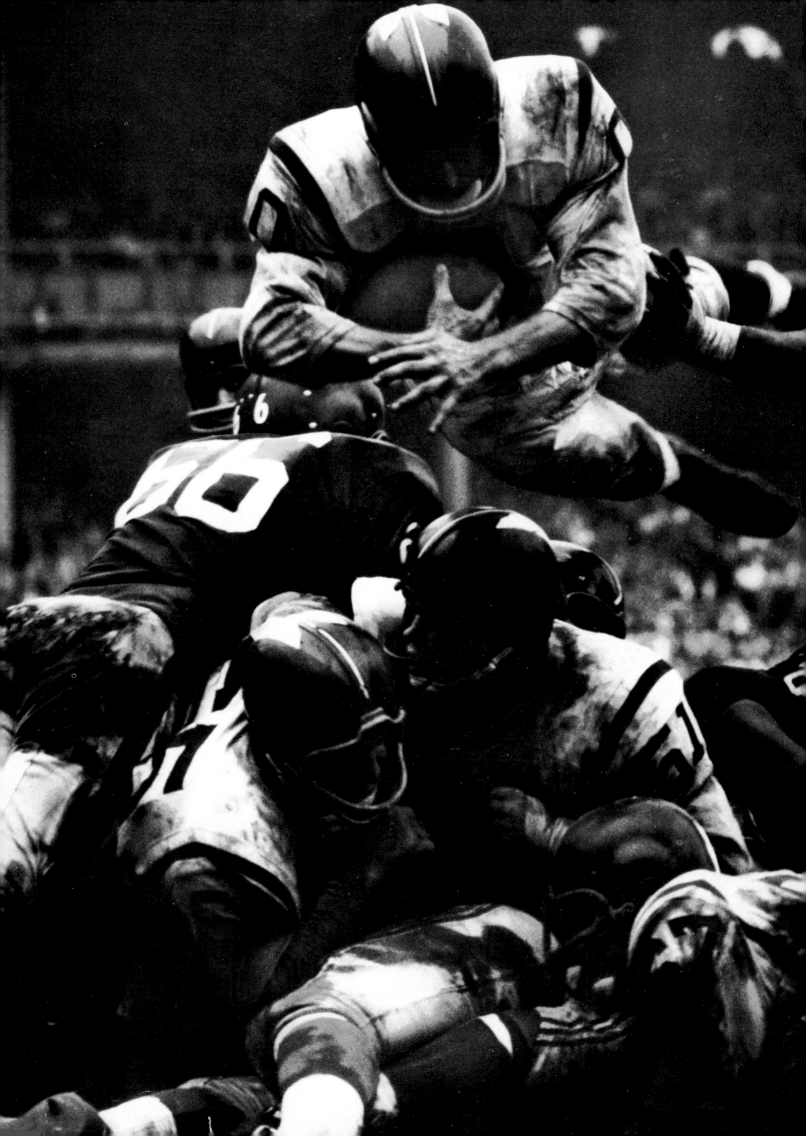

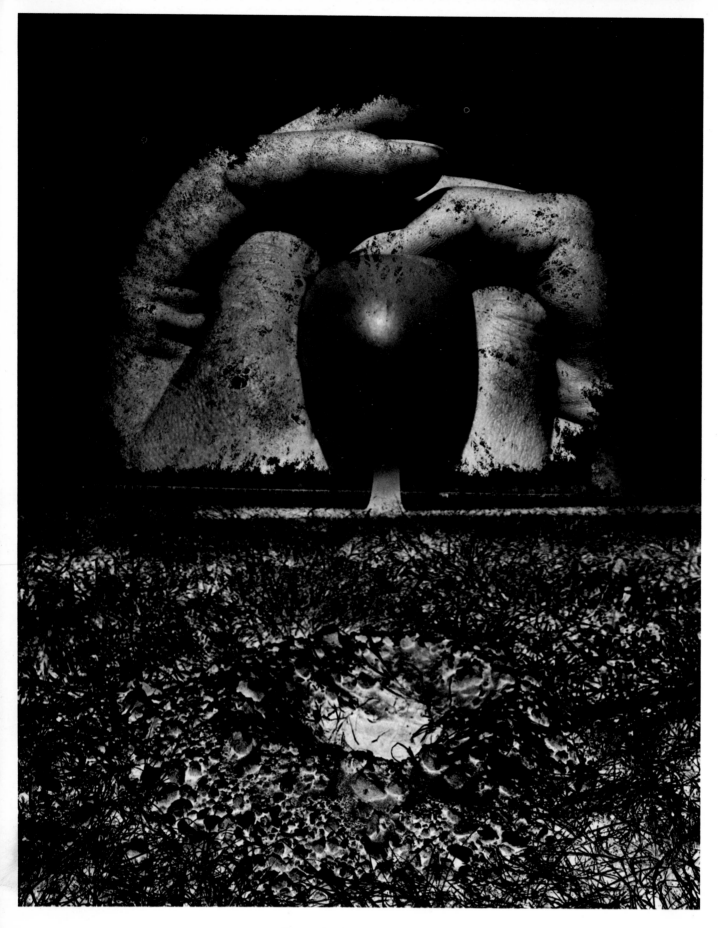

Jerry Uelsmann b. 1934
UNTITLED
*1968. Collection of the Photographer*

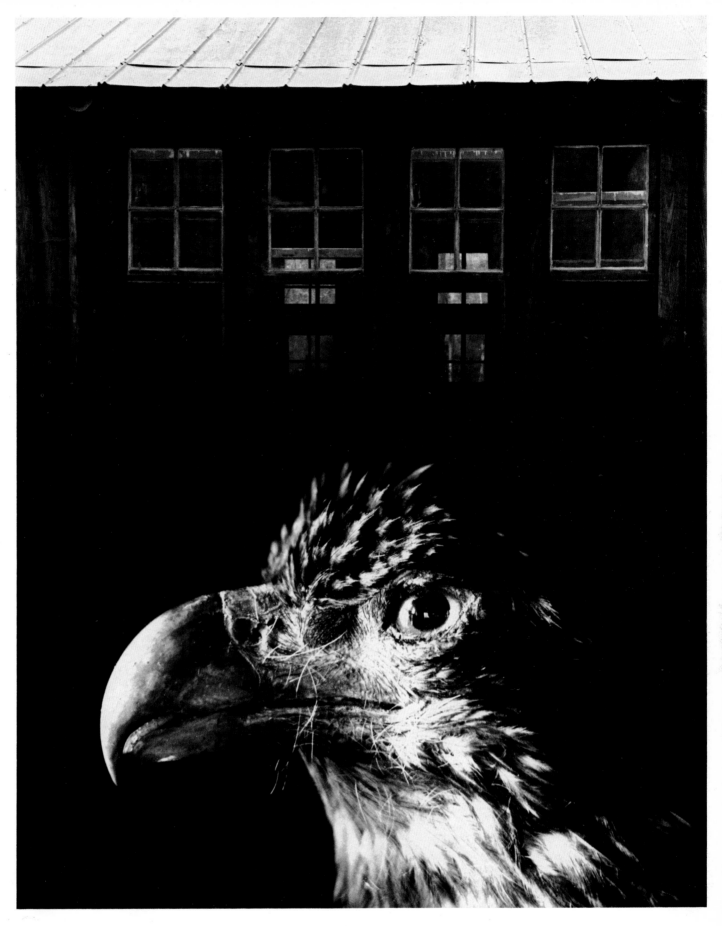

Jerry Uelsmann b. 1934
BLESS OUR HOME AND EAGLE
*1962. Collection of the Photographer*

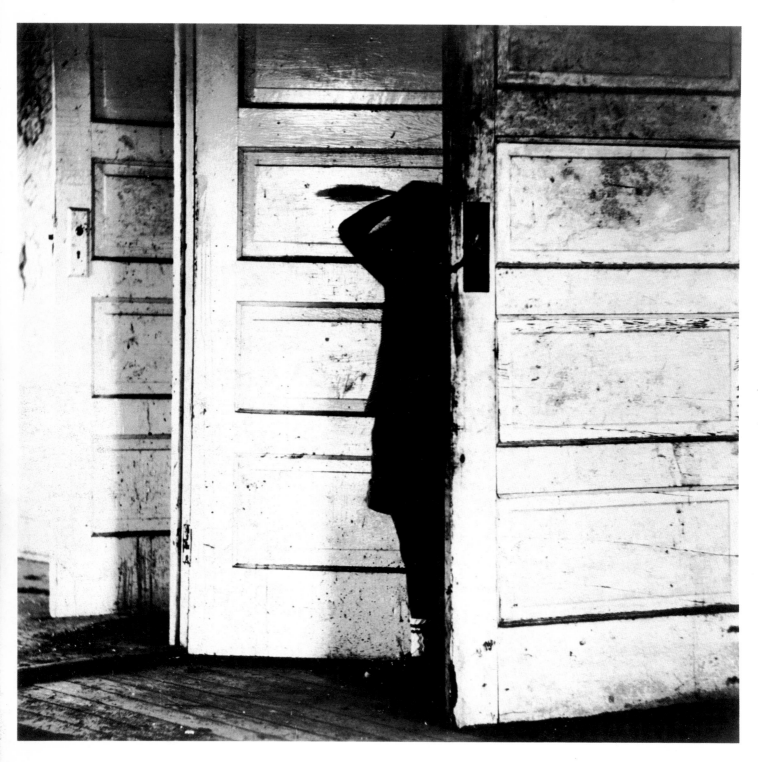

**Ralph Eugene Meatyard** 1925–1972
UNTITLED
*ca. 1965. Collection of Lee Witkin, New York*

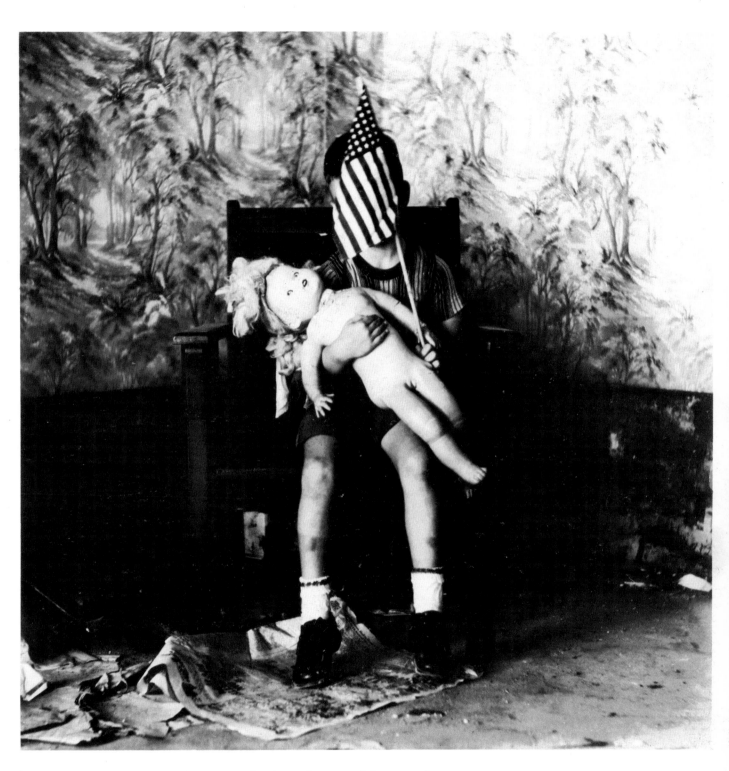

**Ralph Eugene Meatyard** 1925–1972
UNTITLED
*ca. 1965. Collection of Lee Witkin, New York*

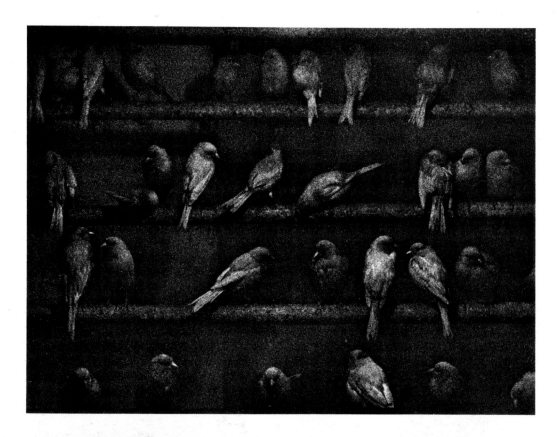

George Krause b. 1937
THE BIRDS
*1965. Collection of the Photographer*

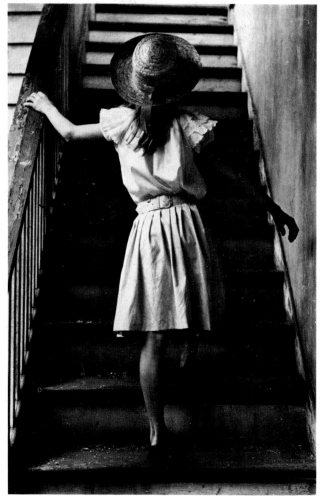

224

George Krause b. 1937
THE STAIRS
*1961. Collection of the Photographer*

Arthur Siegel b. 1913
LUCIDOGRAM #205
*1969. Collection of the Photographer*

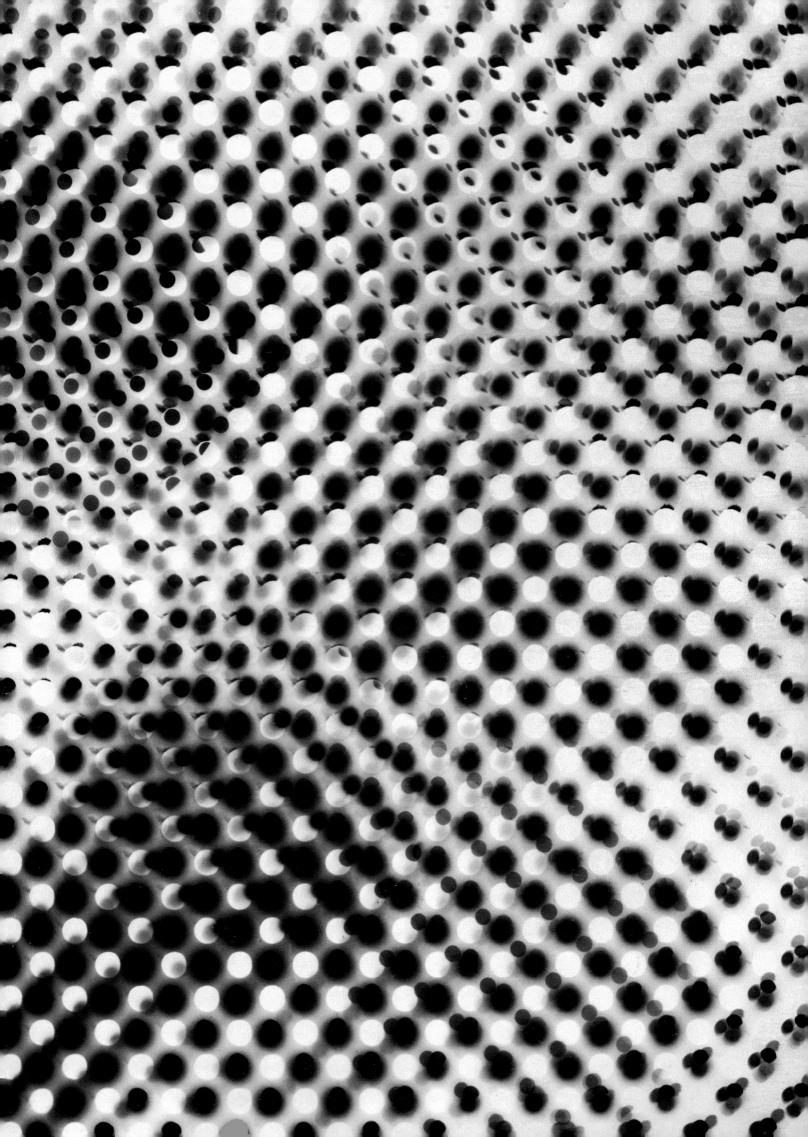

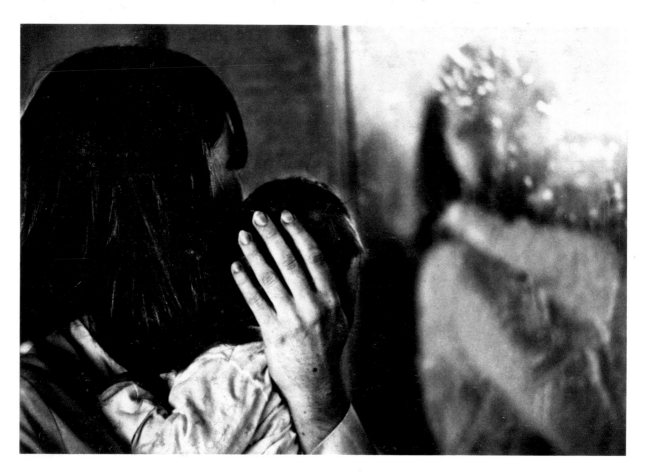

**David Heath** b. 1931
PORTFOLIO 63 : PLATE 5
*ca. 1963. The Art Institute of Chicago*

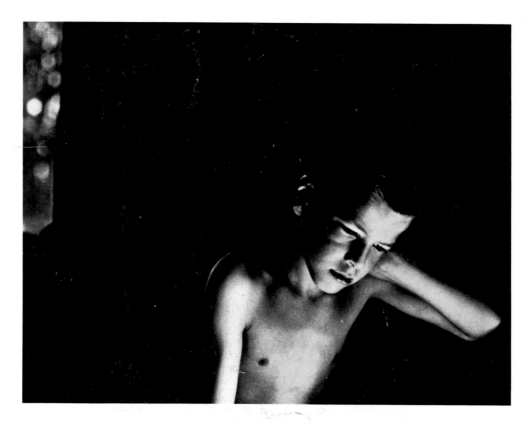

**David Heath** b. 1931
PORTFOLIO 63 : PLATE 20
*ca. 1963. The Art Institute of Chicago*

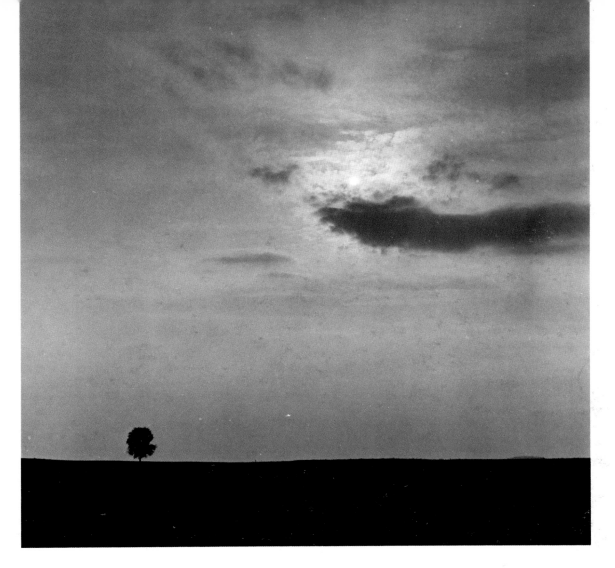

George A. Tice b. 1938
LANDSCAPE AT SUNRISE, LANCASTER, PA.
*1965. Collection of the Photographer*

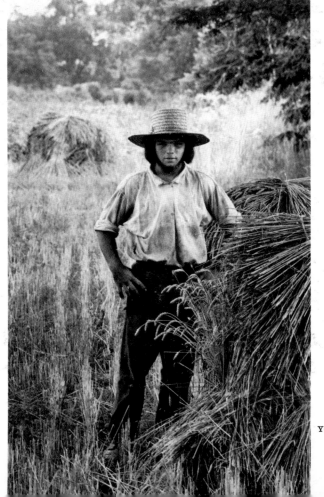

227

George A. Tice b. 1938
YOUNG AMISH MAN, MIFFLIN COUNTY, PENNSYLVANIA
*1967. Collection of the Photographer*

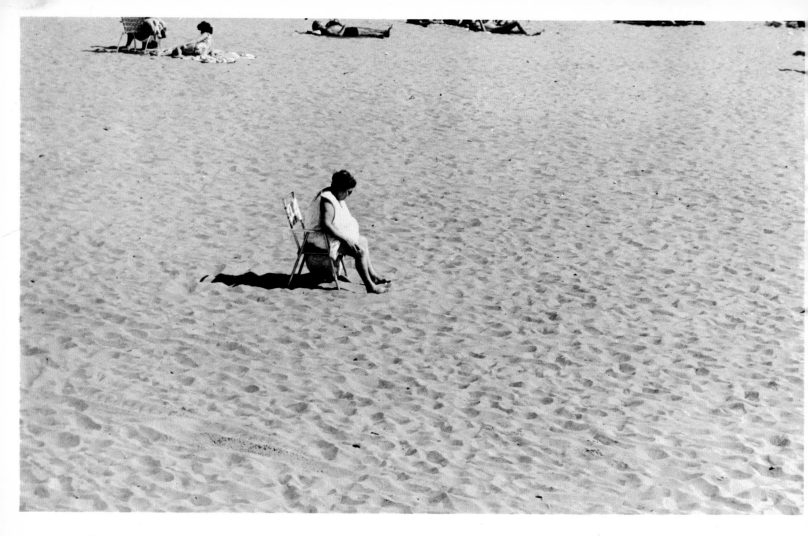

Carl Roodman b. 1934
CONEY ISLAND
*1966. Collection of the Photographer*

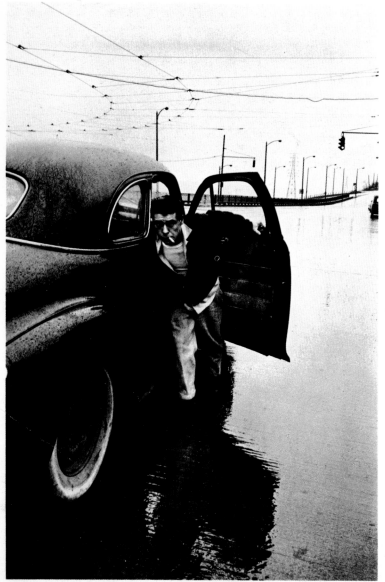

Simpson Kalisher b. 1926
BOY PUSHING A CAR
*1960. Collection of the Photographer*

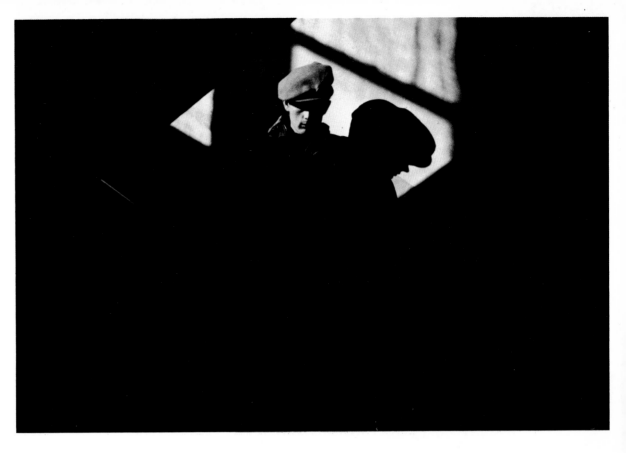

**Dennis Stock** b. 1928
JAMES DEAN IN SHADOW
*1956. Collection of the Photographer*

**Dennis Stock** b. 1928
PUNCH MILLER IN NEW ORLEANS
*1959. Collection of the Photographer*

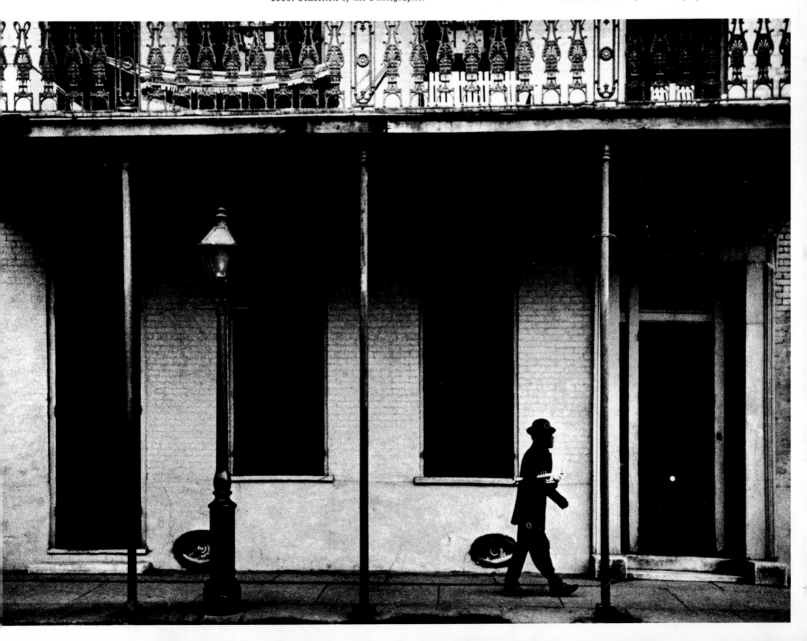

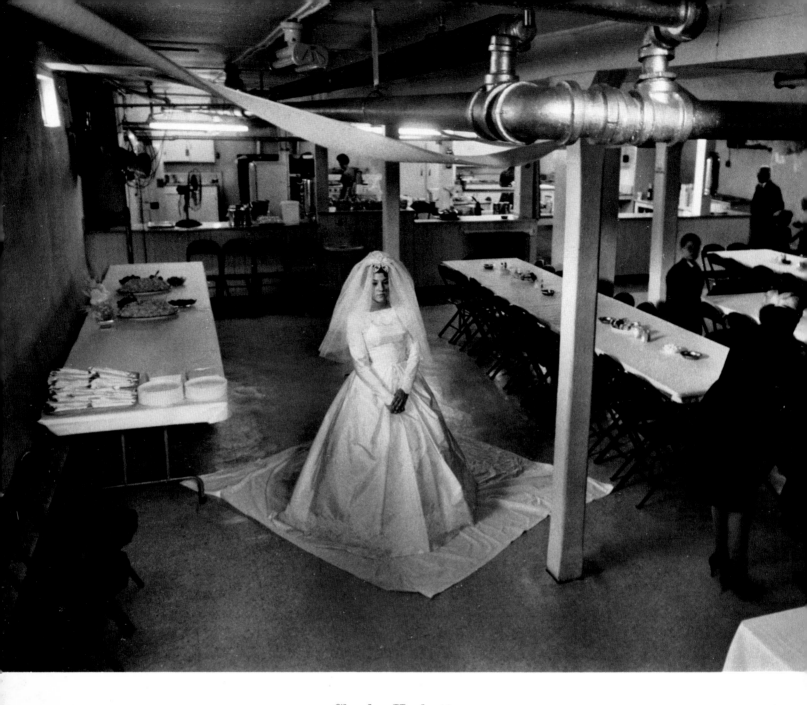

Charles Harbutt b. 1935
BRIDE IN CELLAR
*1966. Collection of the Photographer, courtesy of Magnum Photos, Inc.*

Charles Harbutt b. 1935
TORSO
*1972. Collection of the Photographer, courtesy of Magnum Photos, Inc.*

Charles Harbutt b. 1935
BLIND CHILD GRASPING FOR LIGHT
*1961. Collection of the Photographer, courtesy of Magnum Photos, Inc.*

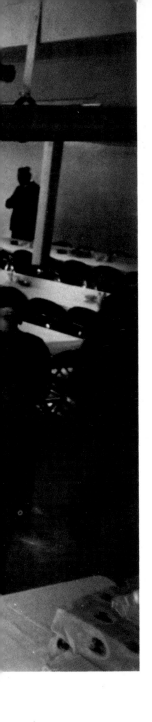
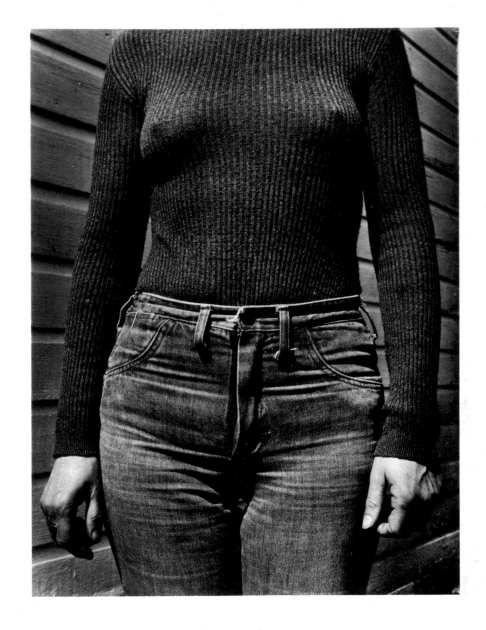
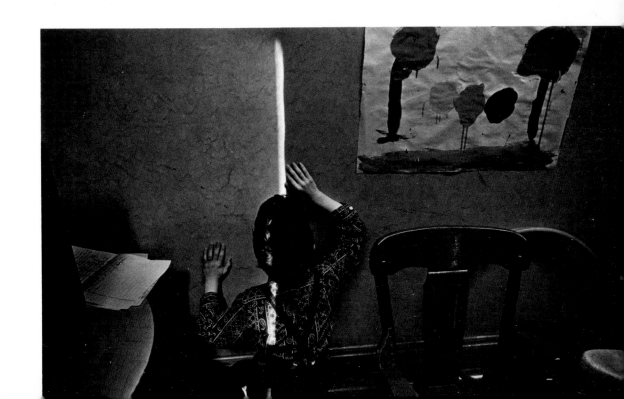

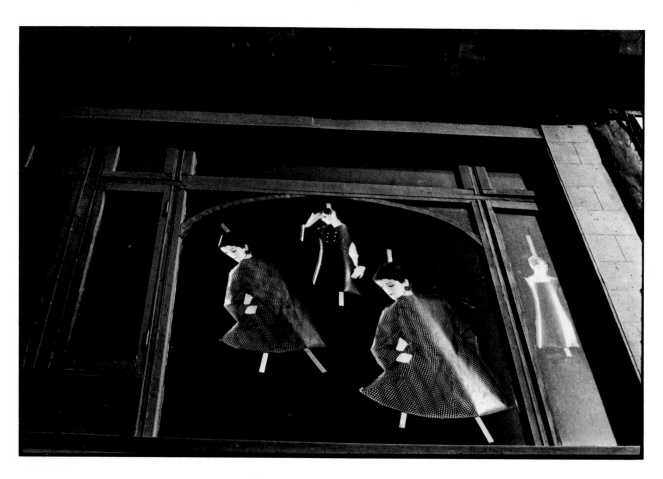

**Nathan Lyons** b. 1930
UNTITLED, NEW YORK
*1967. Collection of the Photographer*

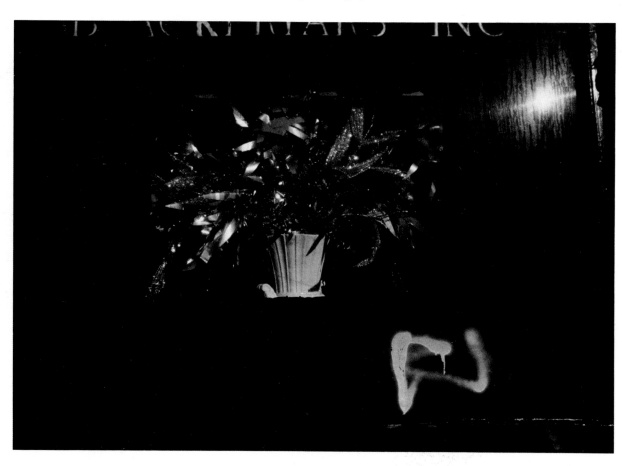

232

**Nathan Lyons** b. 1930
UNTITLED, ROCHESTER
*1967. Collection of the Photographer*

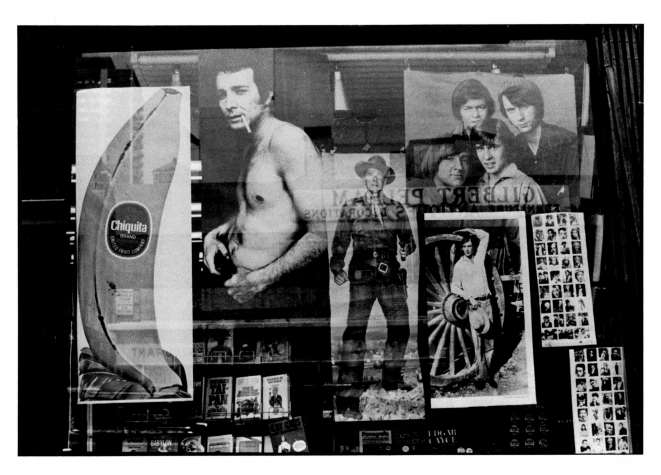

**Nathan Lyons** b. 1930
UNTITLED, NEW YORK
*1967. Collection of the Photographer*

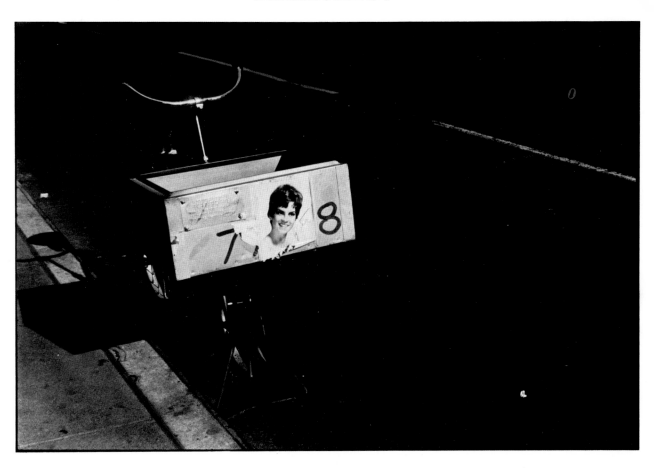

**Nathan Lyons** b. 1930
UNTITLED, NEW YORK
*1965. Collection of the Photographer*

**Brett Weston** b. 1911
ALASKAN GLACIAL FORMS
*1973. Collection of the Photographer*

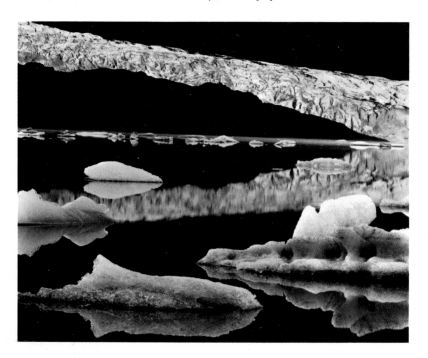

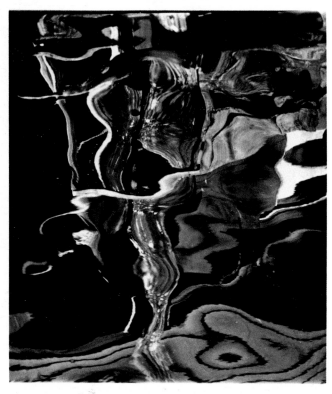

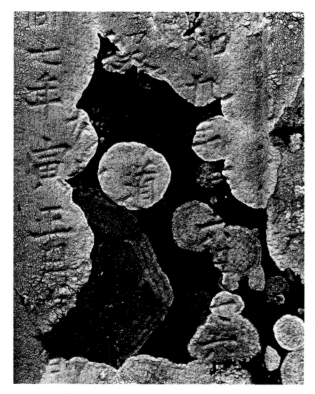

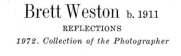

**Brett Weston** b. 1911
REFLECTIONS
*1972. Collection of the Photographer*

**Brett Weston** b. 1911
HEADSTONE, JAPAN
*1970. Collection of the Photographer*

234

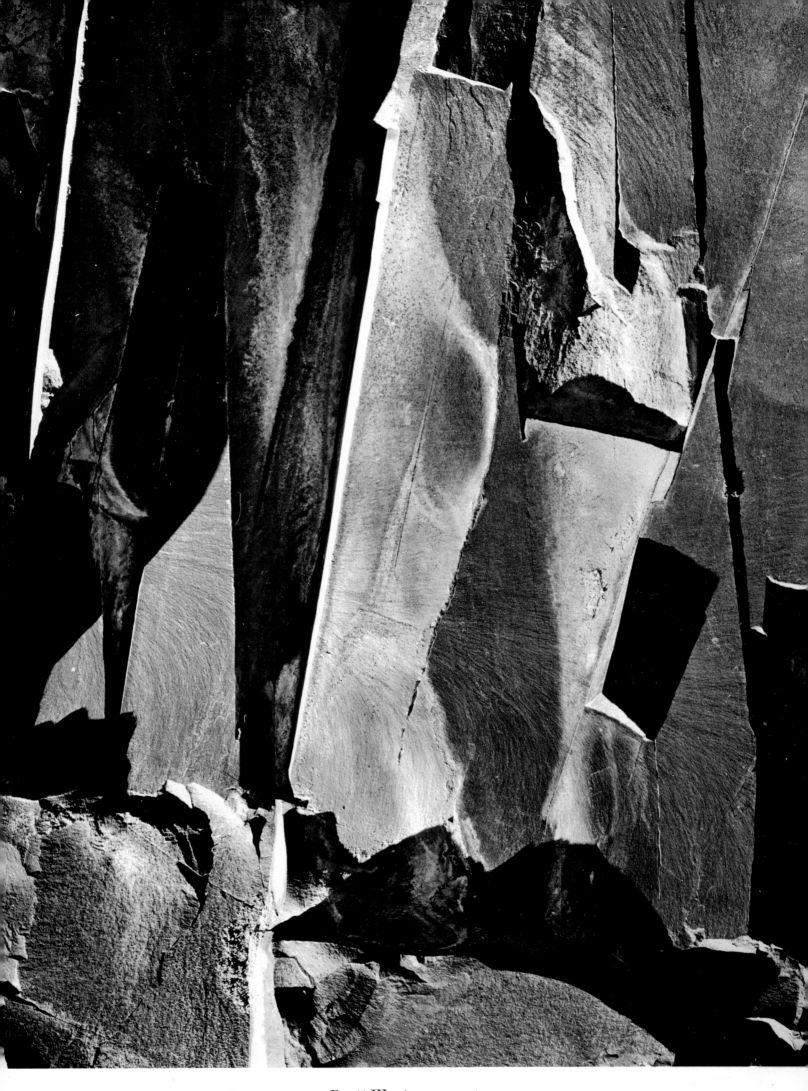

**Brett Weston** b. 1911
ROCK FORMS
*1971 Collection of the Photographer*

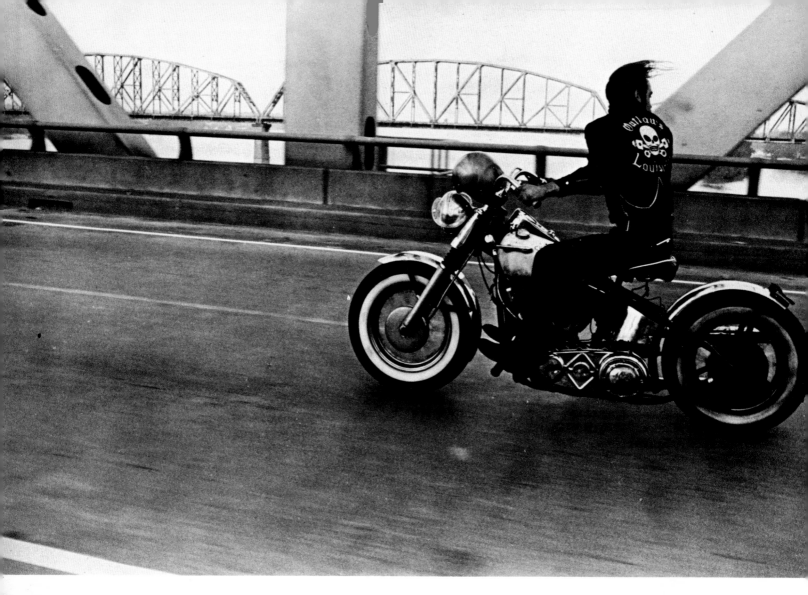

Danny Lyon b. 1942
CROSSING THE OHIO, LOUISVILLE
*ca. 1966. Light Gallery, New York*

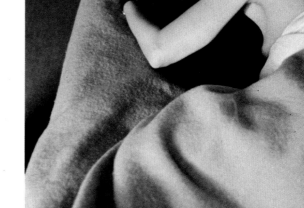

Erich Hartmann b. 1922
RUTH AND CASSANDRA
*1971. Collection of the Photographer, courtesy of Magnum Photos, Inc.*

236

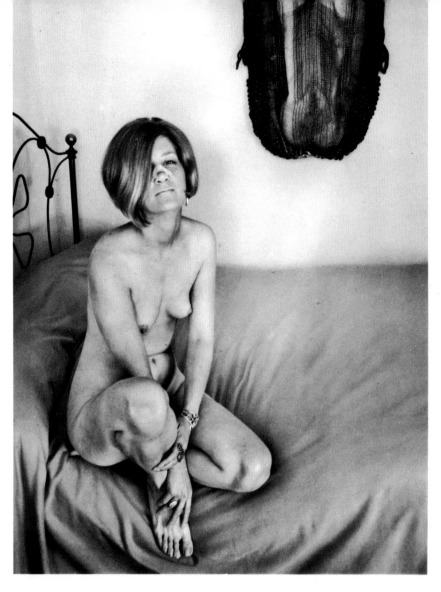

Leland Rice b. 1940
UNTITLED
*1971. Collection of the Photographer*

Leland Rice b. 1940
UNTITLED
*1969. Collection of the Photographer*

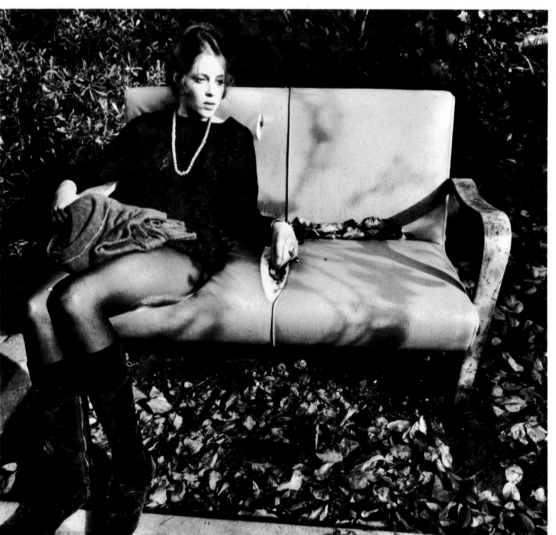

Duane Michals b. 1932
THE APPARITIONS : ADAM AND EVE
*1971. Collection of the Photographer*

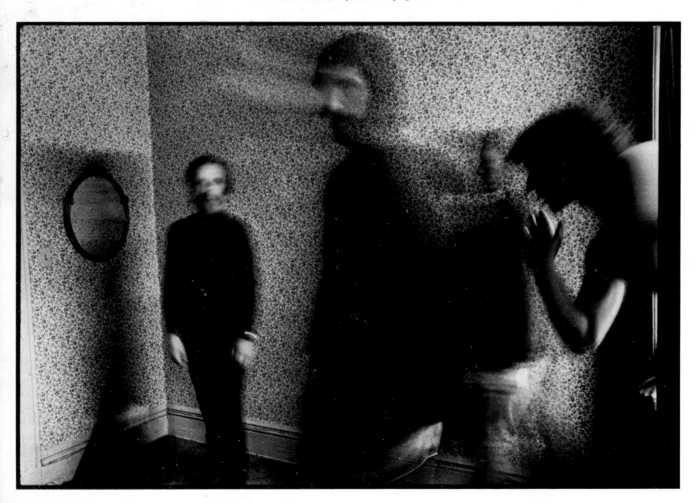

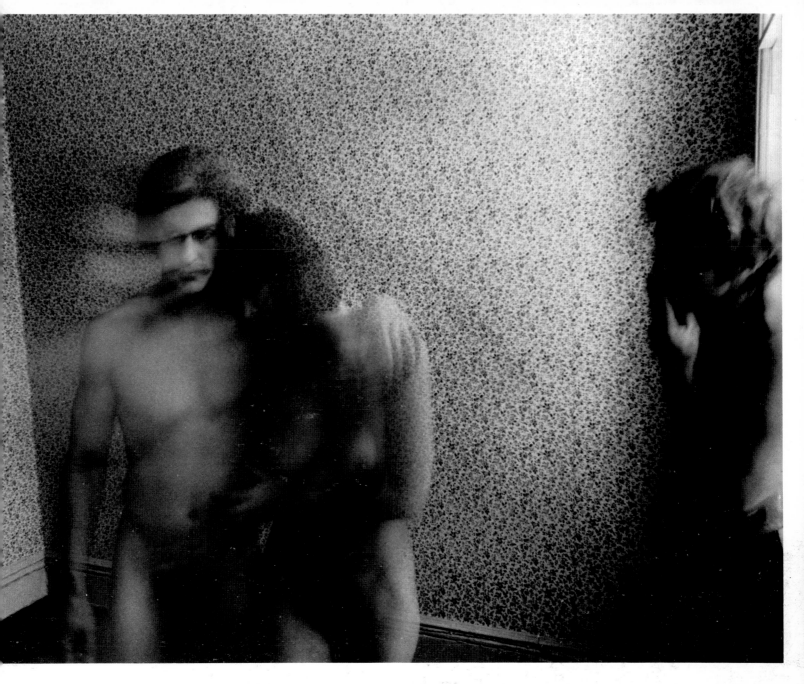

Duane Michals b. 1932
THE APPARITIONS: HIS FRIENDS
*1971. Collection of the Photographer*

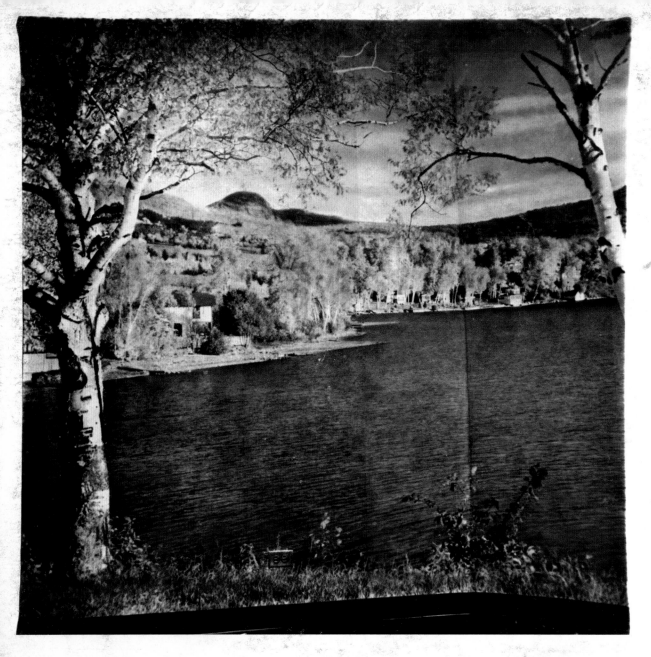

Diane Arbus 1923–1971
A LOBBY IN A BUILDING, NEW YORK CITY
*1966. Courtesy of the Estate of Diane Arbus*

Diane Arbus 1923–1971
UNTITLED (4)
*1970–71. Courtesy of the Estate of Diane Arbus*

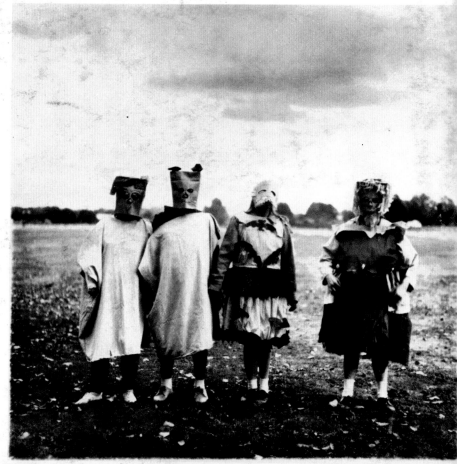

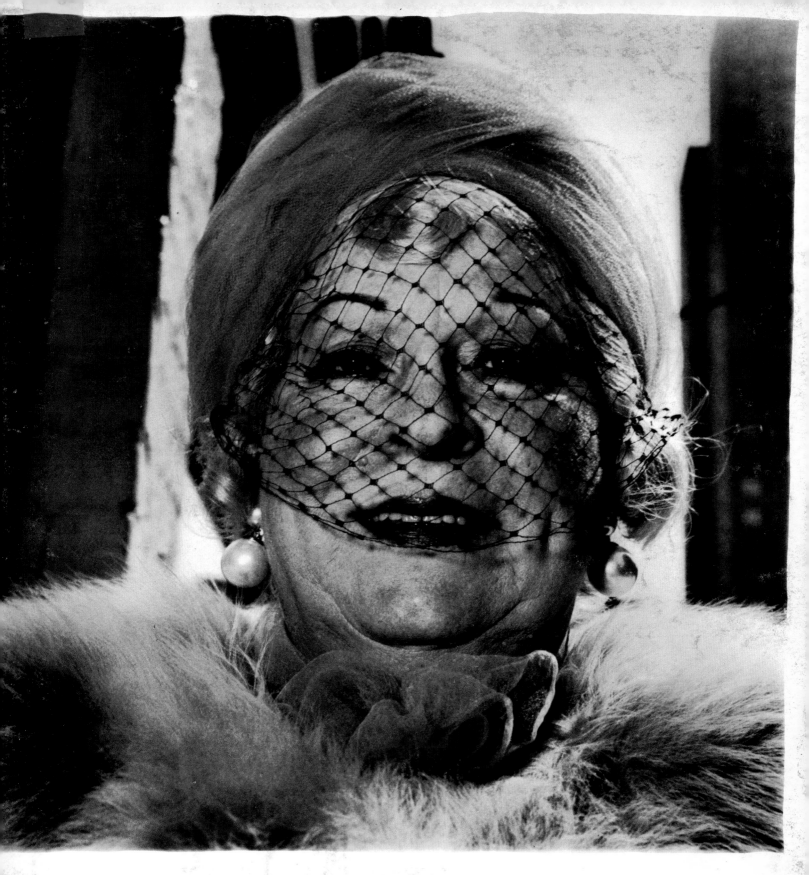

**Diane Arbus** 1923–1971
WOMAN WITH A VEIL ON FIFTH AVENUE, NEW YORK CITY
*1968. Courtesy of the Estate of Diane Arbus*

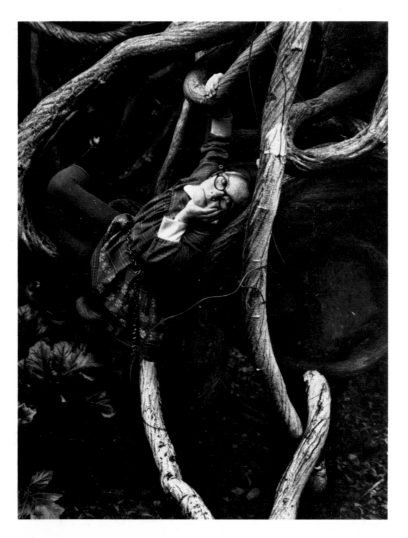

Jack Welpott b. 1923
RACHEL IN THE WISTERIA
*1971. Collection of the Photographer*

Jack Welpott b. 1923
KATHLEEN KELLEY
*1972. Collection of the Photographer*

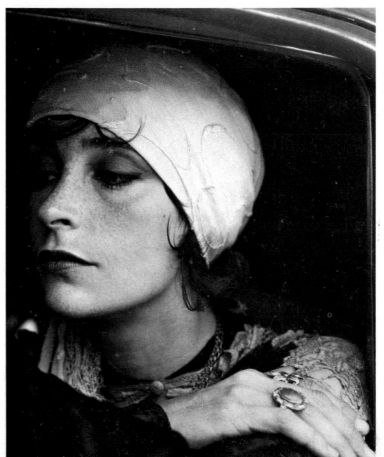

242

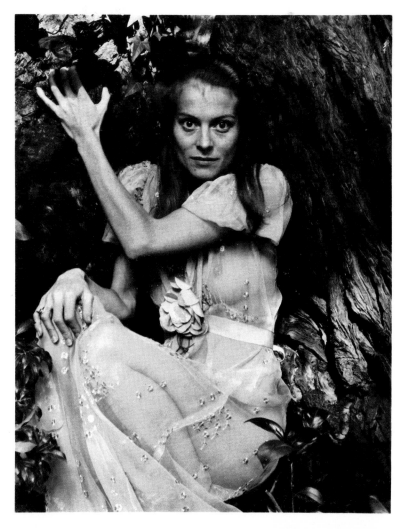

**Judy Dater** b. 1941
TWINKA
*1970. Collection of the Photographer*

**Judy Dater** b. 1941
BARBARA DEZONIA
*1973. Collection of the Photographer*

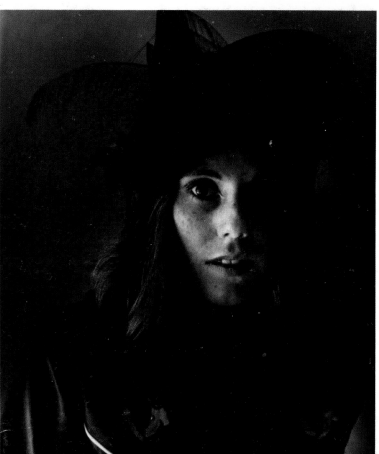

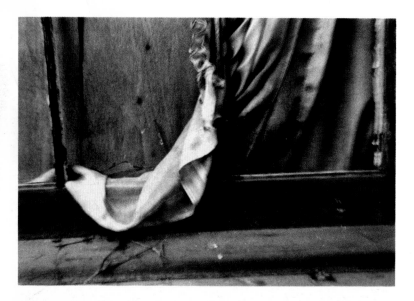

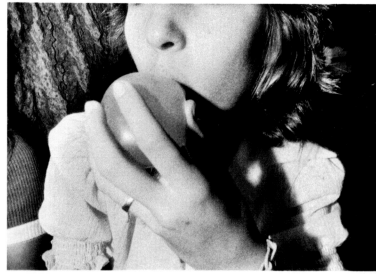

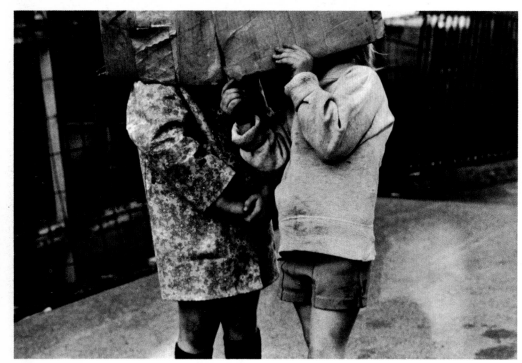

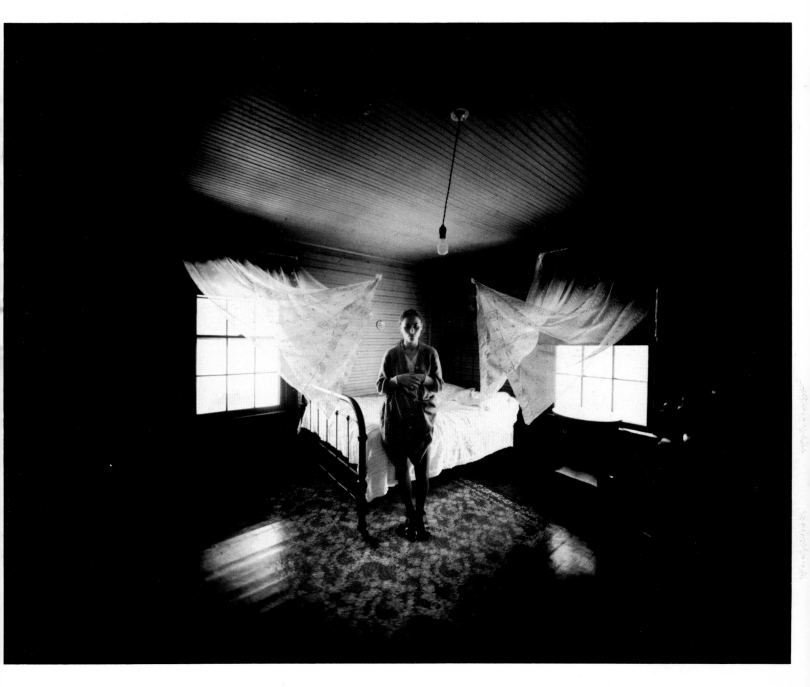

Emmet Gowin b. 1941
EDITH
*1971. Light Gallery, New York*

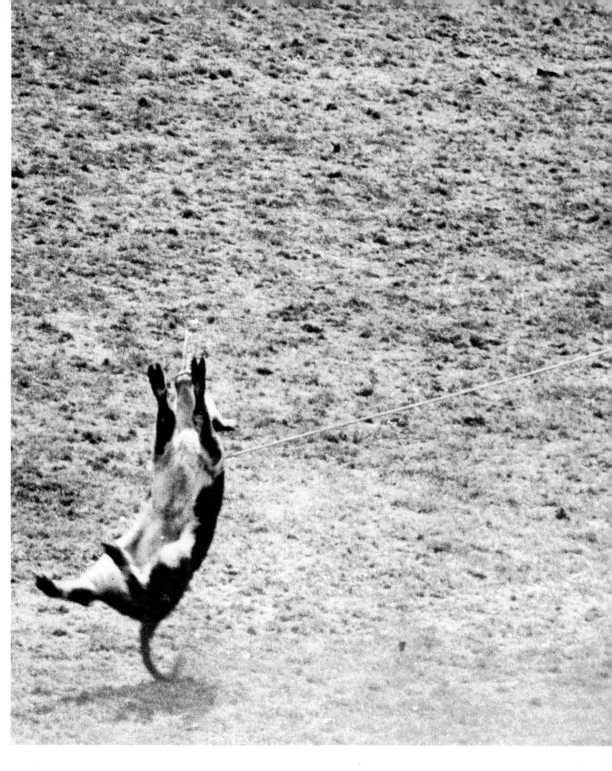

Douglas Kent Hall b. 1938
CALF ROPING, PENDLETON, OREGON
1972. *Collection of the Photographer*

Douglas Kent Hall b. 1938
MESQUITE, TEXAS
1973. *Collection of the Photographer, courtesy of Magnum Photos, Inc.*

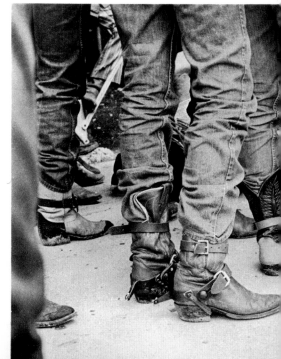

246

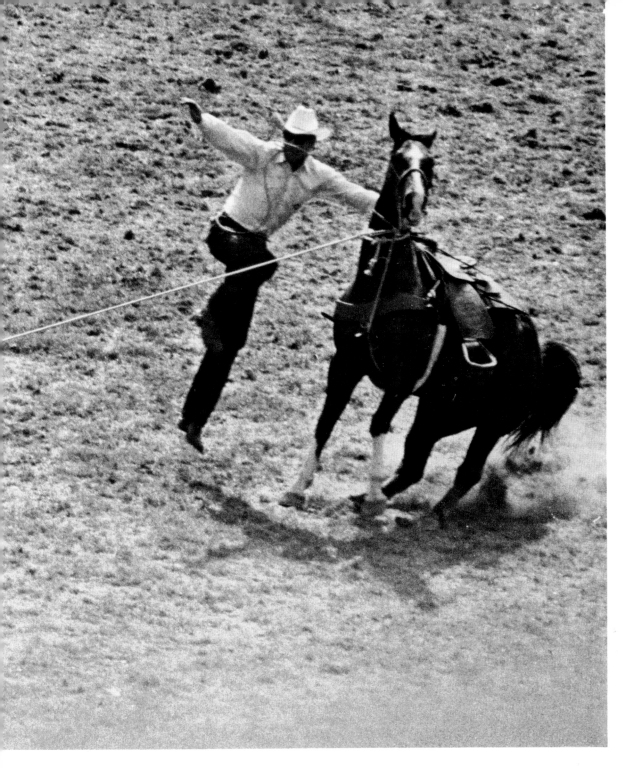

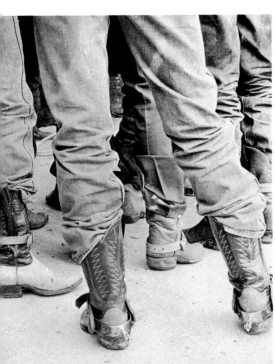

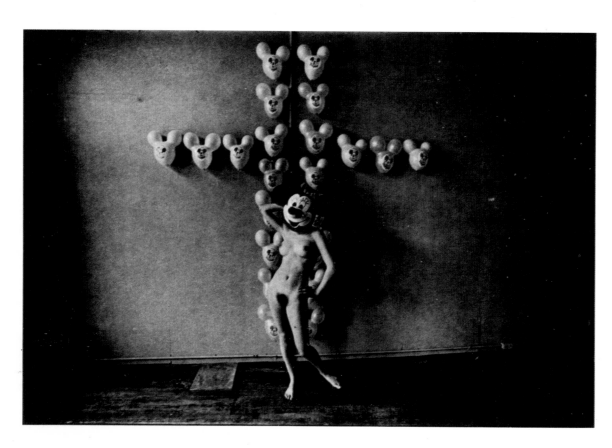

Leslie R. Krims b. 1943
UNTITLED
*1968. Collection of the Photographer*

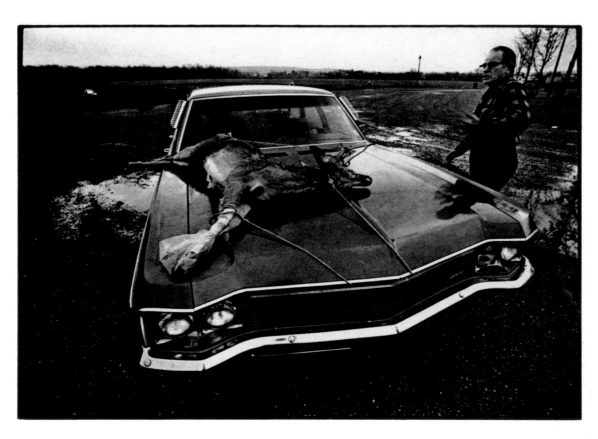

Leslie R. Krims b. 1943
FROM THE PORTFOLIO "THE DEERSLAYERS"
*1971. Collection of the Photographer*

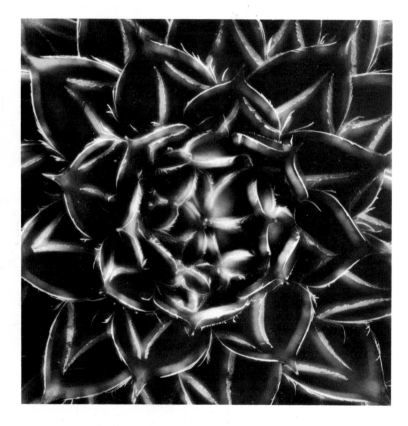

## Don Worth b. 1924
SUCCULENT: AGAVE FILIFERA VAR. COMPACTA, MILL VALLEY, CALIFORNIA
*1970. Collection of the Photographer*

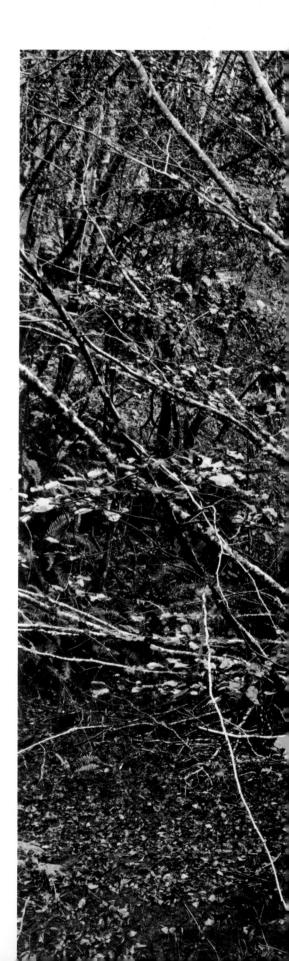

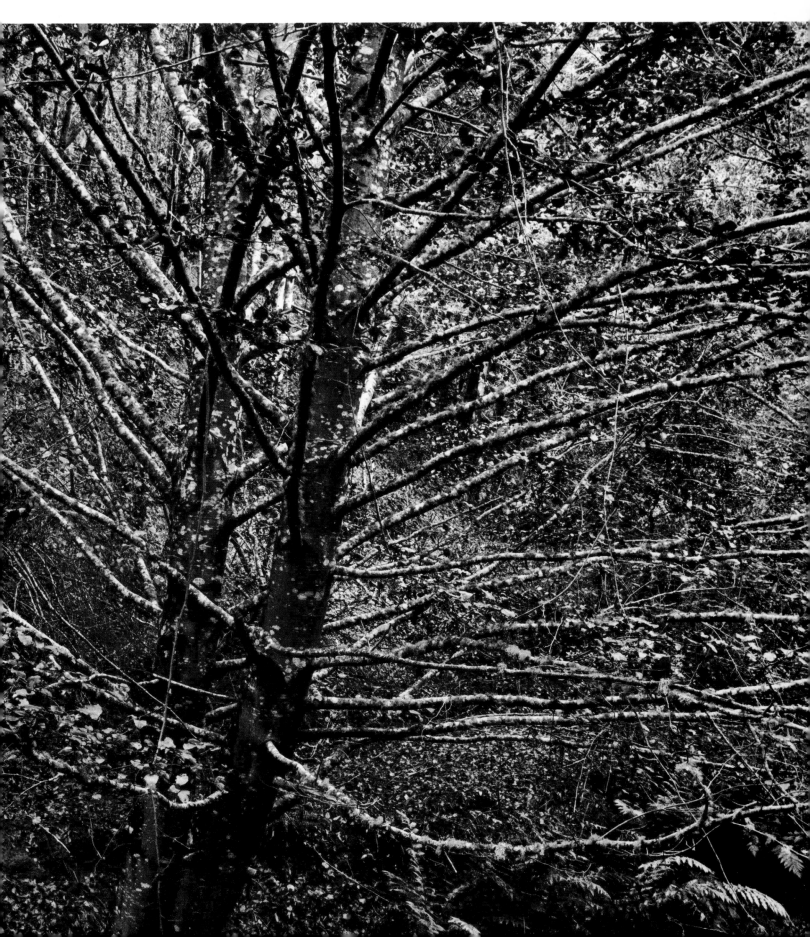

Todd Walker b. 1917
UNTITLED
*1970. Collection of the Photographer*

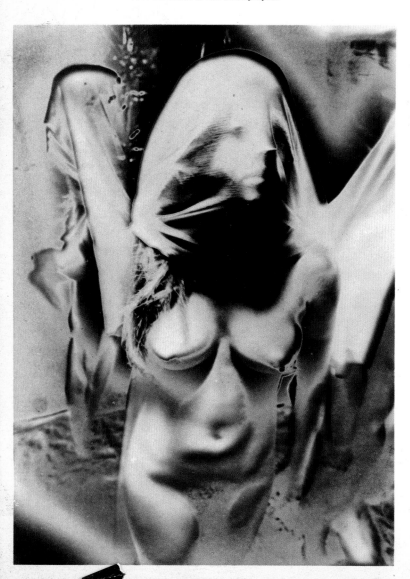

Todd Walker b. 1917
UNTITLED
*1969. Collection of the Photographer*

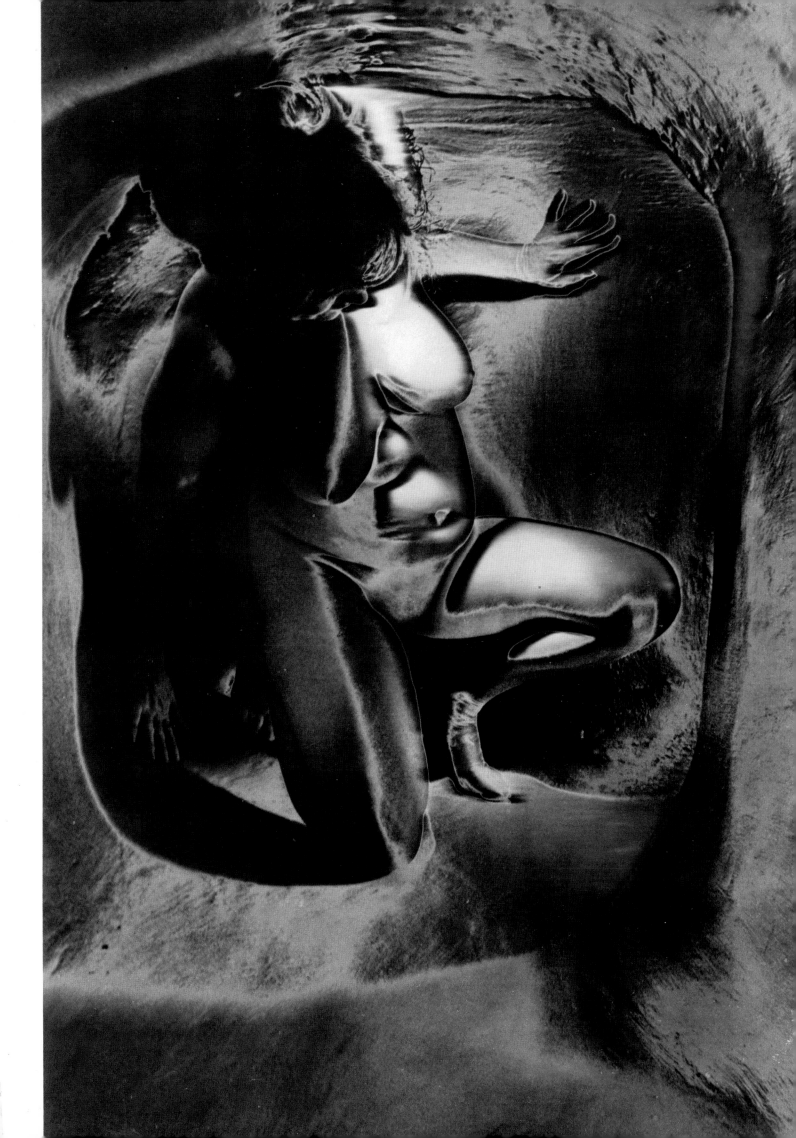

# Index to the Photographers